AF225849

*An Unofficial Guide to*
*New Zebedee*

# AN UNOFFICIAL GUIDE TO NEW ZEBEDEE

People, Places, and Things
in the Lewis Barnavelt series
Created by
**John Bellairs**

◆ ◆ ◆

## By Brad Strickland

*BrushMush Books*
*Snellville, Georgia USA*

*This book is dedicated to the memory of John Bellairs, Frank Bellairs,
Ann and Tony La Pietra, Thomas E. Fuller, Thomas F. Deitz
and to all the fans of John Bellairs everywhere!*

*A half share of royalties from this edition will go to the Marshall District
Library in recognition and furtherance of that institution's continuing support
for John Bellairs's work and legacy.*

This work offers the memoirs, observations, literary analyses, and commentary of the author, Brad Strickland, and is not affiliated with the publishers of the John Bellairs novels or with the production company of the motion picture *The House with a Clock in Its Walls.*

*An Unofficial Guide to New Zebedee* Copyright © 2018 by Brad Strickland. All Rights Reserved.

All rights reserved. No part of this book may be reproduced in any form or by any electronic or mechanical means including information storage and retrieval systems, without permission in writing from the author. The only exception is by a reviewer, who may quote short excerpts in a review.

Cover designed by MOS Graphyx


Printed in the United States of America

First Printing: September 2018
BrushMush Books
Snellville, GA
USA

3 4 5 6 7 8 9 10 11

ISBN-978-1-7324570-1-0

*"I write scary thrillers for kids because I have the imagination of a ten-year-old. I love haunted houses, ghosts, witches, mummies, incantations, secret rituals performed by the light of the waning moon, coffins, bones, cemeteries, and enchanted objects."*
—JOHN BELLAIRS

*"Life is a pure flame, and we live by an invisible Sun within us."*
—SIR THOMAS BROWNE, *URN-BURIAL*

## Contents

## Introduction: How I Came to New Zebedee

The year was 1991. I had written a few books, science fiction, horror, and fantasy for adults, and one young-adult novel. Late in the spring of that year, my agent, Richard Curtis, telephoned me. "What do you know," he asked, "about a writer named John Bellairs?"

"Oh," I said. "You mean the John Bellairs who wrote 'Several centuries (or so) ago, in a country whose name really doesn't matter, there lived a tall, skinny, scraggly-bearded old wizard named Prospero, and not the one you're thinking of?"[1]

Richard laughed and said, "I think you're the man for the job. How would you like to write a couple of John Bellairs novels?"

"Why would I do that?" I asked, completely befuddled. "I mean, yes, I'm a huge fan of his, but Mr. Bellairs probably wouldn't like me poaching on his territory."

"Brad," Richard said gently, "John's dead."

You know that cold, hard feeling you get in your chest when bad news slams hard into you? That was what I felt, as if I'd been told a favorite uncle had passed away without warning.

I stammered something meaningless—"I'm sorry to hear that, I didn't know," words like that—and Richard filled me in on some of the details—John had passed away from heart failure on March 21, at a dismayingly young age (he had turned 53 in January), leaving two novels unfinished, and the publisher, John's son (the late Frank Bellairs), and Richard all wanted the books to be completed. Richard knew my writing style well and knew that I liked to do a little stunt writing in my own works, imitating styles from the past. I don't remember, but he might have read a few parodies I wrote of William Faulkner, Ernest Hemingway, and other heavy hitters in literature (my day job, after all,

---

[1] If you don't recognize this, it's the first line of John's wonderful fantasy novel *The Face in the Frost*. Go find a copy and read it.

was teaching English). Anyway, Richard had talked it over with John's son, and Frank thought I could do it.

I provisionally agreed. Richard warned that before I started, both the publisher and editor had to approve of me. I might have to show them that I could write a book in John's style. Richard thought that might mean doing a sample chapter or two (one problem, he said, was that both partial novels were underwritten and needed new scenes). He said to wait, and he would find out from the publisher just what was required.

I couldn't just wait, so I got moving almost as soon as Richard hung up the phone. The first thing I did was to go out, that very day, to the local bookstore and buy all the young-adult novels John had in print—not just the Lewis Barnavelt books, but the Anthony Mondays and the Johnny Dixons, too.

The second, and most pleasant thing, was to read them all. Richard had told me the two unfinished manuscripts were in the Lewis Barnavelt series, so I concentrated on them. I'm afraid I marked up copies of John's three Barnavelt books rather thickly, finding references to remember. All the while notes on everything went down on a legal pad, things to remember and be sure to get right. I read all three books over one weekend and spent a few days annotating them.

Then—why not?—the next step was to create an index to the three New Zebedee novels: *The House with a Clock in Its Walls; The Figure in the Shadows;* and *The Letter, the Witch, and the Ring.* The first is spooky and enchanting, with a heady mixture of comedy and horror. The second is for me the scariest book John Bellairs ever wrote, and the third is John's ode to Rose Rita Pottinger, his fascinating pre-teen girl adventurer. I propped up the legal pad next to my computer and began transcribing and alphabetizing the notes. Making the index took a week or so.

Then—why not?—while Richard negotiated with Dial Books' publisher Phyllis Fogleman and John's editor Toby Sherry, I very quickly wrote a John Bellairs book. Except not really. Just to demonstrate that I could capture the style and setting, I wrote a faux Johnny Dixon novel called "The Snow Globe," although I changed the setting and didn't use John's characters. The hero was a lot like Johnny Dixon, and his elderly friend was a grumpy old history professor who served on the board of a museum. Sounds familiar, I know. I dashed the story off, not trying to do a polished work, but just to demonstrate a sense of pacing and a literary style. It took two weeks and 120 pages, start to finish. I sent it to Richard, first draft, not revised (something I never do) and said, "If the editor wants a sample, this is a demo."

He called me back in a couple of days: "Toby Sherry likes the book, but she says she can't publish it because it's too close to John's style."

"I never meant for it to be published," I said. "It's just a demo."

Phyllis Fogleman wanted to meet the Bellairs fan who was so rabid that he would write a novel not meant to be published to try to get the chance to write one that would be. First, she sent me a photocopy of John's typescript for "The Ghost in the Mirror." As always, John had worked with a portable typewriter. He had not bothered with a clean manuscript—his, like my demo, was obviously first draft—and had backspaced and x'd out typos or words he wanted to change. He had inked in a few additions, not many.

In June, Phyllis happened to be traveling to Atlanta for a publishing conference—at that time I lived fifty miles north of the city—and we arranged to meet. We sat at a table in a hotel restaurant and she quizzed me: What did the book need? How would I set about to fix it? Could it be done while leaving John's language intact? Could I smoothly mimic John's language and style?

As I recall, I said that first, the villain needed more exposure; he came into the book only at the end, to be quickly dispatched. Second, mention was made of a hidden treasure, but that remained a loose end. If there was a treasure, it had to be found. Third, the book needed a proper conclusion. As it was, it simply stopped—none of the central questions set up in chapters 1 and 2 were ever resolved. I briefly told her what I thought should happen in the conclusion.

She returned to New York and told Toby Sherry that she thought I could do it. Toby then called me and said, right off the bat, "I can't accept that snow-globe book." I told her I knew she couldn't, that it was a demo. "But I do like it," she said.[2] "So how are you going to fix 'The Ghost in the Mirror?' Sell me on your ideas."

Once again I went through the list, in more detail this time because after talking to Phyllis I had written everything down in my legal pad. Toby kept murmuring, "Uh-huh. Okay. Uh-huh."

---

[2] Later I turned it into a Johnny Dixon novel, *The Hand of the Necromancer*, and it finally was published, after all.

When I finished, she laughed. "I made a list of everything I thought should be done," she said. "You just hit every one of them. Get to work."

Richard negotiated the two-book contract and I got to work. Overall, I'd guess the finished novel, *The Ghost in the Mirror*, was roughly 60% John and 40% me. I wove some scenes in the early part of the book—the appearances of the villain early on, the scene with the enchanted book that nearly entraps Rose Rita (because Toby felt "something spooky should happen in this chapter"), the clues to the hidden treasure, a more elaborate comeuppance for the villain, the finding of the treasure, and the discovery that Mrs. Zimmerman and Rose Rita had succeeded in their mission and had earned a reward.

I enjoyed the work and Toby discovered that she had found a writer who played well with editors. She confided to me that John, like many writers, perhaps most, was more than a tad protective of his work and resisted changing things. Toby said he would turn in a first draft and ask, "What do you want me to do to it?" She would carefully go through and make page-by-page suggestions for revision. Then John would argue with nearly every point—though he always went on to make the changes.[3]

No argument from me. My philosophy has always been that an editor is the writer's ally, not a natural enemy. In fact, I really have only one big regret about what I did on that book: John habitually inverted his dialogue tags. That is, he would never write an exchange like this:

"Uncle Jonathan, what are we going to do?" Lewis asked.
"My boy," uncle Jonathan said, "we will just have to wait and see."

What John would have written is this:

"Uncle Jonathan, what are we going to do?" asked Lewis.
"My boy," said Uncle Jonathan, "we will just have to wait and see."

That style—putting the verb first and then the speaker, "said Lewis" instead of "Lewis said"—is old-fashioned and vaguely British. The copy editor didn't like it and normalized John's dialogue tags, and my own, so it was almost always speaker-verb instead of the other way around.

---

[3] The one time that he decided not to take the editorial suggestions with the first Anthony Monday book wasn't a great success. I will have something to say about that in Chapter 11.

To my shame, I didn't put up a fuss, so now when I re-read the novel, its style seems off somehow. I learned better after a book or two and kept the dialogue tags in Bellairsian order from then on.

*The Ghost in the Mirror* went well enough to persuade Toby Sherry to give me the go-ahead to complete a fragmentary manuscript, "The Witch Finder," before *Ghost* had hit the bookstores. When the manuscript arrived, I learned that John had completed only two chapters, and he had written no outline.

Now, on outlining: John was an instinctive writer. When he started a story, he had no idea what was going to happen. He once told a fan, "I roll a sheet of paper into the typewriter, put my fingers on the keys, and let my imagination run wild." He liked to write the way he liked to read, discovering the story as the events revealed themselves.

I cannot write that way. I'm a compulsive outliner—first a one- or two-page plot sketch, then biographies and descriptions of my characters, and then a full outline of everything in the book, at about one page per chapter, single-spaced. At that stage, I don't put in dialogue, but I do indicate conflicts: "Johnny and Fergie run from the monster. Fergie suggests a goofy way to fight it, and when Johnny argues with him, the monster almost gets them." My completed outline also tells me exactly when and how the book will end.

In fact, one of my writing quirks is to write the last scene of a book before I write anything else. The conclusion always changes—always, every single time—but I need to have a sense of where the book is heading, and having the final chapter means there's a goal to aim at.

For *The Witch Finder* manuscript, I had to create the plot from those first two chapters. I did a twenty-page outline, Toby approved, and I wrote that book. Neither took very long, because my enthusiasm was compelling me to hurry and finish.

Pre-sales of *The Ghost in the Mirror* were encouraging, so Toby dug out letters from John that briefly mentioned plot situations for more books (John, who had retired from teaching, had been writing about two per year). Four were in this short-idea form, and she asked me to write those books, too. I believe the first was "The Drum, the Doll, and the Zombie." John's proposal was this:

Professor Coote buys a voodoo drum while visiting New Orleans and brings it home. He has bad dreams about it and brings it to Professor Childermass. Playing with the drum, Johnny and Fergie accidentally summon a zombie that attacks them.

And so was born *The Drum, the Doll, and the Zombie,* the first Johnny Dixon I worked on.

From there I went on to write a good many books in the Johnny Dixon and Lewis Barnavelt series. Never got a chance to do an Anthony Monday, though. More about that in Chapter 11. Remind me if I forget.

Later in the 1990s, I heard from a bookstore owner in Marshall, Michigan, John's home town. Her name was Ann La Pietra, and I will forever be grateful to her. She invited me to come up to Marshall for the annual Bellairs Walk.

Wow. Just wow. Ann's bookstore, The Kids Place, was a little operation, but so warm, so friendly! And Ann introduced me to Marshall, saw to it that I got to tour the original inspiration for *The House with a Clock in Its Walls* (the Cronin mansion), helped me get into the Haunted Opera, showed me where John was born, where his dad's shop was, where the model for the splendidly spooky cemetery was, the waterworks, oh, man, just everything.

Plus, during the Bellairs Walk I got to dress up as Uncle Jonathan. I stood on the front lawn of the mansion and heard the "real" Uncle Jonathan tell the groups that came by all about the mysterious and spooky things that went on inside the house. On my visit, by the way, they insisted that I climb up into the unused tower. I did, and even peeped out through the oval window. I wasn't alone, because about a hundred small bats clung to the walls, but bats don't bother me, and we got along fine.

After that first visit, I returned several times, both alone and with my wife Barbara, and heard many great stories about John Bellairs and his life and adventures in Marshall, the real New Zebedee. If you know the novels, you feel right at home in Marshall, because you recognize the scenery. Oh, granted, John moves some things around, and he invents a fanciful Civil War monument, but you can still recognize New Zebedee when you walk the friendly streets of Marshall. When Ann passed away in 2007, Barbara and I lost a great friend, and Marshall lost a treasure. Rest in peace, Ann.

To cut to the chase, I've come to feel that, though not a native, I'm very much at home in New Zebedee. Its real-life counterpart, Marshall, has been more than kind to me, and the fictional version has served as the setting for nine books I've written or co-written. It has been great fun strolling through both the real place and the imaginary one. That's worth a lot to me, and I owe the town something. Time to pay up.

It occurred to me that readers of the Lewis Barnavelt series might like a guide, even an unofficial one, and that's the excuse for this book. It consists of three parts: a long-winded Introduction; the original "Index to *The House with a Clock in Its Walls, The Figure in the Shadows, and The Letter, the Witch and the Ring*" in preparation for my beginning to play in John Bellairs's yard; and the last section consists of individual chapters on each of the books I wrote solo, with alphabetical entries on the characters, places, and situations peculiar to those novels. It is chock-full of luscious Bellairsian trivia, with a few secrets about how books come to be written and published. I hope the traveler enjoys the stroll down these mysterious streets.

Thanks to John Bellairs, whose imagination ran so wild that it created an unforgettable world of mystery and magic. Thanks to the late Frank Bellairs, his son, and Priscilla Bellairs, his former wife, for allowing me to continue to work with John's characters and places. Thanks to the late Edward Gorey, whose cover illustrations worked so perfectly with the stories. And thanks to you, the Bellairs fan. It's all for you in the end. And remember, one of your number is—

*Yours truly,*
*Brad Strickland.*

◆　◆　◆

# Chapter 1: An Index to John Bellairs's *The House with a Clock in its Walls* (1973); *The Figure in the Shadows* (1975); *The Letter, the Witch, and the Ring* (1976)
### By John Bellairs, all published by Dial Books for Young Readers

When John Bellairs passed away, he was writing a continuation of the Lewis Barnavelt series, with one novel in rough draft and another begun. Lewis hadn't been around for a long time, and *Ghost* was to be the first New Zebedee novel after a lapse of fifteen years. In the meantime, John had been writing two other book series, the Johnny Dixon books, set in Massachusetts and the Anthony Monday books, set in Minnesota.

In fact, the last book that John had completed and (mostly) revised was an Anthony Monday, *The Mansion in the Mist* (1992). At the request of Toby Sherry, the editor, I did a little silent editorial work on *Mansion*, tidying up things like inadvertent repetitions and resolving three or four minor contradictions. These were the kind of last-minute details that John would have cleaned up within a day or two and, on my part, did not amount to revising, so I took no credit on the novel, though working on it gave me a little experience with John's style and writing habits.

Anyway, in preparation for tackling *The Ghost in the Mirror*, I created the following index to the first three volumes, hoping to maintain consistency as I added to John's first-draft manuscript of *Ghost*. I present it to you here as I wrote it, though I have tried to repair a few typos and other errors. This is different from later chapters, since it's what I prepared as my personal guide to the first trilogy of books in the New Zebedee series.

◆ ◆ ◆

**Advertisements**. Barns in the countryside around New Zebedee often carry tobacco signs on their sides: CHEW MAIL POUCH. Barbed-wire fences sometimes have yellow tin signs wired to them advertising DeKALB CORN. BURMA-SHAVE signs run alongside the U.S. highways. The magic parlor organ in the Barnavelt house sometimes gets bored and plays radio ads for CUTICURA, CLARK'S SUPER ONE HUNDRED GASOLINE, and SUPER SUDS (*House*, 162-163 for the texts of the commercials). Rose Rita at one point gets into her head a radio jingle: "Use Wildroot Cream Oil Charlie . . . ." (*Figure, 138*).

*Amulets* / by *F.H. Zimmermann* / *D.Mag.A.* /*A FREE INQUIRY INTO* / *THE PROPERTIES OF MAGIC AMULETS* / *A dissertation submitted to the Faculty of Magic Arts of the University of* / *Gottingen, in partial fulfillment of the* / *requirements for the Degree of* / *DOCTOR MAGICORUM ARTIUM* / *(DOCTOR OF MAGIC ARTS)* / *by* / *Florence Helene Zimmermann* / *June 13, 1922* / *English Language Copy.* Mrs. Zimmermann's doctoral dissertation. In it Lewis learns the magic test that shows him the three-cent piece from Grampa Barnavelt's Civil War trunk is a very powerful magical device (*Figure, 49*)

**Asmodai**. The demon summoned by the ring of King Solomon. When he appears, he brings a feeling of terror; the air becomes cold and thick and the darkness seems to engulf one. His voice is scary, harsh, and whispery (*Letter, 154*).

**Athletic Field**. Somewhere beyond the city limits, past the traffic circle with the fountain (*Figure, 125*). It is near the Bowl-Mor Bowling Alley.

**Automobiles**. Jonathan drives a big black 1935 Muggins Simoon (an imaginary car possibly inspired by the Armstrong Siddeley Typhoon—a simoom is, like a typhoon, a strong wind), with running boards and a windshield that can be cranked open. The dashboard lights are green (*House, 94*). After 1950, Mrs. Zimmermann drives a green 1950 Plymouth, high and boxy with a humpy sort of a trunk. A strip of chrome divides the windshield in two, and on the side of the car little square letters say CRANBROOK, the name of that particular model (*Letter, 26-27*).

**Barlow, Bishop**. Not an ecclesiastical bishop; Bishop is his first name. He is a Realtor, a fat loudmouth who wears sunglasses all the time, smokes smelly cheap cigars, and wears sports clothes that look like awnings (*House,* 108).

**Barnavelt, Charlie.** Lewis's late father (*House,* 10).

**Barnavelt, Grampa.** Jonathan Barnavelt's grandfather, a veteran of the Civil War. His name is on the Civil War Monument. The action of *Figure* begins when Lewis finds a lucky token (a three-cent piece) in Grampa Barnavelt's old trunk. For a description of the trunk, see *Figure,* 17. Also in the trunk are a curved sword with a tarnished brass hilt and Grampa Barnavelt's Fifth Michigan Fire Zouave Lancers uniform. Grampa survived the Civil War battle of Spottsylvania Court House only because he never saw action, having been wounded in the leg by Walter Finzer. The shooting resulted from Barnavelt's winning Finzer's lucky three-cent piece (really a magical amulet) in a poker game *(Figure, 22-23).* Rose Rita ultimately throws the amulet down a well, destroying its magic power and banishing an evil spirit it conjured up (*Figure,* 139).

**Barnavelt House.** Jonathan and Lewis Barnavelt live in an impressive house at 100 High Street in New Zebedee. Jonathan once lived on Spruce Street, near the waterworks, but moved to the present house in 1943. He calls it Barnavelt's Folly: a three-story stone mansion with a turret in front, including a little oval window set like an eye in the bank of shingles at the top of the turret. A chestnut tree grows in the front yard, and a green and white striped lawn glider is underneath it. Surrounding the house: A frilly iron fence topped by iron pompons and sporting in red glass reflectors the number *100.*

**Lewis's bedroom** and his uncle's are on the second floor of the house. Lewis loves it. Among other things, it is crammed with books. A window looks out over the front lawn, and from it Lewis can see the Hanchett House, and in the distance, a hill with a water tower.

On the first floor, **the study** is described on page 30 of *House.* It has sliding doors that open into the dining room. The study comes complete with a secret passage (behind a bookcase) that leads into the china cupboard in the kitchen (*House,* 38). In *Figure,* Jonathan calls one room **the library**; this may or may not be the same room as the study. It has books crammed in, floor to ceiling, and has a set of glass double doors in one wall that open right out into the side yard (53).

Jonathan's cluttered **kitchen** includes a cupboard that conceals a secret passage, as Lewis discovers at a shocking moment in *House.* **The dining room** is also where Uncle Jonathan, Mrs. Zimmermann, Lewis, and later Rose Rita play poker. It features a potted plant that Uncle Jonathan uses as an ashtray (*Figure,* 90). In **the parlor** is the magical parlor organ which has an "infinite replay" setting. In December 1948, Jonathan did not own a TV set (*House,* 113).

The **front hall** contains a blue Willoware vase full of all sorts of canes, bone-handled, ivory-handled, and some concealing swords. Jonathan's wand (his cane) also reposes here (*House,* 52). The front door does not have an electric doorbell; instead, there is a tired, mechanical bell set in the middle of the front door (*House,* 116).

**The cellarway** is where Jonathan keeps his tools and is also the haunt of the Fuse Box Dwarf (*House,* 126-127). In the cellar is the disused **coal bin**; leftover coal there hides a secret door, leading to the passageway where Isaac Izard hid his doomsday clock (*House,* 167). The original owner of 100 High Street, Isaac Izard had his initials stamped, carved, or painted all over the house (*House,* 33).

Other spaces: the **second floor** has lots of spare bedrooms (*Figure,* 90) as well as Jonathan's and Lewis's rooms. The **third floor** is generally closed off to avoid heating empty space, but on expeditions there Lewis finds interesting things, including boxes of chessmen, china doorknobs, and cupboards that he can climb inside (*House,* 124). One room contains another parlor organ, this one unmagical, that Lewis can play. Every room in the enormous old mansion, including those on the third floor, has a fireplace in it (*Figure,* 85). The **attic** is where Uncle Jonathan stores Christmas decorations and lights in Seagram's and Oxydol cardboard boxes (*Figure,* 97). These decorations include a circular mirror (representing an ice pond), dirty cotton batting for snow, and a cardboard village and celluloid deer. At Christmas time, Lewis likes to squint at the lighted tree, making the lights appear to be stars (*Figure,* 98). The **back yard** features a birdbath and four elm trees at the far end (*House,* 53). The exterior of the house--but not the interior--is closely modeled on the Cronin mansion in Marshall, MI.

**Barnavelt, Jonathan van Olden**. Lewis's uncle, who is raising him. Jonathan has a bushy red beard streaked in several places with white. His arms are covered with springy red hair. He likes to wear Big Mac khaki trousers or wash pants (which do not conceal his pot belly), and he favors blue work shirts worn under gold-buttoned red vests. The vests have four pockets: pipe cleaners stick out of the top two, and a chain of paperclips strung between the bottom two secures a gold watch. When he is thoughtful, he clicks the paperclips. On special occasions, like V-J Day or Lewis's coming home from Boy Scout camp, he dresses up in a white linen suit that is rather yellow and smells of mothballs (*Letter*, 182). His bathrobe is cut like a graduation robe and is black with red stripes on the sleeves. He rarely wears a hat, though he does own a dusty old gray fedora that he claims is the proper poker-playing costume.

He smokes a pipe (one of his pipes, given to him by Lewis, is carved in the shape of a dragon's head). Jonathan is a terrible poker player—when he has a good hand, he snorts and chortles and blows smoke out of both corners of his mouth, but when it's bad he sulks and chews his pipe stem.

He is a sensitive about the fact that Mrs. Zimmermann has her doctorate (in Magical Arts), while his own degree is an A.B. from Michigan Agricultural College, in Agricultural Science (specifically Animal Husbandry). He intended to be a farmer until his grandfather died and left him a pile of money. At some point he took up magic, although he calls himself only a parlor magician. Still, he has some real magical powers and can create grand illusions.

Unlike Lewis, Jonathan prefers electric candles to real ones. Languages he speaks include Greek, Latin, French, German, and Middle-Kingdom Egyptian (though Mrs. Zimmermann deplores his French). He is apparently a (somewhat active) Catholic. John's friends have no trouble in seeing Jonathan as John's self-portrait.

**Barnavelt, Lewis.** The nephew of Jonathan Barnavelt and the hero of two of the books. Lewis is a fat kid; in *Letter* he is "pudgy and round-faced." Though bright, he is timid and fretful and something of a worrywart. Lewis's parents both died in an automobile accident when Lewis was ten, in the year 1948. Lewis's father was in the U.S. Army (most likely the Air Corps) during World War II, because he bought a suitcase in London just after the war, and Lewis still uses it. It is cardboard and enormous, and it is covered with ripped and faded Cunard Line stickers.

Before his parents died, Lewis lived in Wisconsin, and he has bad memories of his poor luck in sports there (*House*, 64). Lewis always wears corduroy trousers, the kind that go *whip-whip* when he walks. In *Figure* he becomes a Boy Scout and wears a Scout uniform with a red neckerchief. After his first Holy Communion, he received a St. Anthony medal, which he wore for a while.

In *Figure*, he replaces the St. Anthony medal with the three-cent lucky piece from Grampa Barnavelt's Civil War trunk (57). He has blond hair which he grooms with Wildroot Cream Oil. In the winter he wears coat, hat, and galoshes. He has been an altar boy and often prays when under stress. For specific prayers, see *House*, 4 and 128; an amulet-testing prayer is in *Figure*, 51.

Lewis is a great reader and loves to eat candy or other snacks while he reads, including peppermint patties, chocolate-chip cookies, and Welch's Fudge Bars. He is also partial to Reese's Peanut Butter Cups and strawberry shortcake. Lewis has some modest talents. He can play the parlor organ, although his repertoire is limited (*House*, 125).

He is not normally very athletic or aggressive, but in *Figure*, under the influence of the amulet, he beats up the bully Woody Mingo—though afterwards he feels sorry for Woody and becomes afraid of the amulet.

In the summer of 1950, he goes to Boy Scout Camp to learn how to tie nots, paddle canoes, and hike through the wilderness, wanting to be "a real boy" and make Rose Rita like him more (*Letter*, 11). At the end of the summer, he returns with a suntan and the ability to swim (180). He has also made crafts for everybody: a copper ashtray for Jonathan, a necklace of purply-white seashells for Mrs. Zimmermann, and a leather belt and a necklace slide whittled from wood and painted green with yellow spots for Rose Rita. The lump on the front is presumably a toad; it has eyes, at least (186).

In connection with the Scouts, Lewis acquires some standard equipment. He has a Boy Scout knife (*Figure*, 103), and Rose Rita gives him a genuine official Boy Scout fire-starting kit (*Letter, 5*). By nature he always foresees greater dangers than exist. He doesn't usually believe in old superstitions and sayings, but sometimes he must. He loves his uncle and takes his magic in stride, and in *House*

Lewis even experiments with magic, unfortunately (and accidentally) calling Mrs. Izard back from the grave. He apparently decides to abandon magic as a career, because when he grows up, he becomes an astronomer at Mount Palomar (*House*, 120). Like Jonathan, Lewis is John's self-portrait, himself at a younger age.

**Barnavelt's Folly.** Jonathan Barnavelt's indulgent name for his house at 100 High Street, New Zebedee, Michigan. For a general description, see *House* (24-25). See also *Barnavelt House.*

**Baseball**. Lewis sees his inability to play baseball (because he is uncoordinated and fat) as his greatest problem (*House*, 43-44). In the last chapter of *Figure*, Rose Rita gets a season ticket to the Detroit Tigers' home games for Christmas (of 1949). Jonathan likes the Tigers, and Mrs. Zimmermann is a big White Sox fan. In *Letter* we learn that Rose Rita is not only a good baseball player (she's a deadly accurate softball pitcher), but that she knows a lot about baseball history and trivia, too; she defeats a "lug" in a baseball-knowledge contest. She knows, for example, Ty Cobb's lifetime average; the number of unassisted triple plays; Smead Jolley's great record, four errors on a single played ball; and that Bill Wambsganss of the Cleveland Indians pulled off the only unassisted triple play ever during a World Series game (1920 World Series, game 5—*Letter*, 75). See also *Kell, George.*

**Battle Meadow**. A meadow on Oley Gunderson's farm. When Oley and Mrs. Zimmermann were kids, they found some Indian arrowheads there and gave the meadow its name. Oley found the magic ring there (*Letter*, 16).

**Bedrooms**. These come in for considerable description; they are personal territories and mean a great deal to the characters.

**Lewis's** is on the second floor of the Barnavelt House, and a good description is in *House* (17). Lewis has a new Westclox bedside alarm clock with luminous hands (*House*, 81) and from his window he can see the water tower at the top of the hill, as well as the Hanchett house (113). He has a tall mirror with battlements on the top that match the ones on Lewis's bed, and before the mirror is a beautiful hooked rug made by Mrs. Zimmermann's great-grandmother in an Autumn Leaves pattern. Lewis's fireplace is of black marble and has a fire screen (*Figure*, 86).

**Rose Rita's bedroom** includes a desk and a tall black bureau, the top drawers of which have personal stuff in them, such as a chestnut carved to look like a jack-o'-lantern, a deck of miniature playing cards in a miniature case marked *Little Duke Toy Cards*, an X-Acto knife set, a box of little plastic chessmen with the label *Drueke* on the top, a pair of magnetic toys shaped like the Republican elephant and the Democratic donkey, and, in a worn little blue case labeled *Marshall Field's, Chicago* (with a white label under that bearing Rose Rita's name and address), and in *Figure*, the three-cent piece, the magical amulet that she accepts from Lewis for safe-keeping. She locks the two top drawers and keeps the key pinned inside her black plush beanie (*Figure*, 104).. She has a tank of goldfish in her room (*Letter*, 7).

The second-floor **guest bedroom** in Mrs. Zimmermann's house is purple and pleasant: The wallpaper has a pattern of violet bouquets, and the chamber pot in the corner is purple Crown Derby china. Over the bureau is an H. Matisse painting of a room in which everything is purple, given by the artist to Mrs. Zimmermann during her visit to Paris just before World War I (*Letter*, 19).

The **bedroom in Gert Bigger's store** is not often used. It has an iron bed, painted green, with the wrought iron posies in the headboard touched up in pink. It has a doorless closet with dresses, stockings, and shoes in it. The dresser has a mirror, and on top of the dresser are containers of Jergen's Lotion, Pond's Lotion, and a big blue bottle of Evening in Paris perfume (*Letter*, 146).

**Bessie.** The name Rose Rita gives Mrs. Zimmermann's green Plymouth in *Letter* because its placid expression reminds her of a cow's (36).

**Bigger, Gert.** A big, rawboned woman in a shapeless sack of a dress, and one of Mrs. Zimmermann's worst enemies. Gert has an angry face, and we learn that she has always wanted to be a witch. She holds a grudge against Mrs. Zimmermann (whom she spitefully overcharges for gas). In 1905, when Mrs. Zimmermann was 18, she spent the summer at the Gunderson farm, and she and Gert fought over the same boy, Mordecai Hunks (*Letter*, 32). She appears somewhat pathetic when she complains to Rose Rita that losing "Mordy" ruined her life. The man she married instead beat her and made her miserable (153). Angry at the world, she studied to be a witch, but lacked talent, and until she came into possession of the Ring of King Solomon, she could work no magic. With the ring, she plans to transform herself into a young, beautiful woman. Then she will take all her money and move to a new place. She will live for a thousand years. Unfortunately, the demon Asmodai thwarts her plans by changing her into a young, beautiful willow tree (171-172). Mrs. Zimmerman later explains that such a transformation destroys a witch's powers.

**Bigger's Grocery Store**. In *Letter*, this belongs to Gert Bigger, who aspires to become an evil witch. The store is also a gas station. Dark pine forest is around it on three sides. A white frame house, it has a plate glass window in the front; it is two-storied, with a cellar below and a second-floor bedroom above. On the front window some green letters once spelled out SALADA, but now they just read ADA (a brand of tea). The store functions as a Mobil gas station, with two red gas pumps and near them a sign with a flying red horse on it. The same horse is on the circular ornament on top of each pump. In a woody field nearby is a chicken coop (30-31). Running up one side of the store is a trellis with a thorny vine on it, but Rose Rita wrecks it while trying to break in (135-140). The cellar door, however, proves to be unlocked.

**Bishop Barlow Realtors**. The realty company that handles the Hanchett house rental (*House,* 107). Their telephone number is 865.

**Blucher**. A Prussian general at the Battle of Waterloo (see "Waterloo")..

**Bon Sour One Frank**. A poker term invented by Lewis. When you want to call, you shout "Bon Sour One Frank!" loudly. Lewis takes the term from a misreading of an inscription on one of Jonathan's antique coins.

**Bowl-Mor Bowling Alley**. Beyond the city limits, near the Athletic Field (*Figure,* 125).

**Brush Mush**. One of Mrs. Zimmermann's pet names for Jonathan Barnavelt.

**Burchard, the Reverend Merriwether**, D.D., Litt.D. Author of *A Cyclopædia of Jewish Antiquities.* Rose Rita finds this book in the bedroom of Bigger's Grocery Store. It is big and heavy with a tooled leather cover. The pages are edged with gilt, and the spine and cover have fussy gilded decorations. The book tells about the Temple of Solomon, the Ark of the Covenant, the Brazen Laver, the Seven-Branched Candlestick, and the Ring of King Solomon (*Letter,* 146-

147). Burchard and the volume are John Bellairs's creations and not real.

**Camp Kitch-itti-Kippi**. The summer camp to which Rose Rita declines to go in the summer of 1950 (*Letter*, 4). It was an actual summer camp, now defunct, near Marshall, MI.

**Cane, magic**. Uncle Jonathan's magic cane is a long black rod of some very hard wood. At one end is a ferrule of polished brass, and at the other a glass globe the size of a baseball. It seems to be snowing in the globe; through the flakes one can sometimes see now and then an odd little miniature castle. The globe burns with an icy gray light (*House*, 53). Touching it is like touching a living human arm; life pulses through it (146). When Lewis tires to wield the cane, the globe sizzles and crackles and turns from gray to rosy pink to black and then gray again.

The villainous Mrs. O'Meagher also wields a wand disguised as a magic cane, this one ivory-handled (*House*).

**Capharnaum County Magicians Society**. A club of magicians, including Jonathan and Mrs. Zimmermann. Jonathan uses their blue and gold playing cards for poker (*House*, 13-14).

**Captain Marvel**. Lewis reads Captain Marvel comics, which he purchases at Heemsoth's Rexall Drug Store (*Figure*, 43).

**Captain Midnight Secret Decoder Ring**. Rose Rita has one, she says, that Lewis borrowed (*Figure*, 94). This is a lie to cover up a fight she and Lewis have over the magic amulet. The ring was a giveaway premium related to the old-time radio show *Captain Midnight*, about a pilot who fought criminals and spies. Each show would end with a cipher called out; the ring allowed the listeners to decrypt the cipher and get a clue to next week's episode. The gimmick may have first been used for the older radio show *Little Orphan Annie*.

John's memory was partly right, partly wrong. Collectors say there were no decoder *rings*—just decoder pins or badges. The confusion arose because *Captain Midnight* and other radio shows also offered rings as premiums, usually with gimmicks like a tiny secret compartment for hiding small things, or a built-in magnifying glass, a siren whistle, and so on. This is a very common confusion, and later in the series I even contributed to it in *The Beast Under the Wizard's Bridge*.

**Card games**. In addition to poker, Jonathan Barnavelt plays a form of solitaire called "Napoleon at St. Helena." Mrs. Zimmermann has been known to play "ladies' games" like "Spit-out-the-Window" or "Johnny's Nightshirt." Mrs. Zimmermann teaches Rose Rita and Lewis klabberjass and six-pack bezique (Winston Churchill's favorite card game). Some of these are certainly real; others I have not been able to confirm.

**Carver, Lois**. A girl in Lewis's and Rose Rita's school. She is a rotten softball player, and Rose Rita can always strike her out (*Figure*, 72).

**Cemetery, New Zebedee**. Though it's often just called this, the proper name of the graveyard is "Oakridge Cemetery" (*House*, 91). A beautiful cemetery on a high hill (Cemetery Hill, of course) just outside of town, it features elaborate gravestones and mausoleums. One lot has gravestones all carved to look like wooden logs (64-65). The cemetery is on a long ridge on the other side of Wilder Creek Park, and you have to walk half a mile past the city limits to get to the road that leads up to the ridge (82). The ridge itself is high and flat-topped, cut in two places by a narrow dirt road. It isn't hard to climb. The cemetery gate is an arch, on which are inscribed these words: THE TRUMPET SHALL SOUND / AND / THE DEAD SHALL BE RAISED.

**Charles Atlas booklet**. Charles Atlas was a famous body-builder of the fifties. Lewis orders one of his exercise booklets in *Figure* (44). It arrives at the very end of that story..

**Charm, magic**. Mrs. Bigger pins an evil magic charm inside Mrs. Zimmermann's dress in *Letter* to transform her. It is a small slip of paper with indecipherable red writing on it (79).

**Chicken, white**. Mrs. Zimmermann is temporarily transformed into a white hen by Mrs. Bigger's evil magic in *Letter* (95, passim).

**Christmas decorations in New Zebedee**. In 1949 they were big tinsel-covered bells along Main Street, and the fountain at the traffic circle was turned into a Nativity scene (*Figure*, 97).

**Church**. Lewis, his Uncle Jonathan, and Mrs. Zimmermann apparently are all Catholic, though they do not always attend Mass (*Figure*, 75).

*City of Escanaba, The*. A ferryboat that carries cars across the Straits of Mackinac (*Letter*, 44).

**Clabbernong, Elihu**. Built the Wilder Creek Bridge in 1892 and put something in the iron to keep the ghost of his uncle Jedediah from crossing the stream to get him (*House*, 100).

**Classic Comics**. Lewis reads these; one he has finished is *The Iliad* (*Figure*, 3). This is a slight anachronism, since the first printing of that title was in 1950, and it appeared not as a Classic Comics title, but in the second series by the same publisher, Classics Illustrated.

**Clocks**. In *House*, Jonathan Barnavelt appears obsessed with them. He has filled his house with clocks to drown out the "clock in the walls" (15). The grandfather clock is in the study. It makes a sound like a steamer trunk of tin plates falling slowly and solemnly down a flight of stairs. The *doomsday clock* made by Isaac Izard is an eight-day Waterbury; Lewis smashes it in *House*.

**CLOUD FORMATIONS / AND /OTHER PHENOMENA / *Observed from the Window / by / ISAAC IZARD***. A fictitious manuscript; Lewis discovers it hidden in the third-floor parlor organ (*House*, 127).

**Coins**. Jonathan Barnavelt casually uses his collection of antique coins for checkers, backgammon, and poker chips (*House*, 12). Mrs. Zimmermann kids him about Brasher doubloons. He keeps the coins in a red tin candy box with a picture of the New Zebedee County Courthouse on the lid. For a list of coins, see page 161 of *House*. In *Figure*, a lucky three-cent piece found in Grampa Barnavelt's trunk is a powerful (and evil) magic amulet.

**Corrigan, Tarby**. Tarby is the most popular boy in school. He is a daredevil and a great ball player. He is skinny, with a big fluff of brick-red hair. In *House*, when we first see him, he is recovering from a broken arm. He briefly befriends Lewis and teaches him a little baseball (44). Mr. Corrigan, Tarby's father, runs a hardware store, and the family lives in a huge frame house halfway across town from 100 High Street. Tarby has nine brothers and sisters. Mrs. Corrigan is fat and tired-looking and she sounds crabby (140). As Tarby recovers from his broken arm (and especially after he witnesses Lewis's attempt at necromancy), he turns against Lewis, and by the end of *House* the two are no longer friends.

***Cyclopædia of Jewish Antiquities, A***. Fictitious book. See Burchard, the Reverend Merriwether, D.D., Litt.D.

**Dancing**. Rose Rita thinks dancing might be fun, but she is afraid of being a wallflower (*Letter*, 52). She is somewhat impressed when Agatha Sipes confesses that she likes to go to square dances at the Four-H Building (*Letter*, 127).

**Dedications.** Except for *The Ghost in the Mirror*, each book in the series bears a dedication. For the first three:

*The House with a Clock in Its Walls:* "For Priscilla, who let me be myself." Priscilla Bellairs was John's wife and remains a staunch supporter of his work.

*The Figure in the Shadows:* "For Don Wilcox, David Walters, and Jonathan Grandine. Friends who have been friends indeed." Priscilla Bellairs warmly recalls these friends, all academics and colleagues of John's. They introduced her to John and remained close after she and John married.

*The Letter, the Witch, and the Ring:* "For my son, Frank."

**Detention Home.** This stood on a high hill near the town where Lewis and his parents lived. Lewis's mother once threatened to send him there if he was bad, and the threat terrified him (*House,* 106).

**DiMaggio, Joe.** Not the real Yankees baseball player, but a deranged bum in New Zebedee who calls himself that. He wears a New York Yankees hat and hands out pens shaped like baseball bats and inscribed "Joe DiMaggio." Sometimes "Joe" helps the police check the doors of the Main Street shops, and sometimes he jumps out at kids at night and yells "Boo!" (*Figure,* 81) Locals in Marshall say both he and Hammerhandle are versions of an actual town bum from the late 1940s and early 1950s.

**Dog, black.** Mrs. Bigger, with the aid of King Solomon's Ring, can take on the form of a small, ill-tempered black dog. The story is told in *Letter.*

**Doll Face.** One of Jonathan's pet names for Mrs. Zimmermann.

**Durgy's Pond.** When this freezes over, it is a skating pond for the boys and girls in New Zebedee. Lewis has weak ankles and is afraid of skating, but he tries it to impress Tarby (*House,* 114).

**East End Park.** A small park at the east end of Main Street (the traffic circle and fountain are on the west end). It has a few benches and a flower garden surrounded by a little iron fence (*Figure,* 10).

**Eclipse.** Jonathan Barnavelt "performs" a lunar eclipse for Lewis and Tarby in *House,* 54-56. Magical preparations include a birdbath, three saucepans full of rain water, and Jonathan's magic cane. During the eclipse, those witnessing it gain magical knowledge of their surroundings. The episode frightens Tarby and to some extent alienates him from Lewis.

**Episcopal Church**. This is next door to Lewis's school in *Figure,* and there is a narrow, shadowy alley between the two buildings (4).

**Fat Ears.** One of Mrs. Zimmermann's pet names for Uncle Jonathan.

**Fatso.** One of Mrs. Zimmermann's pet names for Uncle Jonathan.

**Feasel, Jute.** Works for the Capharnaum County Public Works Department. In the winter he drives the snow plow (*Figure,* 129). He smokes King Edward cigars, and the only clean song he knows is "Three Iddle Fishies." Jute curses, even in front of Rose Rita. He knows that Uncle Jonathan a sort-of wizard, but he doesn't mind. Marshall informants say he is based on an actual man-of-all-work employed in the fifties as a handyman by the city, but Jute's foul language is not as strong as his real-life counterpart's.

**Fifth Michigan Fire Zouave Lancers.** The Civil War unit to which Grampa Barnavelt and Walter Finzer belonged. They were the only two members of the unit to return to Michigan alive from the war. *Figure* summarizes their story.

**Finzer, Walter**. He was a soldier in the Fifth Michigan Fire Zouaves during the Civil War, a comrade of Grampa Barnavelt. Finzer lost his three-cent lucky piece to Grampa Barnavelt in a poker game and was so angry that he wounded Grampa in the leg. As a result, both missed the Battle of Spottsylvania Court House, in which their outfit was wiped out. Both survived the war, and Finzer was dishonorably discharged from the Army (*Figure,* 23-24).

**Fondrighter, Mrs.** A mean teacher at school who uses "eyeglasses on a stick" (a lorgnette) and always calls her husband "Jerrold" (*House,* 47).

**Foods**. Lewis and his uncle often consume Cheerios for breakfast, but for other meals Uncle Jonathan and Lewis like more substantial fare. Mrs. Zimmermann is an expert cook and makes delicious chocolate-chip cookies, doughnuts, and apple cider. Jonathan likes breakfasts of American fries, waffles, eggs, sausage, coffee, and milk (when he's not eating Cheerios). Lewis loves a wide array of snack foods, and meals are almost always rather festive times in the Barnavelt house.

**Fried cakes**. Mrs. Zimmermann's name for doughnuts. The recipe came to the USA from the Netherlands and is not yeast-based.

**Frizzy Wig**. One of Jonathan Barnavelt's pet names for Mrs. Zimmermann.

**Frumpy**. One of Jonathan Barnavelt's pet names for Mrs. Zimmermann.

**Fuse Box Dwarf**. A magical illusion created by Jonathan, taking the form of a tiny little man. He hides behind the paint cans in the cellarway and pops out when someone passes by, screaming, "Dreeb! Dreeb! I am the Fuse Box Dwarf!" Lewis thinks he is more to be pitied than feared. (*House*, 121)

**Gallagher, Marie**. Rose Rita's best friend before Lewis met Rose Rita (*Letter*, 4).

**Geer, Miss**. The librarian in the New Zebedee public library. She is an old woman with arthritis, and she moves slowly, but she is kind and likes Lewis (*Figure*, 82).

*Grand Traverse Bay*. A ferryboat that takes autos and passengers across the Straits of Mackinac (*Letter*, 84).

**Grinning Griselda**, the resuscitated cadaver. An illusion, a trick that Mrs. Zimmermann says she can play, but it is terrifying (*House*, 69).

**Grouchy**. One of Napoleon's lieutenants at the Battle of Waterloo. In *House*, Uncle Jonathan mischievously mispronounces his name, but Mrs. Zimmermann corrects him. See "Waterloo."

**Gunderson Farm**. Once belonged to Sven Gunderson, then to Sven's son Oley, and finally to Oley's cousin, Mrs. Zimmermann. For a description of the farm, see *Letter*, 37-38. The farmhouse has two adjoining bedrooms at the top of the stairs, each with its own small dark bedstead (41). It has a spooky barn, where Mrs. Zimmermann parks her car Bessie, and the front yard has a huge old mulberry tree.

**Gunderson, Oley**. Mrs. Zimmermann's late cousin. He owned a farm in northern Michigan (near Petoskey, right up at the north end of the Lower Peninsula), which Mrs. Zimmermann inherits on his death. He discovers what may be King Solomon's Ring there. On May 21, 1950, he wrote Mrs. Zimmermann a letter telling her about finding the ring in Battle Meadow and leaving his farm to her. He died soon after (*Letter*, 14-15). Mrs. Zimmermann calls him a "queer old duck." In the letter, he says he has no relatives except her, and he indicates they were not always on friendly terms. Oley's father was Sven (*Letter*, 16). He kept his magic ring locked in a drawer of his desk, hidden in a Benrus watchcase (the ring itself was inside a small ring box). Gert Bigger stole the ring (*Letter*, 38 ff).

**Hag Face**. One of Jonathan Barnavelt's many pet names for Mrs. Zimmermann, this occurs once as "Haggy Face," the editor's preferred form ["not as harsh"].

**Haggerty, Miss**. Lewis's and Rose Rita's sixth-grade teacher in *Figure*.

**Hammerhandle**. A menacing hobo who lived in a tar-paper shack on the outskirts of New Zebedee. He supposedly could foretell the future and made a living by carving ax, hammer, and pick handles (*House*, 108-109). He had a harsh, scraping voice and liked to talk about the World's Last Night, the imminent end of the world. He was Mrs. Izard's henchman, and presumably she killed him; "the blood of a hanged man" is one of the ingredients for the Hand of Glory Mrs. Izard wields. See Izard, Selenna, and DiMaggio, Joe.

**Hanchett son**. He is a lawyer in Osee Five Hills. His parents move in with him (*House*, 108).

**Hanchetts**. The friendly, middle-aged couple that formerly lived across the street from Uncle Jonathan. They move out in December, 1948, and Selenna Izard rents their house (*House,* 106). Their house has a spirea hedge out front. They will probably move back in after Selenna has been dispatched and their home has been purified of its contact with evil spirits.

**Hand of Glory**. A magical item wielded by Selenna Izard in *House*. Made from a dead man's hand, it has a hypnotic power and can "freeze" anyone who sees it. Based on actual supernatural lore.

**HARDESTY'S** *Universal Omnium Gatherum / Perpetual Calendar, Date Book, Almanac, and Book of Days*. A fictitious book in Jonathan Barnavelt's study. He consults it before performing a lunar eclipse. Notice type style: HARDESTY'S is all caps, roman; then all other lettering is italic and as given.

**Hartwig, Mr.** The gym instructor at the Junior High A big, cheerful man, he likes kids, and he likes Lewis (*Figure*, 42).

**Helen, Aunt**. Lewis's living aunt. He doesn't much like her and would not like to live with her. She has a personality like a leaky inner tube. She sits in an easy chair and whines about her asthma all day. She is married to Uncle Jimmy (*Figure*, 86). She may be Jonathan's sister who lives in Osee Five Hills and whom Jonathan occasionally visits (*Letter*, 128).

**Henny Penny**. A pet chicken Rose Rita once owned (*Letter*, 95).

**Holabaugh, Carl**. One of the boys that Tarby Corrigan plays baseball with in *House*. He is a tall kid.

**Homer.** A town not far from New Zebedee. Lyon Lake and Mrs. Zimmermann's cottage are out on the Homer Road. Homer and Lyon Lake are both real.

**Hookah.** Jonathan Barnavelt occasionally smokes one that is shaped like a Spanish galleon, with the crow's nest being the bowl. A description of the action is on pages 31-32 of *House*.

**Hospital, Ironwood**. After a magical attack by Gert Bigger, Mrs. Zimmermann spends three days there. The description is in *Letter* (71 ff).

**Hospital, New Zebedee**. An enormous old mansion that once had been owned by a rich old lady. When Lewis spends a night there, his room is in the attic. Description is in *Figure* (144).

**Humphries, Dr.** The Barnavelts' family doctor. Lewis likes him a lot. He has a voice like a bass viol, and he makes jokes to put people at ease. He always carries a black leather bag full of rattling square pill bottles (*Figure*, 144-145). He is Mrs. Zimmermann's doctor, too (*Letter*, 85).

**Hunks, Mordecai**. Lived near the Gunderson farm. In 1905 Gert Bigger and Mrs. Zimmermann fought over him. Mrs. Zimmermann and Mordecai dated for one summer, but then broke up, and he later married someone else (*Letter*, 35). In a junk shop Mrs. Zimmermann and Rose Rita discover a photo of him together with Mrs. Zimmermann, inscribed "Florence and Mordecai, Summer, 1905." Mrs. Bigger has maliciously obliterated Mrs. Zimmermann's face in the photo (48). Mordecai is handsome, with a handlebar moustache. In the photo, he is playing the banjo. Mrs. Bigger's pet name for him was "Mordy" (153).

**Izard, Isaac**. The former owner of Jonathan Barnavelt's house until his death in 1943. He had his initials, II, carved or painted or stamped all over the house. Izard was a warlock who was fascinated by the end of time. Unlike Uncle Jonathan or Mrs. Zimmermann, Izard was a wicked wizard, a very evil man. His wife died suddenly and was buried in the family mausoleum in Oakridge Cemetery by mysterious outsiders. Izard himself died in the middle of a wild thunderstorm. The Izard mausoleum is on the side of the ridge away from town, the side looking across a deep valley. The mausoleum has an Omega on the cornice in lieu of a name. In *House,* Izard is described as an unpleasant-looking old man, with an almost-bald head covered with a few strands of hair, deep-set eyes, and a hawkish nose (150). He created the doomsday "clock in the walls" in order to end  the world.

**Izard, Selenna**. The wife of Isaac Izard. Lewis and Tarby inadvertently raise her from the dead (*House,* 86-87). Her most striking physical feature is her glasses, which appear as two gray luminous ovals. She uses the alias of "Mrs. O'Meagher" later in the book (116). She wields an ivory-headed cane as a magic wand (153) and uses a Hand of Glory to paralyze Uncle Jonathan and Mrs. Zimmermann (170) while she tries to bring about the end of the world with her husband's doomsday clock.

**Jimmy, Uncle**. Married to Lewis's Aunt Helen. (*Figure,* 86).

**Joan of Arc** (1412-1431**).**  A visionary and much beloved French heroine. When comforting Rose Rita  in *Letter* (188), Mrs. Zimmermann holds her up as an example of an active woman who even commanded male troops in France's struggle against England during the Hundred Years' War (1337-1453, and yes, that's 116 years. Blame historians, not me).

*John L. Stoddard's Lectures: Vol. IX, Scotland, England, London.* A book Lewis reads in *House* (18-19). The *Lectures* are a real fifteen-volume set of books, and were so popular that they can be readily found in used-book stores.

**Kalamazoo Mental Hospital**. Near enough to New Zebedee so that occasionally a crazy person gets loose and scares people in town (*Figure,* 116).

**Kell, George**. A baseball player Lewis admires. Lewis saw him play in Detroit at Briggs Stadium.

**Laberdeen, Carol Kay**. A pretty but unpleasant girl in the sixth grade whose father is on the school board (*House,* 47).

**"Lard ass."** Woody Mingo calls Lewis this in *Figure,* 33 and passim. Editor says this is too harsh for use in *Ghost.*

**Lutz, Tom**. One of the big wheels in Lewis's school (*Figure,* 3). He fights Dave Shellenberger at the beginning of the book, and though he witnesses the fight, Lewis is afraid to get near it.

**Lyon Lake.** A small, pastoral lake outside of town. A few lake cottages cluster on its shore. A real place, south of Marshall; very built up now. In the early fifties, the site of a destructive tornado.

**Magic items in Jonathan Barnavelt's house.** A stained-glass window in the back staircase of the south wing changes scenes (*House,* 24-25; in *Figure,* 33, we learn that the trait is common to all the stained-glass windows in the house). A coat rack with a mirror stands in the front hall; the mirror changes scenes and can pick up radio station WGN on its beveled edges. The mirror may occasionally show one's face; more often it displays Roman ruins in the desert, Mayan pyramids, or Melrose Abbey in Scotland (*House,* 25-26, 121; *Figure,* 33). Uncle Jonathan's magic cane usually stands among other canes in a big Willoware vase in the front hall as well. The Christmas tree ornaments are also magical, sometimes reflecting the room, sometimes showing ancient ruins on unknown planets (*House,* 120). Jonathan gives Lewis a magical Easter egg; when he looks into its peephole, instead of seeing Easter chicks and ducklings, he may see any battle in history he wants to observe (*House,* 120). Lewis has a toy Magic Eight Ball that actually becomes enchanted in *House* (163) to reveal the location of the clock in the walls.

**Magic items used by Gert Bigger.** These include a funeral pall, a big wooden cross, some brown beeswax candles, a tarnished silver censer, a gilded incense boat, an aspergillum (holy water sprinkler), and the Ring of King Solomon (*Letter,* 173). Probably only the latter was really effective, but it allowed her to use the others.

**Magicians.** There seem to be quite a few living ones in New Zebedee. Historical magicians mentioned in *House* include Regiomontanus, Albertus Magnus, and Count Cagliostro. *Figure* refers to Simon Magus, who owned an amulet that let him fly through the air and make himself invisible.

***Malleus Malificarum.*** "The Hammer of Witches" is an esoteric book on witchcraft, "written a long time ago by a monk." Mrs. Zimmermann has a copy (*Letter,* 80). It was written in 1487 by a German, Heinrich Kramer, under a Latin form of his name, Henricus Institoris. Though not defrocked, Kramer had been discredited as a clergyman and dismissed by his bishop. His book became a best-seller for its era and later perhaps influenced both Shakespeare (*Macbeth*) and King James II (*Demonology*) in their writing.

**Mattie, Aunt.** Lewis's Aunt Mattie is dead. Her house always smelled of kerosene (*House*, 117). She once told Lewis that in his brown sweater and corduroy trousers he looked like a balloon ascension (*Figure*, 4). He remembers her as "mean Aunt Mattie."

**Medina, Sidonia, Duke of.** Commander of the Spanish Armada. See *House*, 173-176.

**Mingo, Woody.** A bully who torments Lewis. He is just a little wiry guy, but he is tough and carries a jackknife in his pocket and reportedly has threatened kids with it. He steals Lewis's Sherlock Holmes hat (*Figure*, 8). He gets into a fight with Rose Rita (35) but contents himself with pulling her hair because she's a girl. Later during a football game, he picks a fight with Lewis, who, driven by the three-cent lucky piece (an amulet) bloodies Woody's nose.

**Moss, Eliphaz.** The evil spirit in *Figure* is his. He burned to death on April 30, 1849, in his house out near the Homer Road. Mrs. Zimmermann's grandfather had a farm near there. Moss came out of the burning house afire and threw himself down the well, where they left him. His hired man was Walter Finzer, who probably set the fire. Finzer certainly stole the three-cent coin amulet, a magical token with powers of calling and possession, from Moss.

**Murray's Hill.** A hill in New Zebedee where in the winter children go to sled. Lewis and Rose Rita sled there together (*Figure*, 75).

**Nancy Drew mysteries.** Rose Rita is apparently fond of them (*Letter*, 59).

*Necromancy*. A big black leather-bound book in Jonathan Barnavelt's library. The frontispiece shows Dr. John Dee and his assistant, Michael Kelley, raising the spirit of a dead woman at midnight in an English churchyard (*House*, 67-68). Note: the actual engraving shows Kelley and an onlooker, not Dee. There are no identifiable books of this title and description, but the engraving is readily available in many standard works on magic and demonology.

**New Zebedee *Chronicle*.** The local newspaper (*House*, 36, 91). In *Figure*, a ghostly paper from April 30, 1859 (Walpurgis Day), wraps itself around Lewis's ankles outside the Masonic Temple on Mansion Street (119).

**New Zebedee, Michigan.** The county seat of Capharnaum County. This is where Uncle Jonathan and Lewis live, and it has its own Magicians Society (see "Capharnaum County Magicians Society").

In 1948 it had a population of 6,000. New Zebedee is full of tall, elaborately decorated old houses. The stores on Main Street have false fronts, and on one block there is an abandoned opera house in the upper stories. Main Street runs from west to east, from a traffic circle surrounding a park with a circular fountain in the center to East End Park. In most of its geography, New Zebedee closely resembles Marshall, Michigan, John Bellairs's beloved home town.

**Notre Dame football team.** A regular fall topic of conversation between Lewis and Rose Rita (*Figure*, 89).

**O'Meagher, Mrs.** The alias that Selenna Izard uses when she rents the Hanchett house across High Street from Uncle Jonathan's house (*House*, 116). The name is a pun on "Omega," the last letter of the Greek alphabet, and often used as a symbol for endings or death.

**Omega.** The marking on the mausoleum containing the bodies of the Izards in the New Zebedee cemetery (*House*, 69).

**Osee Five Hills.** A town near New Zebedee. Uncle Jonathan has relatives there; they may be Aunt Helen and Uncle Jimmy. In *Letter*, Rose Rita says that Jonathan has a sister there (128). Unlike Homer, this is not a real town, according to Marshall informants. The name is biblical, an alternate spelling of the prophet Hosea. The Book of Hosea includes mention of worshiping "in the hills."

**Pentacle, Magic. Magic.** A protective figure (a circle enclosing a five-pointed star) used by witches and wizards when they are doing magic. Rose Rita knows what they are and recognizes one drawn by Gert Bigger (*Letter*, 101).

**Photographs.** Mrs. Zimmermann says that witches and warlocks hack up pictures when they want to get rid of somebody (*Letter*, 49).

**Pitcher, Molly.** Folk hero based on the real Mary Ludwig Hays, whose husband was a soldier in Washington's army during the American Revolution. She accompanied him and worked as a cook, nurse, and servant for the camp. In the Battle of Monmouth, she carried water to the battlefield, and when her husband was wounded, she took his place loading and swabbing a cannon. A British cannonball reportedly ripped through her skirts but passed harmlessly between her calves, and she said, "That could have been worse," showing courage under fire. Mrs. Zimmermann uses her as an example of a courageous woman as she is comforting Rose Rita (*Letter*, 188).

**Postcard.** No longer much used, these are four-by-six-inch cards with postage generally already affixed (picture postcards are the exception). Cheaper to mail than a letter, they carry their messages on the side opposite the address, and of course the message cannot be private. In *Figure,* Lewis receives an ominous postcard with the Latin message *Venio,* which warns "I am coming."

**Pottinger cousin.** He lives on a farm near New Zebedee. He was 14 in 1949, and he taught Rose Rita how to drive a tractor (*Letter,* 62).

**Pottinger, George.** Rose Rita's father. Usually he is not home during the day, but he's there on Saturdays (*Figure,* 113). He can be crabby, but then he can relent and become cheerful almost at once. In *Letter* he thinks Mrs. Zimmermann is "the town screwball" and argues with his wife about her.

**Pottinger, Louse.** Rose Rita's mother. She is absent-minded (*Figure* 111) and does not like to listen to Rose Rita's occasional ill-tempered outbursts (*Letter,* 5). In *Letter,* she defends Mrs. Zimmermann against her husband's charge that she is "the town screwball" and points out that Mrs. Zimmermann is the best friend of "old what's-his name, the bearded character with all the money. The one who does magic tricks. . .." (25).

**Pottinger, Rose Rita.** Lewis meets her in school. She lives at 39 Mansion Street with her mom and dad (*Figure,* 114). She knows the names of all the kinds of cannon (saker, minion, falconet, demi-culverin, etc. *House,* 178).

Physically, she is tall, a good head taller than Lewis. She is nearsighted and wears glasses, which she must have changed pretty often (*Figure,* 108) by her optometrist, Dr. Wessel. Her hair is long, dark, and stringy, and in *Figure* she wears a black plush beanie with an ivory stud. The beanie is covered with enameled buttons of cartoon characters from Kellogg's Pep cereal boxes (5). Sometime after Christmas, 1949, she stopped wearing her beanie because it started to seem silly (*Letter,* 6). In *Letter* she is described as "tall for thirteen," having grown a lot in the last year (63).

Though she wears a skirt and blouse to school, she runs home to change to sweatshirt and jeans. When traveling, she uses a worn black valise as a suitcase. Her summer wear includes underwear, shirts, and jeans, and she does not include dresses, blouses, or skirts when she packs for travel in *Letter* (26). While on this trip, Mrs. Zimmermann buys her a salt-and-pepper shaker set shaped like a fielder's mitt and a ball (the ball is the salt) to use as desk decorations (47). She is a great ball player (she pitches softball), and has a wonderful knowledge of baseball facts (*Letter*, 76). After she wins a baseball-knowledge contest from a "lug" in *Letter*, he tells her she's "a pretty damn funny kind of a girl," and the taunt bothers her.

A tomboy, Rose Rita fights with Woody Mingo in *Figure*, and Lewis is too timid to help (33). Although she has attended one funeral at the Catholic church in New Zebedee (158), the tone of the passage suggests that she is not Catholic.

At the end of *Figure*, Mrs. Zimmermann gives her a magic nasal inhalator (143). In the summer of 1950, she refuses to be a girl scout or campfire girl (*Letter*, 3). Early in *Letter* she thinks of herself as skinny and homely and wishes she were a boy (6-7). Rose Rita has a lively imagination and reads a lot, including *Treasure Island* and Nancy Drew mysteries.

Unlike Lewis, she easily rises to demanding occasions: in *Letter*, she drives the Plymouth when Mrs. Zimmermann is taken ill and does well enough until a witch frightens her. The car winds up in a clump of juniper bushes (64 ).

Bright and inventive, Rose Rita makes up lies on short notice both in *Figure* and *Letter* to cover problems (taking the amulet away from Lewis in the first book and getting help when Mrs. Zimmermann disappears in the second one). She can get carried away, however; in *Letter*, she exaggerates the trip to the Upper Peninsula (to Lewis) so much that Mrs. Zimmermann complains she ought to write books. Later, Rose Rita tells Mrs. Sipes that she is an orphan, her parents having died after having been bitten by a rabid beaver (*Letter*, 118-120).

For a while she uses the alias "Rosemary Potts" in *Letter*. She is briefly put under a death spell by Gert Bigger in that book. It involves silver dollars placed over her eyes and a funeral pall being spread over her (149-158). The appearance of the demon Asmodai disturbs and breaks the spell (presumably because the demon turns Mrs. Bigger into a tree).

According to John's friends and relatives, Rose Rita was based on a real friend of John's from Marshall, also named Rose Rita.

**Potts, Rosemary.** The alias Rose Rita uses when she is with the Sipes family in *Letter*.

**Pruny, Pruny Face**. One of Jonathan Barnavelt's pet names for Mrs. Zimmermann, reminiscent of "Prunella," a name Emerson Eells applies to his sister in *The Mansion in the Mist*.

**Public Library.** Lewis likes to do his homework here. It is a pleasant place to work, with old scarred tables and green-shaded lamps. Lewis goes there a lot, just to browse or to look things up. Closing time for the library is 9:00 p.m. (*Figure*, 80). The library has glass doors. Miss Geer, an old lady with arthritis, is the librarian and is fond of Lewis (82).

**Ridpath, John Clark**. Author of *History of the World*, a (real) book Lewis is familiar with. He knows what Napoleon looks like because of a picture from this volume. See Waterloo.

**Ring of King Solomon**. In *Letter*, Mrs. Zimmermann's cousin Oley believes he has found this. Mrs. Bigger steals it from Oley's house. According to the *Cyclopædia of Jewish Antiquities*, the ring gives the bearer the powers of teleportation, sorcery, divination, and changing himself and his enemies into animals. The bearer may become a black dog; his enemies take various forms.

The information purportedly comes from Flavius Josephus (*Letter*, 151), though Josephus' description of it is different and belongs not to the era of Solomon, but to the Medieval period.

The ring's greatest power is that it can summon the demon Asmodai, who can grant long life and great beauty–though Asmodai is a tricky devil. Rose Rita briefly possesses the ring and almost uses it to make a wish (apparently to be transformed into a boy); Mrs. Zimmermann appears just in time to prevent this (165-168).

Mrs. Zimmermann isn't sure that the ring actually was King Solomon's, but its powers suggest it might be. She thinks Vikings may have brought it from the Old World, because she has found iron rings like the ones Vikings used in breastplates in a cupboard in Oley's kitchen—presumably, he discovered these on his farm. Mrs. Zimmermann is not affected by the ring's evil attraction because she is happy being just what she is, she says, and she melts it down and then sinks it in Little Traverse Bay (183-186).

**Roads**. Several are named in the books.

Twelve-Mile Road runs into Wilder Creek Road, which leads into New Zebedee (presumably from the south—*House*, 96). At the intersection of the two roads are a white wooden church with smeary stained-glass windows, a Civil War cannon, and a general store with a window on which SALADA is stenciled. An iron bridge made of crisscrossing black girders takes Wilder Creek Road over the creek itself. The bridge is floored with boards and was built by Elihu Clabbernong.

The Homer Road is a winding country road between New Zebedee and the very small town of Homer. One drives south on the Homer Road to get to Mrs. Zimmermann's cottage on Lyon Lake (*Figure*, 76). At one point outside of town, Homer Road runs through Eldridge Corners, where there is a gas station. It then crosses the railroad tracks and comes into town (76).

U.S. Route 9 takes up at the fountain where Main Street leaves off and heads west. In *Letter*, Mrs. Zimmermann and Rose Rita take U.S. 12 to U.S. 131, then straight north through Grand Rapids. For a description of scenery, see pages 27-28.

**Roman galley**. Rose Rita and Lewis are making an intricate model of one in *Figure*. Lewis draws a picture of Duilius, the great Roman admiral, on the sail and he adds the motto *In hoc signo vinces*, copied from a Pall Mall cigarette package (48). The motto comes from the legend of Constantine's vision of the Cross, and it means "In this sign you will conquer." The vision led to Constantine's conversion to Christianity.

**"Rugbug."** A famous fox trot composed by Maxine Hollister. It is one of the tunes that Uncle Jonathan's magical parlor organ plays (*House*, 58). I have not been able to confirm this as a real song.

**Sandflies**. These pester Rose Rita while she and Mrs. Zimmermann are driving a back road near Ironwood on the Upper Peninsula in *Letter* (61).

**School**. When he is in the sixth grade, Lewis goes to school in "a tall old brick building with shaky wooden staircases." His classroom is on the second floor. The building is next door to the Episcopal Church, with a narrow alley between them (*Figure*, 34). Seventh and eighth grades are in Junior High. The junior-high kids go to school in a big black stone building next to the high school. They had lockers in the halls like the high-school kids, and they even had their own gym where they had Saturday-night dances (*Letter*, 6).

**Shellenberger, Dave.** One of the big wheels in Lewis's school. He and Tom Lutz are always the captains of the sports teams. In *Figure*, Dave is the captain of the football team that Lewis plays on when he beats up Woody Mingo (66).

**Sherlock Holmes.** Lewis is an admirer of Sherlock Holmes, though once Uncle Jonathan tells him he would make a better Watson (*House*, 28). On the Fourth of July, 1949, Jonathan gives Lewis a green-plaid Sherlock Holmes hat, which he loses to a bully (*Figure*, 6). Later Jonathan gives him a replacement. The "Witchfinder" fragment begins with Lewis and Jonathan in London, searching for the site of Sherlock Holmes's flat at 221-B Baker Street.

**Shops in New Zebedee.** Only a few are mentioned; one is Heemsoth's Rexall Drug Store (*House*, 5) on Main Street, which is where the bus stops, and where Lewis and Rose Rita sometimes go for Cokes (*Figure*, 111). Across from the drug store is a church tower with a clock and bell; the belfry is arched and the clock has a luminous face and iron numerals (*House*, 7). Another shop is Kresge's Ten Cent Store, also on Main Street (*Figure*, 6). On their trip north, Mrs. Zimmermann and Rose Rita stop at Big Rapids and visit an A&P for supplies (*Letter*, 28).

**Sin-and-Flesh Creek**. This intriguingly-named stream runs through Capharnaum County. It is bigger leaving New Zebedee than it is coming in, and Jonathan thinks its growth is caused by an underground stream that feeds into it (*House*, 59). There is a real Sin and Flesh Brook in Rhode Island that may be the basis for the name.

**Sipes, Agatha**. Known as "Aggie," she is about Rose Rita's age. She has long, straight dishwater-blonde hair, a long face, and dark eyebrows that curve upward in a sad, worried expression. She looks like the Jack of Clubs (*Letter*, 105-108). When Gert Bigger temporarily turns Mrs. Zimmermann into a chicken, Aggie's family takes Rose Rita in. Aggie believes in ghosts, witches, and magic spells, even though "you're not supposed to" (107). She is a farm girl with five brothers and one sister. Her room is flouncy, frilly, and pink, with a teddy bear in a rocking chair (126-127). She likes square dancing. Rose Rita sees her as a pretty straight arrow, but Aggie helps Rose Rita break into Bigger's Grocery.

**Sipes Family**. A farm family in the northern part of the Lower Peninsula of Michigan, it is made up of a father, mother, and seven children. Rose Rita stays with them for about one day when Mrs. Zimmermann is missing in *Letter*. Mrs. Sipes is no slouch; she doesn't for a moment buy Rose Rita's lie about her parents' dying from the effects of a rabid beaver's bite (113).

**Sipes, Leonard**. Brother of Agatha Sipes. He has dark hair, is skinny, and is sarcastic about Rose Rita's sad story regarding a rabid beaver (*Letter*, 118-119).

**Sipes, Mrs.** Mother of Agatha Sipes. She is kindly, nosy, and looks like her daughter. Rose Rita's lies don't fool her (*Letter*, 113).

**Spanish Armada**. Jonathan creates an illusion of the Armada for Lewis on Halloween Night, 1948 (*House*, 173-176).

**Stevenson, Robert Louis**. Author of *Treasure Island*. Rose Rita reads the classic pirate novel in *Letter*.

**St. Ignace**. The town in the Upper Peninsula of Michigan where a ferry takes passengers across the Straits of Mackinac (*Letter*, 84).

**Streets in New Zebedee. Main Street** is the chief thoroughfare. It runs east and west; at the eastern end is East End Park. Nearby is the Civil War Monument, a fantastic stone structure shaped like an artist's easel. Each of the joints and corners of the easel has a soldier or sailor standing on it, and the flat part is covered with the names of Capharnaum County residents who died in the Civil War. A small stone arch nearby is the Civil War Monument Annex, with names the carvers couldn't fit on the main monument (*House*, 23-24). East End Park is a real park in Marshall; the Civil War Monument as described in the book is imaginary. At the western end of Main Street is a fountain that spumes "a crystal willow tree from within a circle of marble columns." At night this fountain is lit and changes color from red to orange to yellow to blue to green to red (144). The fountain is in the middle of a traffic circle, and at Christmas a Nativity scene is erected in the little circular park. These details are true of the circle and fountain on Michigan Avenue in Marshall. Main Street is only three blocks long. The G.A.R. Hall is at one end, presumably the eastern one, near the Civil War Monument (*Figure*, 8). Marshall's G.A.R. Hall, now a museum, is directly east of East End Park on Michigan Avenue.

**Green Street** leads off Main, just across from the alley between the Episcopal Church and the elementary school. Green Street eventually intersects with **High Street** (*Figure,* 8).

**Mansion Street**, a long, tree-lined avenue, leads off Main from near the drug store. Rose Rita Pottinger and her parents live at 39 Mansion Street, and somewhere on the street is the Masonic Temple, a tall, four-story brick building with a dark archway in the front (*Figure,* 117). Streets and the Masonic Temple are radically relocated from the Marshall originals, but they exist.

**High Street** leads off Mansion, and at the top of the hill, Jonathan Barnavelt and Lewis live in Number 100.

**Spruce Street** is where the waterworks are; Jonathan lived there prior to 1943. Actual waterworks are in a heavily industrial/RR area, no residences anywhere close.

**U.S. Route 9** takes up at the fountain, where Main Street leaves off, and leads west out of town. On all these streets, the city limits signs are square and made of tin.

**Superstitions.** Oddly, the only one elaborated on is "If you drop a knife, then company is coming" (*Figure,* 75). There are many childhood superstitions, and one feels that Lewis and Rose Rita should know more.

**Telephone numbers**. At first New Zebedee is not a dial system. The operator asks, "Number, please?" when you lift the receiver. Bishop Barlow Realtors: 865 (mentioned in *House*). Jonathan Barnavelt: 865 (*Letter,* 97). Either the numbers changed between 1948 and 1950, or John Bellairs made a mistake, or he played a joke.

**Terminus Movers, Inc**. The moving company that moves Mrs. Izard into the Hanchett house, across High Street from Jonathan's house (*House,* 108). The name is rather ominous.

**Texaco.** A former cat, now a skeleton buried in Jonathan Barnavelt's back yard. Lewis gains magical knowledge of it and its former owner during Jonathan's magical eclipse of the moon in *House,* 58.

**Three-cent Lucky Piece**. This belonged to Walter Finzer, who lost it to Grampa Barnavelt . It is smaller and thinner than a dime. On one side is the Roman numeral III, and on the other a six-pointed star with a striped shield inside it. "United States of America" is stamped around the outside of the star, and under the bottom point is the date 1859 (*Figure,* 25). The coin is a real one, and examples of it bring high prices from collectors. Mrs. Zimmermann cannot detect its magic, but it is in fact a powerful amulet. Lewis tests it and decides to wear it. It gives him vivid dreams of battle and victory and helps him imagine that he is Blackbeard the Pirate or Tom Corbett, Space Cadet. See "Finzer, Walter."

**Ticonderoga No. 2 pencil**. The kind Lewis uses.

**Time frames of the novels**. Unlike later works in the series, the first three novels cover specific date ranges.

*House with a Clock in its Walls* begins a few weeks before school starts, in August, 1948, and ends in April, 1949. Lewis is ten years old.

*The Figure in the Shadows* begins in September, 1949. Lewis and Rose Rita have been friends since April, 1949 (5). The action ends just after Christmas, 1949.

*Letter, the Witch, and the Ring* begins in the summer of 1950 and ends a few weeks later.

**Tobacco**. Jonathan's favorite pipe blend is "Turkoman's Terror," an imaginary brand (*House,* 51). Mrs. Zimmermann at first smokes a magical brand of cigars she materializes from thin air. Later in the series, both of them give up smoking.

**Umbrella, Magic**. Mrs. Zimmermann's wand is disguised as an ordinary, rather shabby black umbrella with a crystal as the handle. When she uses it, it transforms into a tall staff with a bright purple star filling the globe, which becomes the crown of the staff. It is effectively destroyed in a magic struggle at the climax of *Figure.*

**Upper Peninsula of Michigan**. Mrs. Zimmermann and Rose Rita plan an auto tour there in the summer of 1950 (*Letter,* 17). Among the sights they see are Mackinac Island, Tahquamenon Falls, the Pictured Rocks, and the towns of Ishpeming, Germfask, and Ontonagon (44-45), all real.

*Venio.* "I come"; the Latin message that Lewis receives several times from the mysterious stranger in *Figure.* It first appears on pages 28-30 on a postcard delivered at midnight. Next it shows up on a sheet of lined notebook paper that Lewis finds one afternoon on his way to Rose Rita's house. In a minor narrative slip-up, the stranger begins to approach before Lewis summons him.

**Waterloo, Battle of.** An illusion of the battle, not quite a re-creation, is created by Jonathan Barnavelt for the amusement of Lewis, on

Halloween Night, 1948. Since it is an illusion, Jonathan can switch events and let the French win for a change, upsetting the Duke of Wellington to no end. The full description of the illusion and the historical figures associated with it are in *House* (78-80).

**Wellington.** Commander of the British forces at Waterloo.

**Wessel, Dr.** An optometrist in New Zebedee. He keeps comics in his waiting room, along with a hat rack. He doesn't like his patients to wear beanies during their examinations (*Figure*, 108-109).

**Wilder Creek.** A stream on the outskirts of New Zebedee, separating Wilder Creek Park and Oakridge Cemetery (q.v.). A bridge built by Elihu Clabbernong (q.v.) crosses it. The creek eventually empties into Lake Michigan (*Figure*, 102). See also Roads.

**Wilder Creek Park.** A park near (south of?) New Zebedee. Uncle Jonathan remembers eclipsing the moon there on the night of April 30 (Walpurgis Night), 1932 in *House* (51). The cemetery is on a ridge on the far side of the park from town. If it existed, this park would be roughly in the same place as the street where John was born. The cemetery is real, though the ridge it is on is not as high as John recalled; the town is not visible from any point in the real cemetery.

**Zimmermann cottage.** In addition to her house and the farm she inherits from a cousin, Mrs. Zimmermann owns a summer cottage on Lyon Lake, between New Zebedee and Homer, by way of Homer Road (*Figure*, 76). The last few pages of *Letter* take place at the cottage (180). If there is a Jonathan/Lewis scene added to *Ghost*, as discussed with Dial, this might be a good location for it.

**Zimmermann, Florence Helene.** Jonathan Barnavelt's next-door neighbor on High Street. Mrs. Zimmermann is a witch (and better at magic than Jonathan). She has gray hair and favors baggy purple dresses. She is a little over 60 in *House*. She wears eyeglasses (*House*, 38) and carries a silver pocket watch on a long chain (40). She loves the color purple, and it shows up in her furnishings, her clothing, and even her ink and stationery (*Letter*, 179-180).

Mrs. Zimmermann wears a non-magical ring with a purple stone in it (*House*, 156), which she raps on things when she is trying to think (*Figure*, 124; *Letter*, 43). The ring is a trinket that she got at Coney Island (*Letter*, 43). She smokes long, twisted cigars, which she keeps in a silver case. She snaps lighted matches right out of the air, then makes them vanish to avoid littering. She often cooks breakfast for Jonathan and Lewis, because Jonathan is a terrible cook. She herself loves to cook, especially desserts and treats, and she also bottles her own prune brandy (*House,* 124). At night, especially after parties, Mrs. Zimmermann drinks hot milk to get to sleep, though she hates the taste (*Letter,* 10).

Mrs. Zimmermann was apparently well-traveled as a young lady; she visited Europe (and spent at least a full year in France) before World War I, and in 1922 she received her doctorate in magic from the University of Göttingen in Germany. At some point, she lived in Chicago for a while (*Letter,* 72).

She married Honus Zimmermann, who has passed away, leaving Mrs. Zimmermann a widow—in 1950, she has been widowed for some years (*Letter,* 54). However, she says she "was happy as a wife, and now I'm happy as a widow. So try different things. See what you like best" (54).

After 1950, Mrs. Zimmermann drives a boxy green 1950 Plymouth Cranbrook that she special-ordered from the dealer (the color was a mistake, but she was too lazy to insist that the car be re-painted purple) that Rose Rita names Bessie (*Letter,* 26-27).

Mrs. Zimmermann likes card games and is a whiz at pinball (*Letter,* 28). She loves to spend hours shopping in junk shops, and sometimes she must be dragged away by force (*Letter,* 45).

When she is working magic, she wields a tall black staff with a clear globe on top; inside the globe burns a magenta star. When her magic is not at work, the staff becomes an umbrella with a crystal knob as the handle, though a tiny magenta spark always lurks deep within the crystal (*House,* 155). The umbrella itself looks quite ordinary, a small black umbrella with rust streaks running down it (*Figure,* 124). Her wand is shattered in a deadly encounter with an evil spirit in *Figure* (175), and almost all her power goes with it. She says she cannot re-enchant a replacement umbrella that Jonathan gives her for Christmas of 1949, and says she is "back in the bush leagues" of magic, except for minor tricks like snapping matches out of the air (*Letter,* 18).

She gives Rose Rita the first magical item she created, a nasal inhalator (PEERLESS*Reg U.S. / Pat. Off / NASAL INHALATOR) that glows purple, like phosphorescent chalk. It is glass with a gold metal cap, and was made to protect children from evil creatures; it also has healing powers (*Figure,* 140-141). It is based on a brand of Benzedrine nasal inhaler, though since it was already an antique in the book, it undoubtedly had no medicine left inside it—a good thing, because Benzedrine was an amphetamine and became a controlled substance in 1970.

Mrs. Zimmermann is fluent in a dozen languages and can understand a few dozen more, including Bengali, Finno-Ugric, Basque, Old High Norse, and Geeze. She is especially adept at comprehending and casting magical spells in different tongues— each language imparts its own spin to the spells she uses.

Her final practical exam for her doctorate at the University of Göttingen included the identification by touch of various objects, and she had to determine whether they were magical (*Figure,* 27). Her doctoral dissertation is entitled *Amulets* and is an exhaustive study of the varieties and properties of magical items.

In the summer of 1950, Mrs. Zimmermann inherits her cousin Oley Gunderson's farm (*Letter,* 14). Later that summer, Gert Bigger briefly uses the Ring of Solomon to turn Mrs. Zimmermann into a white chicken. The spell is temporary and lasts for about twenty-four hours. Once recovered, Mrs. Zimmermann uses a powerful magic illusion to persuade Rose Rita to give up the Ring (168-169). Though lacking magical ability—at least she is weaker than she was before the events of *Figure*—she can still cast an illusion spell to make herself look "pretty darned terrifying."

Late in *The Letter, the Witch, and the Ring,* she says that not having her magic power is a relief (185). She explains to Rose Rita that the lure of the magic ring did not affect her because she's happy just being herself (187). Note: Mrs. Zimmermann may be trying to comfort Rose Rita and thereby overstating her contentment. In the *Ghost* manuscript, she obviously misses her magic, but the question of whether she recharges her power is never clearly answered; this has to be addressed. The groundwork for a possible restoration of powers is laid, but the conclusion doesn't touch on whether or not it works.

Editor's information is that John intended to restore her powers, but end of book will need a complete revision to clarify. Mrs. Z. Is based on two real people, according to Marshall informants, a teacher John liked and an older relative, both deceased.

**Zimmermann, Honus**. The deceased husband of Florence. We know little about him. He probably had no magical abilities—none are hinted at in the book. John may have named the character after Honus Wagner (1872-1955), a famous baseball player, because Bellairs was a great baseball fan. Conjecture: Honus Zimmermann died sometime between 1940 and 1943, before Jonathan moved next door to Mrs. Zimmermann. When we meet her, she has been a widow for some years.

**Zimmerman house**. A two-story house next to Jonathan's mansion on High Street, Mrs. Zimmermann's place is simply a bungalow with a screened-in front porch. It is full of strange things, and most of them are purple (including rugs, wallpaper, the staircase runner, the toilet paper, and the bath soap). Mrs. Zimmermann obviously attracted admiration from artists when she was young; among her pictures are a surrealistic painting of a dragon done for her specially by Odilon Redon (*House*, 61) and a painting of a room in which everything is purple, done by H. Matisse and given by him to Mrs. Zimmermann during her visit to Paris just before World War I (*Letter*, 19). The *Ghost* manuscript adds a Monet, a small painting of purple water lilies. In Marshall, a house across the street, not adjoining, the Cronin mansion is sometimes identified as hers.

**Zimmermann niece**. She lives in Muskegon and for years kept the magic nasal inhalator before sending it back to Mrs. Zimmermann (*Figure*, 141).

◆ ◆ ◆

## Chapter 2: *The Ghost in the Mirror*
### By John Bellairs, Completed by Brad Strickland
### (Dial Books for Young Readers, 1993)

This is the fourth book in the Lewis Barnavelt/Rose Rita Pottinger series, and the first one completed by Brad Strickland following the death of John Bellairs. It is the second Bellairs book to feature time travel (done by magical means, not by using technology like a time machine) and one of many of John's works to deal with ghosts and the supernatural. Like *The Letter, the Witch, and the Ring,* it was mainly a solo adventure of Rose Rita's. Lewis does make an appearance in the last chapter, though.

◆ ◆ ◆

*Summary:*

The time is the summer of 1951, the place New Zebedee. A year and a half after the events of *The Figure in the Shadows,* the good witch Mrs. Florence Zimmermann has become depressed. Though she saved the day in the climax of that adventure, the cost was great: She has lost almost all of her magic, although, like Jonathan, she can at least still create magical illusions. As this story begins, Mrs. Zimmermann has been seeing strange portents and omens in her house, focusing on a particular mirror and always appearing in the middle of the night.

Rose Rita, like her elderly friend, is upset and feeling blue. Uncle Jonathan and Lewis are off on a trip to Europe, and though Jonathan invited both Rose Rita and Mrs. Zimmermann to come along, around the first of June Rose Rita fractured her ankle and couldn't go. Kowing how upset Rose Rita was, Mrs. Zimmermann stayed home to keep her company.

After keeping the visions she sees in the mirror to herself for many days, at last Mrs. Zimmermann admits to Rose Rita that something eerie is going on—eerie but not evil. The friendly witch tells Rose Rita that she thinks the things she sees in the mirror are related to the late Granny Wetherbee, who initiated a young Florence into the study of magic.

Weeks pass, and the ghost of Granny appears in the mirror and asks Florence to travel to the place where she—Granny—was born to set right an ancient evil. That place is in rural Pennsylvania, and when the time comes, Rose Rita, her ankle now out of its cast, goes with her. As they drive toward a tunnel in the Cumberland Mountains of Pennsylvania, Rose Rita feels a sense of dread—with good reason.

Mrs. Zimmermann's car speeds into the tunnel in the middle of summer—and comes out on the other side in the depths of a snowy winter. It also plows into a snowdrift. Worse, there is no sign of the tunnel or the highway—both have vanished. The two friends, who did not pack winter clothes, struggle through the snow until a kind farmer and his daughter give them a ride in their wagon to a farmhouse, where they learn the year is no longer 1951, but 1828. Somehow in traveling through the tunnel, they have gone back in time.

Soon they discover the problem that they have been sent back to deal with: the Weiss family, who are Pennsylvania Dutch, are facing wicked rumors about their practicing dark magic and are on the verge of being evicted from their farm near Stonebrook, Pennsylvania. As Mrs. Zimmermann tries to help, though, she suffers a magical attack and memory loss. It will be up to Rose Rita to try to discover the villain behind the evil plot to evict the Weiss family.

◆ ◆ ◆

*Behind the Scenes:*

This was the first Bellairs manuscript I completed. Toby Sherry, who had been John's editor, worked very closely with me as I added material to what John had done, occasionally (and mostly in minor ways) tweaking what he had written so the new material would fit in. It was a task I took seriously, and sometimes I felt a little daunted and a little sad. At that point I had never visited Marshall, Michigan, but I closely studied the first three books in the Barnavelt series (the first chapter in this guidebook are the preliminary notes I made to get ready to write *Ghost*), and I tried not to violate anything that John had established in the initial trilogy.

Sometimes, though, I did make requested changes in the manuscript, though with some reluctance. As Mrs. Zimmermann drives them toward a tunnel in the Cumberland Mountains of Pennsylvania, Rose Rita looks ahead with fear. John Bellairs had written, "To Rose Rita the entrance of the tunnel was forbidding—it might as well have been the yawning mouth of hell." The publisher thought that was too strong (though in an earlier book, Lewis had cursed in stronger language) and my editor told me to cut the sentence or change it. Not wanting to drop it entirely, I softened it: "To Rose Rita the entrance of the tunnel was forbidding—it might as well have been the yawning mouth a tomb."

I remember a few puzzlements I had involving references in the Barnavelt series that were unfamiliar to me. For example, John mentioned a sign on a store that just read "SALADA." I had no idea what that was, nor did anyone I asked. Later, I discovered it was a brand of tea that was popular in the Midwest, but unknown here in Georgia. Since then, the brand seems to have expanded into our supermarkets. I like to think that John's mention of it helped spur interest.

Mrs. Zimmermann's car is a Plymouth Cranbrook. Not being a car person, I asked a friend to help me with that one, and he produced not only photos, but a model he had made of a 1950 Plymouth Cranbrook, which turned out to be a magisterial, dignified-looking automobile. It was even the proper color for the book. Thanks to the late Thomas F. Deitz for that one.

A small slip-up came when the jacket designers didn't get the word to add my name to the cover, but that didn't upset me. I did get a writing credit on the title page, so my work was credited along with that John Bellairs and Edward Gorey—great company.

This book, alone of the series, bears no dedication. John had not submitted one—that usually came last—and I didn't feel it was my place to presume. It really should have been dedicated to Toby Sherry, the editor who had worked with John on so many books and who for a long time was my editor at Dial as well. I salute her here, anyway. After all these years, she is still one of our good friends, and whenever we visit New York, we try to see her.

One high point came after my editor asked for a spooky scene to be added at a point where the action lagged. I invented Rose Rita's discovery of a dangerous magic book. If one begins to read it, the reader is unable to tear his or her eyes away until the book destroyed the reader's mind and possibly ensnared the person's soul. Rose Rita must think hard and fast in a dangerous situation.

Edward Gorey, who remains the best-known artist to illustrate John's books, received my initial uncorrected manuscript—time was tight—and chose that scene for the book jacket's front cover, and on the back cover he illustrated one of John's scenes, Rose Rita fleeing from a nightmare army of the dead. When I saw the book jacket for the first time, I admit I wept a little.

◆ ◆ ◆

## *The Ghost in the Mirror:* People, Places, and Things

**Albertus Magnus.** Also known as Albertus of Cologne and St. Albert the Great, Albertus (1193-1280 AD) was a Dominican friar famed for his great learning. He was a prolific writer, leaving behind books on many subjects, including alchemy and astrology. In *Ghost*, Grampa Drexel consults his books for information about magic mirrors (a subject Albertus in real life did not seem to cover).

**Amnesia.** Mrs. Zimmermann suffers a magical attack when an unknown evil force seizes control of her mirror. Afterwards, she has lost her memory. Grampa Drexel treats her for this.

**April 1.** According to Pennsylvania Dutch legend, this is the unluckiest day of the year. On April 1, evil hex magicians are at their most powerful. Mrs. Zimmermann recalls that on April 1, 1828, something terrible happened to the Weiss family.

**Aziel.** An Enochian demon. Enochian was a private language created by Dr. John Dee and Edward Kelley, who recorded a list of angelic and demonic powers in books written in that language. In their system Aziel was the demon who guarded hidden treasures. In *Ghost*, Grampa Drexel finds his symbol engraved on the back of Mrs. Zimmermann's mirror and realizes that it was created by a sorcerer who desired to use an *erdspiegel,* an "earth mirror," to locate hidden treasure. See "Erdspiegel."

**Barnavelt, Jonathan.** He and Lewis are off-stage for much of the novel, traveling in Europe. They do appear in the final chapter, where they hear the fantastic tale of the time-travel adventure and hint that they, too, have a story of mystery and magic to tell.

**Barnavelt, Lewis.** Lewis and his Uncle Jonathan are off on a long European vacation (see *Vengeance of the Witch-Finder*) for most of the story. They both make a late appearance in the last chapter, where they learn about the adventure Mrs. Zimmermann and Rose Rita have been through.

**Barns:** On the drive to Pennsylvania Dutch country, Rose Rita notices that barns with painted ads on the sides (one for Mail Pouch Chewing Tobacco) give way to red barns with hex symbols painted on every wall. Mrs. Zimmermann explains these are to ward off bad luck or evil magic. By the way, companies used to offer to paint farmers' barns for free if they would allow an ad on a side visible from a roadway. Tobacco products, coal, beer, soft drinks, and tourist attractions (among other things) were advertised this way. I don't remember ever seeing a sign on a barn reading "Chew Mail Pouch" (and I would have been baffled if I had), but I do recall many, many barns telling motorists to "See Rock City!"

**Baseball:** Both Mrs. Zimmermann and Rose Rita are fans. They often listen to Detroit Tigers games on the radio. At a crucial moment in the story, they are listening to a game between the Boston Red Sox and the Cleveland Indians that is tied and has gone into extra innings. In the sixteenth inning, a player named Clyde Vollmer makes a memorable home run. This was based on a real game, played on July 28, 1951.

**Bessie.** Mrs. Zimmermann's pet name (courtesy of Rose Rita) for her 1950 Plymouth Cranbrook automobile. It is green—she ordered a purple one, but the company made a mistake—until eventually she magically redoes it in her favorite color.

**Braucherei.** In hex magic, this is positive, healing, good magic. A *braucher* is a good sorcerer, as opposed to a hex witch or *hexmeister.*

**Brunning, Mr.** In 1828, he is the Weiss family's regular pastor. Mrs. Weiss tells a story of how one winter he was absent and his replacement, not being used to Pennsylvania winters, slipped on ice and broke his leg.

**Capharnaum County Agricultural Fair.** Comes to the New Zebedee Athletic Fields every fall. One ride is the Alpine Adventure, a toboggan-themed roller coaster.

**Cottage Rock.** An enormous, tall boulder that marks the edge of the Weiss farm. Rose Rita finds a dangerous, cursed item near it.

**Circle, magic.** A magic circle drawn on the ground or floor can protect a magician inside it from outside spells. Rose Rita draws one when she and Heinrich Weiss go to confront the villain. Generally the circle will contain a pentacle (five-pointed star) and magic words or symbols.

**Crystal spheres.** Grampa Drexel is a *braucher*, a good magician, who creates these spheres—clear though sometimes colorful crystal balls—and charges them with positive magic. He gives Rose Rita one that, he says, might help Mrs. Zimmermann recover her lost magical powers.

**Deutschmacher's Motel:** Mrs. Zimmermann and Rose Rita stay here one night on their extended trip to Pennsylvania for a game of chess, relaxation, and exposition. It was a motel that offered separate cabins for the guests, and it did serve a hearty Pennsylvania Dutch breakfast.

**Dienst, Edgar.** A young man from a town some distance away from Steinbrücke. He courted and married the eldest Weiss daughter, Trinka, when she was eighteen years old (about four years earlier than the story).

**Donniker Treasure.** During the Revolutionary War, the town of Donniker, Pennsylvania, collected gold to support General Washington's troops. The gold was entrusted to three men, including Heinrich Weiss, the father of Hermann Weiss. Unfortunately, Hessian troops tracked down the three and hanged two of them. Heinrich was imprisoned by the British and died before the war ended. However, he did manage to smuggle out a letter he had written in English, not German, with encoded clues to lead to the place where he and his friends hid the treasure. Although everyone, even Hermann Weiss, thinks the old man was insane and the letter is meaningless, Henrich's grandson and namesake—the ten-year-old Heinrich Weiss—is sure that if he could find the treasure, he could solve all his family's problems. Rose Rita promises to help.

**Drexel, Grampa.** In 1828, he is Mrs. Weiss's stepfather, who lives with the family. Frail, elderly, and not in the best of health, he is the victim of rumors in the area that call him a hex witch who practices evil magic. In truth, he is a good magician. He does know some helpful and harmless spells, and when Mrs. Zimmermann desperately needs help, he offers it.

**Erdspiegel.** In hex magic, an "earth-mirror," a mirror that can locate treasures or reveal hidden things. Grampa Drexel identifies Mrs. Zimmerman's mirror as one of these, although she had never known that before the time-travel incident.

*Fraktur.* An elaborate, highly decorative style of handwriting. The secret to finding the Donniker treasure is encoded in this kind of script, written by the first Heinrich Weiss in the days of the American Revolution.

**Frolic.** In Pennsylvania Dutch territory, a frolic was a country dance. When Hilda and Rose Rita talk about dances and frolics, Rose Rita remembers a humiliating time when she dressed up for a school dance, but no boy—not even Lewis—asked her to dance even once.

**Fuller's Hill.** A hill outside of Stonebridge, PA. In John Bellairs's manuscript, it had no name. I named it after my friend and cowriter on several non-Bellairs books, the late Thomas E. Fuller.

**Games:** Mrs. Zimmermann and Rose Rita play checkers, backgammon, and chess. Mrs. Zimmerman is an especially wily chess player and hard to beat.

**"Gold-Bug, The"** by Edgar Allan Poe. Rose Rita recalls this treasure-hunting story and its coded message when she and Heinrich try to decode a clue to the Donniker Treasure's location.

**Grace Lutheran Church.** In New Zebedee. In 1951, the pastor was the Reverend Bunsen.

**Harrisburg, PA.** Mr. Weiss has a brother who lives near this town. The Weiss family contemplates moving there to get away from their troubles, though the move would bankrupt them.

**Helmholtz.** One winter the Reverend Mr. Helmholtz temporarily replaced the Weiss family's regular pastor, Mr. Brunning. Unfortunately, Pastor Helmholtz promptly slipped on the ice on Fuller's Hill and broke his leg.

**Hex doll.** A cloth, wooden, or wax effigy of a person created by an evil magician to curse the victim. It is like a voodoo doll in that sense. Hilda Weiss believes some evil wizard or witch may have cursed her ailing Grampa Drexel with such a doll.

**Hex magic:** *Hexerei,* as Mrs. Zimmermann explains it, is Pennsylvania Dutch magic. An evil hex witch put curses on people, leading to misfortune or death. "Hex witch," by the way, did not imply that the magician was a woman—a hex witch might also be male. Hex signs, colorful symmetrical designs, were counter-charms against hexes (curses) and the Pennsylvania Dutch decorated and protected their barns with them. Good sorcerers were called *brauchers,* and they were most often, but not always, male (see *"Braucherei"*). Their magic concerned itself with healing and helping those in trouble.

**Hockendorf family.** Neighbors of the Weiss family, they are suspicious and fearful of Grampa Drexel and are among the local people who want to drive the Weisses out.

*Inner Sanctum.* An old-time radio show, very spooky. Mr. Pottinger likes to listen to it, and Rose Rita recalls that its plots often dealt with amnesia.

**Kleinwald, Mrs.** A neighbor of the Weiss family. When Rose Rita speaks to her, the woman seems to despise the Weisses, and especially Grampa Drexel, whom she calls an evil wizard.

**Mirror, Magic.** A wall mirror that hangs above a bookcase in Mrs. Zimmermann's living room, it is mahogany framed and rectangular, about eighteen inches by two feet. Though an ordinary mirror, it becomes a means by which the witch Granny Wetherbee (long dead) can somehow communicate with Mrs. Zimmermann.

**Mount Kidron Road.** In 1828, an unpaved country road in rural Pennsylvania. By 1951 it has become a modern paved highway.

**Mummix.** A Pennsylvania Dutch stew with beef and potatoes. Rose Rita is initially put off by the name, but she finds it's really very tasty.

**Nebby.** A mule belonging to the Weiss family. He is dark brown and always looks grumpy.

**Niklaus.** The Weiss family horse, he is a sturdy, handsome chestnut gelding.

**Nuttenhaus.** The Weiss family lawyer, who tells them there is no law to protect them against hateful gossip.

**Pennsylvania Dutch:** Mrs. Zimmermann explains that they are not actually Dutch, but of Germanic descent. She talks about their origins and customs as she and Rose Rita drive toward the town of Stonebrook, Pennsylvania. Later, when living with the Weiss family, Rose Rita gets some first-hand information about them, their beliefs, and their traditions.

**Pennybaker, Otto.** Mrs. Zimmermann says he was her first boyfriend when she was about Rose Rita's age. The two of them used to go sledding on Fuller's Hill near Stonebridge, PA, when Mrs. Zimmermann visited as a teen.

**Pilcher, Mrs. (Zina).** A neighbor of the Weiss family, a chubby, innocent-looking woman. She seems friendly when Rose Rita first meets her, but she refuses to talk about hexes or hex magic. I gave her the first name Zina, but at some point, the editor took it out.

**Pottinger, Mr. and Mrs.** Rose Rita's parents. Though Mr. Pottinger has been known to call Mrs. Zimmermann "the town screwball," they feel sorry because their daughter missed the trip to Europe with Lewis and Uncle Jonathan, and they give permission for Rose Rita to join Mrs. Zimmermann on a trip to Pennsylvania after Rose Rita's ankle has healed.

**Pottinger, Rose Rita.** At 14, she is a tall, gawky girl with thick glasses and straight black hair. Though she is still wearing her beanie with cartoon buttons pinned to it, along with jeans and sweatshirts, she is beginning to want to dress up now and then. She secretly wishes she were prettier. In *Ghost,* she breaks her ankle on the first of June and is in a cast for about six weeks, until the middle of July.

***Pow-Wows; or, the Long-Lost Friend.*** Usually called *The Long-Lost Friend,* this is a real book written by a Pennsylvania Dutch master magician, John George Hohman, and first printed in 1820. It contains ordinary recipes, formulas for folk medicines, prayers, directions for preparing magic potions and ointments, and magic spells that supposedly do things like making a person incapable of moving, to make the magician incapable of losing when playing cards, to create a magical shield against evil spells, and so on. Bellairs noted that Grampa Drexel owned this and other magical books. I added a short scene in which Rose Rita discovered the same books in the possession of another, unsuspected wizard.

*Shadow, The.* An old-time radio show featuring a hero who can make himself invisible, this was one of Mr. Pottinger's favorites. It is a mystery with weird overtones.

*Sixth and Seventh Books of Moses, The.* A book of magic. Grampa Drexel owns a copy, but warns Rose Rita not to read it, because it contains some evil spells as well as many good ones. This is a real volume, which claims to be an ancient work written by Moses. In fact, it first appeared in Germany during the 18th Century. It was a popular book among German immigrants and their descendants. See also "Pow-Wows."

**Stoltzfuss, Adolphus.** In 1828, a neighbor of the Weiss family. A widower whose farm is the smallest in the area, he is about seventy, tall, thin, and bad-tempered. He is furious because he thinks Mrs. Weiss's stepfather, Grampa Drexel, is a hex witch who has cast spells to burn buildings and change the weather.

**Stonebridge, PA.** The town where, back in 1898, Mrs. Zimmerman met the eighty-two-year-old Granny Wetherbee. Eventually the latter began to teach her the rudiments of magic. In 1828, the town was called Steinbrücke, which means "Stone bridge" in German.

*Time Machine, The.* Novel by H.G. Wells. Rose Rita has read it and thus knows a little bit about time travel.

**"To the Sons of Liberty."** A poem, supposedly by Henrich Weiss the elder, written in 1778 about the Revolutionary War. The verse contains a coded guide to where Weiss and his friends hid the Donniker Treasure. Since John Bellairs had not included a discovery of the treasure, and I didn't want to cut anything he had written, I made up the poem as a crucial clue.

*Treasure Island*, by Robert Louis Stevenson. Rose Rita has read this book and remembers its treasure map when she and Heinrich look for the Donniker Treasure.

**Umbrella, magic.** Mrs. Zimmermann's magic umbrella was destroyed in *Figure*. In this book, she creates a replacement.

**Weiss farm.** In 1828, a pleasant farm with a rambling two-story farmhouse and many outbuildings. Mrs. Zimmermann and Rose Rita are guests there for some time.

**Weiss siblings.** In 1828, Hermann and Susana Weiss have a large family: Heinrich, ten, is the youngest son; his sister Hilda is twelve, and then come the twins, Rebecca and Sarah, sixteen. There are also two older brothers, Jacob and Hans, and the eldest daughter, Trinka, is now in her early twenties, married to young Edgar Dienst and living away from the farm.

**Weiss, Heinrich.** In 1828, he is ten, the youngest of the Weiss children. Pale and jumpy and nervous, he reminds Rose Rita of her friend Lewis back home in New Zebedee. He knows of a rumored treasure supposedly hidden somewhere nearby and thinks if the Weiss family could find it, their troubles would be over.

**Weiss, Hermann.** In 1828, he is a struggling Pennsylvania Dutch farmer whose family is having terrible problems as the neighbors spread untrue rumors that they practice hex magic.

**Weiss, Hilda.** Twelve years old in 1828, she is blonde, anxious-looking, and frightened, deeply troubled about the nasty stories people have spread about her family. When Mrs. Zimmermann first sees Hilda, she remembers having glimpsed her face in the magic mirror.

**Weiss, Susanna.** In 1828, she is Hermann's wife. A portly woman with gray-blond hair, she is very talkative, asking ten or twelve questions at once. Rose Rita soon learns to pick out just one to answer.

**Wetherbee, Granny:** She has passed away long before 1951, but her spirit appears as a ghost in the mirror. She was already elderly when Mrs. Zimmermann was a girl. Granny was a witch who specialized in earth magic, including herbs, roots, and divining rods. Physically, she has a wrinkled-apple face, deep-set black eyes, wispy white eyebrows, pink cheeks, and pale downturned lips. Mrs. Zimmermann remembers her as having a sour temper but, under it, being a kind person. As the story goes on, we learn what turned her bad-tempered and the secret of her identity.

**Witchcraft trials:** Mrs. Zimmermann speaks about witch trials in Pennsylvania. One she mentions is the trial of Margaret Mattson, who in 1683 was tried for hexing (cursing) her neighbors. She was found not guilty of witchcraft but guilty of having a reputation as a witch. Mrs. Zimmermann says the most recent trial of an accused witch in Pennsylvania took place as late as 1949, but that is fictitious.

**Zimmermann house:** We pick up a few details. The guest-room bed has a comforter embroidered with violets, and on the wall is an original oil painting of purple water lilies done by Monet and given by him to Mrs. Zimmermann when she was in France in 1913. Mrs. Zimmermann's master bedroom is on the second floor. In it, Mrs. Zimmermann has a wind-up Westclox alarm clock with luminous hands.

**Zimmermann, Florence.** We learn that she is 64 years old and that she received her first instruction in the magical arts from a sour old woman she calls "Granny Wetherbee." Granny always called her "Florrie." In this book she is still smoking her thin cigars (cheroots). We learn that she began to study magic when she was about fifteen years old, long before she took graduate degrees in magical arts in Germany. She lived in France for two years, 1912-1913, and was widely acquainted with artists there. She is a retired schoolteacher and has a comfortable income. She had an older sister, Anna, wife of the lawyer Harold Crippen, who lived in Pennsylvania and whom she used to visit every year, but the sister passed away in 1939.

◆ ◆ ◆

**Division of Labor:**

John Bellairs normally wrote a complete rough draft of a novel, sent it to the editor, and began work on a new book. Commonly, his first drafts were sketchy and short (*The Secret of the Underground* Room is very close to a first draft, because John was ill at the time he revised it and lacked the energy to do his customary thorough revision). After a month or two, the editor would ask John to write a second draft, elaborating and expanding some scenes, incorporating suggestions and editorial corrections, and making sure plot points were all resolved. John relied on the editor to point out places where events needed to be explained or needed to pay off in some way and always obliged. He did not have that chance with this novel, because he passed away at his home in Haverhill, MA, on April 8, 1991, of a heart attack, not long after the publishers had received his manuscript.

Therefore, they called me in and asked me to do the revision that John would have done for himself. Since people wonder how much each of us wrote on the books I completed, this is the count for *Ghost:*

**Chapters 1-7:** These are almost all John's work, with me adding a few tweaks here and there, including one short scene (only a page or so) and a few scattered sentences making connections for later plot development. I probably did most of this writing to elaborate on the hidden treasure, to which John made one throwaway reference and which he never brought up again.

**Chapter 8:** Both John's and my writing figure in this chapter. A major concern was to deal with the hidden treasure. The editor suggested that we needed some baffling clue, so that once the characters understood its meaning they could quickly locate the treasure. I researched *fraktur* (the decorative Germanic calligraphy) and wrote the poem "To the Sons of Liberty" to plant this clue. From this point on, efforts to decipher the poem are my work, as is the later account of the treasure hunt.

**Chapter 9:** Almost all of Chapter 9 is by me; the description of the meal and Grampa Drexler's discussion of Aziel are by John . Rose Rita's encounter with the enchanted book at Cottage Rock are my additions. The editor wanted a spooky scene at that point of the book. Grampa Drexel's gift to Mrs. Zimmermann was prepared but never delivered to her (at least on the page), and the editor wanted to make sure that happened because it explains a crucial point of the novel.

**Chapter 10:** This is a combination. Because in John's first draft nothing was done about finding the treasure, I made Heinrich and Rose Rita's use of the magic spell and the mirror about that. In the original, they were just using the mirror to locate whoever was doing evil things to the family. The scene of them being trapped and the villain's reveal was the first time in John's manuscript that the villain showed up.

**Chapters 11-13:** These are a combination, but mostly my writing. Originally, in five manuscript pages Mrs. Zimmermann (acting alone) showed up, quickly dispatched the villain, Granny Wetherbee made her final appearance in the original mirror, and then Mrs. Zimmermann and Rose Rita rushed back to Bessie and saw that the vanished tunnel had reappeared. They drove through it, emerged in 1951, and Rose Rita said, "We're back. We're really and truly back!" and there the book abruptly ended in what is now Chapter 11.

However, that felt rushed and left several plot points dangling: Did Mrs. Zimmermann recover her magic powers? Did the Weiss family discover the treasure? Did their neighbors ever learn that someone else, not Grampa Drexel, had been hexing them, and did they forgive the family? The publisher wanted these questions answered.

I expanded Chapter 11 to make the confrontation between Mrs. Zimmermann and the villain more of a dangerous struggle. I dealt with the existence of two mirrors that were the same one—one from 1828 and one from 1951—and moved Granny Wetherbee's farewell to Chapter 12.

I wrote all the rest of Chapters 12 and 13 to wrap up the loose threads of the plot and bring Uncle Jonathan and Lewis into the book so readers could resolve the question of whether Mrs. Zimmermann's powers had been restored—and if so, how was that done? That involved Grampa Drexel's gift, a certain umbrella, and a knick-knack from a junk store.

In summary, Chapter 1 is all John's, and of the others, many chapters are 90% Bellairs, 10% Strickland, while others are reversed, and a couple are almost all by Strickland.

◆ ◆ ◆

## Chapter 3: *The Vengeance of the Witch-Finder*
### By John Bellairs, Completed by Brad Strickland
### (Dial Books for Young Readers, 1993)

As soon as I finished *The Ghost in the Mirror,* I began puzzling over the fragment of manuscript that John had left of "The Witch Finder," the fifth book in the New Zebedee series—though admittedly it didn't look as if it had much of New Zebedee in it. As usual, John had not prepared any kind of summary or outline, so we had two chapters, set not in New Zebedee but in England.

Aha! I saw what John was doing: He was telling the story of what happened to Jonathan and Lewis on their European trip *at the same time* that, back in America, Mrs. Zimmermann and Rose Rita were setting out on the adventure described in *The Ghost in the Mirror.* With clues from the first two chapters, I had to generate a plot and characters to people it. This was more of a challenge than polishing up *Ghost.*

As a means of linking the two novels, in the last chapters of *Witch-Finder,* I re-told the reunion scene that takes place when Rose Rita and Mrs. Zimmermann have returned from their jaunt to Pennsylvania (and the past) and Lewis and Jonathan from Europe. However, this time around, the narrative is more from Lewis's point of view. That might cause some readers to have a mild case of *déjà vu.* I have to say, though, that although the repetition of elements was my idea here—I wrote the relevant scene in each novel—it struck me as the kind of playful narrative experimentation that John enjoyed.

Anyway, I hope it is true to his style and his spirit and that it doesn't trouble readers. It was kindly intended.

◆ ◆ ◆

*Summary:*

What the first couple of chapters revealed: In the summer of 1951, Lewis and Uncle Jonathan are on an extended tour of Europe, but early in their journey they are in London, England. Jonathan treats Lewis, the

Sherlock Holmes fan, with a visit to Holmes's home territory, Baker Street. They meet a friendly British policeman, and Uncle Jonathan picks up an ancient Egyptian carving of a scarab beetle as a gift for Mrs. Zimmermann—though he says he really wishes his gift could be the return of his friendly neighbor's magic powers. Chapter two sees uncle and nephew on a train, bound for West Sussex, where Jonathan's "umpteenth cousin," Pelham Barnavelt, lives in a real English manor house. Unfortunately, World Wars I and II have left Pelham relatively poor, so he lives modestly. The prospect of staying in a British manor house excites Lewis, but when he sees the mostly empty, run-down structure, his excitement turns to shock. The last line is his reaction: "It looks so evil."

Working with that information, I wrote Chapters 3-15, inventing characters and throwing Lewis and Jonathan into a plot that pitted them against the spirit of an angry and unforgiving man who in his earthly life had been a seeker and destroyer of witches. Since Lewis had no foil—no Rose Rita character to talk and conspire with—Bertram Goodring, the son of Pelham's cheerful housekeeper/cook, takes that role. I tried to think of Bellairsian menaces, too, adding a sinister hedge maze and puzzles for the two boys to solve. And I knew I wanted to aim for a final chapter that reunited Jonathan and Lewis with Mrs. Zimmermann and Rose Rita.

And so the book emerged.

◆ ◆ ◆

*Behind the Scenes*:

The publishers and I went round and round seeking a good title. The manuscript was "The Witch Finder," which gave me a clue for the Big Bad, but that seemed flat, and publishers are leery of books with "witch" in the title—though this was a witch FINDER. Some we rejected: "The Mystery of Barnavelt Manor"; "The Sinister Spirit"; "The Return of the Witch-Finder"; "The Wrath of the Witch-Finder." Finally the editor suggested "The Revenge of the Witch-Finder" (the last two words picked up a hyphen somewhere and wouldn't let go of it). That was almost right, but to me "Vengeance" sounded more Bellairsian.

I tinkered with names. I don't know where John got "Pelham," but it irresistibly reminded me of Pelham Grenville Wodehouse—better known as P.G. Wodehouse, one of my favorite writers. In creating Mrs. Goodring's son, I used the name of one of Wodehouse's funniest characters, Bertram "Bertie" Wooster. Also, in the first two chapters the small town in West Sussex wasn't named—it was just "a small town" or "a village." I gave it the name "Dinsdale," from a Monty Python sketch involving a gangster named Dinsdale who is terrified of an imaginary giant hedgehog, Spiny Norman. Just a little inside joke, and all these years later I'm still waiting for someone to laugh at it.

Once more, Edward Gorey provided a deliciously spooky book jacket, with the front showing Lewis and Bertie on a midnight expedition to a mysterious, crypt-like structure and the back illustrating a terrifying nightmare scene of Lewis discovering the skeleton of his friend. I dedicated this book to my (and John's) literary agent Richard Curtis, who always was helpful in working out publishing details and was (and remains) a good friend.

Though one rather crabby review of the book complained that the whole first chapter was a meaningless digression about Sherlock Holmes and should have been omitted from the book, I don't believe that's true. After all, it provides a crucial link that returns at the end and brings help at the climax of the novel—but what do I know? I'm only the writer. Once again, I was too timid about insisting on dialogue tags being reversed—"said Lewis" got changed too many times to "Lewis said"—but I noticed them in this book more and began to feel that regularizing them to standard current American practice detracted from the style and made it seem less like Bellairs.

By the time *Vengeance* was ready for the press, my editor at Dial, Toby Sherry, was scouring through letters from John that mentioned possible topics for other novels. She and I worked well together, and she was ready for me to write a book with no Bellairs chapters at all—just the suggestion of a situation. That would soon come.

◆ ◆ ◆

## *The Vengeance of the Witch-Finder:*
## People, Places and Things

**Amulet of Constantine.** A fictitious magical artifact that has the power of breaking and reversing evil spells. It has been hidden away for many generations. In the seventeenth century, Lewis's ancestor Martin Barnavelt used it to stop Malachiah Pruitt's hypocritical witchcraft persecutions.

**Austin 7.** Cousin Pelham Barnavelt's automobile. This is based on an actual British automobile, tiny and cramped by even 1950s standards. It is boxy, old, slow, and uncomfortable, but the best he can afford, and it does take him where he wishes to go.

**Barnavelt, Martin.** The master of Barnavelt Manor during the years of the English Civil War and Commonwealth (1642-1660). Martin had a huge library and was an avid researcher and reader. Bertie tells Lewis that Martin was persecuted by the Puritan government on charges of sorcery. For a period of many years, he suffered eviction from his own house, first because Pruitt the Witch-Finder commandeered the manor as his headquarters and then after the Restoration of the monarchy in 1660 because the government suspected (correctly) that he was a Catholic. Martin managed to avoid execution, though he found it difficult to reclaim his property. He had only a few years to enjoy it when he did, passing away in 1668.

**Barnavelt Manor.** The ancestral home of the Barnavelt family in England since at least the sixteenth century. It is a huge gray stone house, turreted and with leaded windows with steep, slate-shingled roofs. Though it is large and includes several outbuildings, it has a forsaken, dilapidated look, and almost all the rooms are shut off and empty. It looks frightening to Lewis when he first sees it, and somehow evil.

**Barnavelt, Sir Arthur Pelham ("Pelly").** Thoroughly British, he is a lean, elderly, remote cousin of Jonathan's. He is the current owner of Barnavelt Manor, though he is relatively impoverished and has a challenging time keeping it up. Pelham became acquainted with Lewis's late father Charlie when Charlie was in the U.S. Army Air Corps and was stationed near Dinsdale. Through

Charlie, Jonathan got to know Pelly, and the two have corresponded for a few years.

**Barnavelt, Tobias.** Jonathan's great-great-great grandfather and at one time the occupant of Barnavelt Manor. His younger son, who could not by law inherit his father's estate, emigrated to the United States in 1795 and became Jonathan's and Lewis's ancestor.

**British Museum.** Jonathan and Lewis visit the famous old London museum in Chapter 1. Established in 1753 to display the collections of Sir Hans Sloane, scientist and doctor, it opened to the public in 1759. Under George II, it officially became the British Museum by Act of Parliament.

**Buckingham Palace.** The official residence of the kings and queens of England since 1837, this grand structure is in London. Lewis and Jonathan visit it in Chapter 2.

**CARE package.** Following World War II, an American organization, the Cooperative for American Remittances to Europe, began to assemble and send packages of necessities to people in Europe who, in the grim days of 1946, were struggling to survive after World War II had made even basic food scarce. Each C.A.R.E. package included contents like meat, margarine, lard, fruit preserves, honey, raisins, chocolate, sugar, powdered eggs and powdered milk, and coffee. The term was picked up and used as a kind of slang in America—if you sent a college student a package of clothes, food, books, or the like, you might call it a "CARE package." In Chapter 3, Jonathan tactfully gives Cousin Pelly a package with a few delicacies in it, since in Britain food was still being rationed until mid-1954.

**Cromwell, Oliver.** The leader of the Puritan forces that rebelled against King Charles I in 1642 (the English Civil War). After the king was captured and executed in 1649, Cromwell became the new leader of England, not as king, but under the new title of Lord Protector. England was a republic (called the Commonwealth) for eleven years before Cromwell died and, two years later, the people of the country, weary of the stern theocratic rule of the Puritans, demanded that the late king's son, also named Charles, be recalled from exile and crowned king. The Restoration of the British crown in 1660 made him King Charles II and ended the Puritan-dominated government.

**Deerstalker.** This is a British hunting cap, with ear flaps and ribbons that tie at the crown when the flaps are not in use, and a bill both in front and back. Lewis owns one—his Sherlock Holmes hat. It's really his second one, because the first one had been taken by a bully in *Figure.* He wears it as he pretends to be Sherlock Holmes, and Bertie comes along to play Watson.

**Dinsdale.** A small (fictional) town in the British county of West Sussex. Barnavelt Manor is nearby.

*Dracula,* **by Bram Stoker.** Lewis has read the classic vampire novel and references it.

**Dwiggins, Henry.** A Police Constable in London, a friendly young man who helps Jonathan and Lewis find the likely spot where Sherlock Holmes's flat would have been. A fellow Sherlock Holmes fan, Dwiggins even gives Lewis his address so they can keep in touch.

**European trip.** From London, Lewis and Jonathan go to Paris, where they spend several days visiting the Louvre, strolling the Champs-Élysées, and visiting the Eiffel Tower. Though a hearty eater normally, Lewis begins to have trouble with the rich French food, and with his uncle he walks for miles each day, sightseeing. They continue to Marseilles, a French seaport on the Mediterranean, and then on to Italy. They visit Rome and the Vatican, Naples (in the shadow of Mt. Vesuvius), and the dead city of Pompeii, which frightens Lewis. They go on to Venice, and then Vienna and north into Germany. Their Continental travels near an end in Göttingen, where Mrs. Zimmermann went to the university decades earlier to learn all about magic. Then they plan to return to England for a last visit to Barnavelt Manor before going home.

**Goodring, Bertram.** "Bertie" is about a year younger than Lewis, and very chubby. He wears dark glasses because when he was only six, in the last years of the war, he was blinded when a German rocket bomb exploded near him. He needs a delicate and difficult operation to recover his sight, but that must be done in a special Swiss clinic, and the costs of travel and the operation seem out of his mother's reach. He lives with his mother, Mrs. Goodring. His father was a soldier who died in WW II. He knows only a little about the United States, mostly from radio programs and movies, and he is eager to make an American friend. Lewis is a little shy around him, but soon realizes he has good qualities, and the two become friends.

**Goodring, Mrs.** Pelham Barnavelt's only remaining woman servant, a combination maid and cook. She is red-haired, jolly, and good-natured, and she does her best to stretch the food budget at a time when the British still faced rationing, shortages, and long queues for things like tea and coffee. She is a war widow—her husband, Bertie's father, died in combat. When Pelham learned that, he invited her and her son to come to the Manor, because Bertie's grandfather had been a faithful servant working for Pelham's father. Though paying her was a stretch, he felt a loyalty to her, and in turn she was grateful to have a means of supporting her son and herself.

*Gutenberg Bible.* Lewis sees a copy of this ancient and extremely valuable book in Pelham Barnavelt's library. It was the first book printed by Johannes Gutenberg, using moveable type, in Germany around the year 1450. It is in Latin, is huge, and only fifty or so copies survive. Pelham probably did not realize how valuable it was.

**Hedge maze.** A badly overgrown one is on the grounds of Barnavelt Manor. As Lewis learns, it has a sinister secret at its heart.

**Heemsoth's Rexall Drug Store.** This New Zebedee landmark, first mentioned in *House*, reappears in the last chapter. It is based on Hemmingsen's Rexall Drug Store on Michigan Avenue in Marshall, MI.

*History of the Barnavelt Family and the Rebellion Against King Charles I, A.* A fictitious book, written by James Barnavelt, son of Martin Barnavelt. Privately printed in 1721, it included genealogies, descriptions of family crests, and a biography of Martin Barnavelt. It also describes Malachiah Pruitt, who like the real Matthew Hopkins, was a professional witch-finder, traveling from town to town to accuse people of practicing magic.

Convicted persons were hanged or burned at the stake. In 1649, with the power of the Puritan government behind him, Pruitt took over Barnavelt Manor, forcing the owner and all the servants to live in the sheds and barn. Pruitt then set up a torture chamber in the cellar. The book says Pruitt would allow accused witches just one way to save their lives: they had to pay him a huge bribe and name other people as witches.

In 1651, Pruitt brought Martin Barnavelt up on charges of sorcery—though in the book his son says that Martin's only offense was being Catholic at a time when Catholics were persecuted. During the trial, Pruitt apparently became so worked up that he suffered a stroke. Pruitt's less fanatical helpers set Martin free, but they did not return ownership of the Manor to him. Pruitt lingered, speechless, and finally died in 1653. Reading the old book, Lewis finds a paper concealed behind the endpapers: a map of the hedge maze, showing something at its center.

**Holmes, Sherlock.** As we saw in *Figure,* Lewis is a fan of the famous fictional detective. He and Police Constable Dwiggins find the most probable spot where Holmes's apartment, 221-B Baker Street—if it were real—would have been located. Lewis demonstrates a thorough knowledge of Conan Doyle's stories, citing several: *The Hound of the Baskervilles;* "Silver Blaze"; "The Adventure of the Dancing Men"; "The Adventure of the Blue Carbuncle"; "The Adventure of the Naval Treaty"; and "The Adventure of the Empty House." One story element is borrowed directly from "The Musgrave Ritual." With young Bertie Goodring acting as his Watson, Lewis even pretends—in a very serious way—to be Sherlock Holmes.

**Inviting the vampire.** Though the evil spirit threatening the Barnavelts is not a vampire, it is inadvertently invited into the Manor. Lewis remembers vampire lore: One of the Undead cannot enter a dwelling unless invited in by one of the inhabitants, and that eventually explains why the ghost of Malachiah Pruitt can finally cross the protective boundary that Martin Barnavelt placed around his house nearly three hundred years earlier.

**Jenkins.** A man-of-all-work, Pelham Barnavelt's sole remaining male servant. Stout, bald, somewhat gruff, and a little stoop-shouldered, he wears a rusty-looking black suit and speaks in a slow, sorrowful tone. He is almost as old as Pelham and is by nature suspicious of strangers. Jenkins is fiercely loyal to the

Barnavelt family, for all his grumbling. His first name, not mentioned in the narrative, is Herbert.

*Lore of Model Railroading, The.* Lewis sees this dull book in Pelham Barnavelt's library, ironically next to the terrible book of magic *The Necronomicon.*

*Macbeth.* Lewis recalls seeing a performance of this Shakespeare play in Ann Arbor, Michigan, probably at a student performance put on by the theater department of the University of Michigan. The three evil witches impressed him deeply. By the way, there is an old theatrical superstition that if an actor mentions the name of the play inside the theater, bad luck will immediately befall the production. Actors learn to call it "The Scottish play."

**Moon omens.** Lewis glimpses a terrible transformation of the moon into an evil, leering, skull-like face. It is a portent of supernatural wickedness to come.

*Necronomicon, The.* Fictitious volume of eldritch lore written by the Arabian poet Abdul Alhazred, this grimoire is often mentioned in horror stories by H.P. Lovecraft and his followers. It's supposed to be one of the rarest books in the world with only five copies extant, but in Lovecraft's Mythos stories (both by him and his followers), copies of it pop up all the time. Lewis sees one in Pelham Barnavelt's library, but doesn't know what it is and doesn't read it. By the way, Lovecraft loved the word "eldritch," a word meaning "uncanny, eerie, inexplicable."

**Nightmares.** Both Lewis and Bertie have some doozies. One of Lewis's involves the hedges and plants around Barnavelt Manor coming horribly to life and seizing hold of him. In another he discovers Bertie's skeleton—the poor boy is dead. Only the skeleton is animate and laughs at Lewis.

**Old Growly.** A gigantic, invisible, menacing guardian spirit-dog protects the vault in the center of the maze. In folklore, such a creature is called a "shuck." Lewis and Bertie call this one "old Growly" to hide their fear of it.

*Persecution, for Witch-Craft, of Martin Christian Barnavelt Writ by Himself, Anno 1688, The.* A diary kept by Lewis's ancestor, explaining how the witch-finder Malachiah Pruitt had a vendetta against him. When poltergeist activity sprang up that seemed to prove Pruitt's accusation of witchcraft against two innocent women was valid, Martin was the only one who noticed that Pruitt himself was performing magical gestures to produce the phenomena, and he threatened to expose the witch-finder as a fraud. As a result, Pruitt had him arrested and held in solitary confinement until after the two women were hanged and then brought Martin to trial on false charges of evil sorcery.

**Pipe.** In this book, Uncle Jonathan is bothered because smoking is making him short of breath, and he is cutting down, planning on quitting altogether before long. In fact, the publisher had decided that YA novels should not show characters smoking. I realized that Mrs. Zimmermann's twisty cheroots would have to go as well. This was foreshadowing that the pipe and cigars would gradually go away.

**Prester, Matthew.** A visitor to the Barnavelt estate, he rents the derelict gatekeeper's cottage. Yet something about him seems wrong, and Bertie doesn't trust the man, nor does the man-of-all-work, Jenkins, who says that if Mr. Prester really is a London businessman as he claims, "my sainted Aunt Sarah was a foxtrotting pepperpot!" He's right; Prester is a disguised bad guy.

**Pruitt, Malachiah.** The witch-finder of the title. He was active during the English Civil War and the Commonwealth Period (1642-1660) and was a fraud. He accused innocent people of witchcraft and essentially served as prosecutor, judge, and jury, enriching himself by causing others pain and misery. As Martin Barnavelt discovers—and Lewis confirms—Pruitt used evil dark magic himself. His spirit lingers, and he is still furious and vengeful toward all Barnavelts. Though he is dead and can only partially materialize, he wants to destroy the family—and, why not, become King of England; maybe even of the world.

**Scarab.** In an obscure little shop near the British Museum, Jonathan picks up an ancient Egyptian stone scarab, still showing flecks of blue and black enamel, as a gift for Mrs. Zimmermann, who collects talismans.

**Spiney, Norman, Sergeant.** A policeman from the village of Dinsdale, near Barnavelt Manor. He comes to help the Barnavelts late in the novel. His name is a nod to *Monty Python's Flying Circus,* the British sketch comedy show. In one episode, a gangster named

Dinsdale is terrified of an imaginary giant hedgehog named Spiny Norman. Just a little joke. Very little.

*The Strand.* A British magazine, the one in which most of Sir Arthur Conan Doyle's Sherlock Holmes stories appeared. Lewis is delighted to find a complete set of the magazine, bound into volumes, in the Barnavelt Mansion's library.

**Torture Chamber.** In life, the witch-finder Malachiah Pruitt had one built in the cellars of Barnavelt Hall during the time he claimed the house as his own. In the story, the ghost of Pruitt conducts a grueling witch-trial of Jonathan Barnavelt in the hidden torture room.

**Tower of London.** In former years, a prison and place of execution for noble or upper-class felons (or maybe just people the monarch didn't like very much). It is on the Thames, at the eastern boundary of the City of London. Lewis and Jonathan tour it in Chapter 2. Lewis learns some interesting facts about the beheading of Anne Boleyn.

**Van Olden.** The last name of Lewis's grandmother. She died before he was born, and he never knew her. Jonathan's middle name comes from her maiden name: Jonathan van Olden Barnavelt.

**Vault.** A low brick vault, two feet tall and ten feet on each side. The concrete top of the vault has a dome about the size of a large mixing bowl. When he and Bertie find it, Lewis worries that it might be a tomb. They loosen a brick in the vault . . . and something escapes from it, something that can hypnotize and control people who are not on guard against it.

◆ ◆ ◆

**Division of Labor:**

This was the last book I worked on that contained chapters by John Bellairs. Except for minor tweaks, Chapters 1 and 2 are John's. I did add the name of a village, though.

Chapters 3-15 are mine. As mentioned, John left no indication of the plot, and we had only the provisional title "The Witch Finder" (no hyphen) to go by. Since the story involved an English manor house going back, apparently, to the sixteenth century, and since in the seventeenth century England came under the domination of a Puritan government that actively persecuted alleged witches, I decided that the witch finder of the title would be the ghost of a real one.

Malachiah Pruitt is loosely modeled on Matthew Hopkins (1620-1647). During the English Civil War (1642-1649), the Puritans seized control of large areas of England. They believed in witches, magic, and the biblical injunction "Thou shalt not suffer a witch to live" (Exodus 22.18). Witch trials were notoriously stacked against the accused. Reversing normal English jurisprudence, in a witch trial, the accused person was assumed to be guilty and had to prove his or her innocence. Proving a negative is close to impossible. Generally, the one way for an accused witch to escape with his or her life was to confess (falsely), repent (of something the person had never done), and name other people as being witches. If you know about the Salem Village witchcraft trials in America in 1692, you have an idea of how Hopkins operated.

Hopkins fraudulently claimed to be the "Witchfinder General" of England, but Parliament never gave him that title and in fact it did not exist. Yet from 1644-1647, operating in East Anglia and other districts of England, Hopkins personally prosecuted and gained guilty verdicts in 300 cases of alleged witchcraft. The victims were hanged or burned at the stake.

Hopkins wrote a book that purported to describe how to identify and punish sorcerers and witches, *The Discovery of Witches* (1647), which the Puritans of New England later used as a guide in their own witch persecutions. Like the fictional Malachiah Pruitt, Hopkins enriched himself by his persecution of undoubtedly innocent victims.

◆ ◆ ◆

## Chapter 4: *The Doom of the Haunted Opera*
### By John Bellairs, Completed by Brad Strickland
### Dial Books for Young Readers, 1995

*The Doom of the Haunted Opera* is the sixth book in the New Zebedee series, and the first one without any of John Bellairs's original writing in it. I wrote it from a very short suggestion left by John of a possible story situation.

That hinged on the existence in Marshall of a very real abandoned opera house. Though it has been stripped of most of its furnishings, it hasn't been demolished, for the very good reason that it perches on the second floor of some businesses on Michigan Avenue, the main street of the town. Exploring it might be a little dangerous—the stage has been torn out, and the floor has some rough places—but it's unlikely to harbor ghosts.

Lucky for me, I got the chance to explore this hidden bit of Marshall history. It has a kind of grandeur about it still—a magnificent ruin, a shadow of its former self.

Still, it's a very atmospheric place, the kind of location that gives a writer ideas.

◆ ◆ ◆

*Summary:*
Uncle Jonathan receives a letter telling him an old friend and fellow magician has died down in Florida and has made Jonathan the executor of his estate. He requested that Jonathan and Mrs. Zimmermann come to Florida to sort through his collection of amulets, some of them powerful and dangerous.

It is early March, though an unseasonable winter still lingers, and school is in session, so Lewis can't go. Instead, he will remain in New Zebedee and a friendly, elderly woman, Hannah Holtz, will come and stay in the Barnavelt mansion to keep house and watch after him.

Meanwhile, Lewis and Rose Rita have a report to do for school on some historic event or site in New Zebedee. They learn of the long-deserted New Zebedee Opera House, on the second floor of some businesses downtown, and decide to research that. While touring the old theater, they discover the music and libretto for an opera, *The Day of Doom*, by Immanuel Vanderhelm.

The local historical society decides to perform the opera for the very first time. And that sets off a chain of mysterious, magical, and horrifying events.

◆ ◆ ◆

*Behind the Scenes:*

With *The Vengeance of the Witch-Finder*, we had exhausted all the unfinished manuscripts that the publisher had on hand. The editor, though, found some references—not even proposals—for other potential books in John's letters.

The first of these was a Johnny Dixon: "Professor Coote buys a voodoo drum while visiting New Orleans and brings it home. He has bad dreams about it and brings it to Professor Childermass. Playing with the drum, Johnny and Fergie accidentally summon a zombie that attacks them."

Working with that and with John's characters and setting, I wrote the novel. By the way, I also visited the real-life town that John used as the model for Johnny's fictional Massachusetts town of Duston Heights. The real town is Haverhill, north of Boston, and for the Bellairs fan it is worth a trip.

That novel became *The Drum, the Doll, and the Zombie* (1994). *Doom* grew from another similar bare suggestion: "Ghosts haunt the Eagle Opera House. They are conjured by the music of a musician who is also a sorcerer."

As I mentioned in the introduction, in 1993, Ann and Tony La Pietra, residents of Marshall, had invited me up for the John Bellairs Walk. It was, and still is, a town festival celebrating Marshall's famous writer, and I was very happy to go, though on that occasion my wife Barbara was teaching school and could not spare the time to come along on the trip. Ann, the owner of The Kids Place bookstore, saw to it that townspeople ushered me around to see all the John Bellairs sights—including the cemetery (not as atmospheric as John's version), the waterworks, even Lyon Lake.

I had been pondering the "Eagle Opera House" note, and Ann told me there was indeed a real, ruined opera house in the heart of downtown Marshall, but hardly anyone was aware of it. That was because it had been built on the second floor of a block of businesses.

Around the turn of the 20th Century, the Eagle had been a flourishing theater, hosting famous opera singers, touring troupes of actors, and even Houdini, the famous magician, escape artist, and investigator of paranormal claims. However, in 1903 a tragic fire broke out in the similarly-constructed Iroquois Theater in Chicago, causing the deaths of more than six hundred people. Like the Iroquois, the Eagle Opera House had severely restricted access, with only one means of escape. In a wave of closings, theaters across the country built on similar plans went out of business—as did the Eagle Opera House.

Ann couldn't arrange for me to visit the theater on that visit, but six months or so later she called and said that the store owners agreed I could tour it if I wanted to. This time my wife and I flew up for a research trip and got to walk through the ruined Opera House. Chillingly, as we ascended the dusty, long-disused stair, we arrived on the top landing and saw lying on the floor ahead of us *a dead body*!

All right, it was the body of a pigeon that had wandered in and perished perhaps thirty years earlier, from the look of it, but even so, it most definitely was a dead body. The lighting up there was sketchy, because no one normally goes into the space, so the old stage and house lights were gone. A few work lights gave a sort of candlelight glow to the place. We went into the auditorium wondering what we might see.

The sight that greeted us was the ruin of a spectacular theater. All the seats had been removed, the balcony was gone, and the original stage had been demolished, although we could see where it had been. The dressing rooms remained intact, though bare of furnishings, with incredible old posters and playbills still on the walls. I took lots of photos, made lots of measurements, and even before we went home, began to plot the next book. In fact, I recall sitting up in bed, with the room's one lamp—a floor model—perched in a chair beside me so I could hold my yellow legal pad on my knees. I sketched in a scene of the climax of the book, and even on the flight back to Atlanta I was scribbling away.

Some things about the stories were changing, not entirely because of me. The publisher had laid down a general ban on tobacco and smoking in books for younger readers, so Uncle Jonathan's pipe tobacco and Mrs. Zimmermann's cigars were phasing out.

Also, the editor asked me to follow the practice that John had already established with the Johnny Dixon series—make the years indeterminate, just some time in the 1950s, and freeze the ages of the characters. The Johnny Dixons were a longer series than the Lewis Barnavelts, and John had decided that Johnny would always be "about thirteen."

The editor said she and John had talked that over, and he had thought it would be all right to stop Lewis's aging in the same way. That, by the way, seems to be common in mystery fiction. One of my favorite mystery writers is "Ellery Queen" (in real life, two cousins Manfred B. Lee and Frederic Dannay) whose character—also named Ellery Queen—remained 35 years old over fifty years of novels.

We switched to that approach with Lewis, too. From this time forward, the stories would not be set in a specific year, but "in the 1950s," and Lewis would always be "about thirteen." Unlike Harry Potter, Lewis was destined never to become a troubled, angsty teen, a school dropout, and later a married man with children. I'm sure even to this day he's a heavyset, rather anxious, chubby boy who is about thirteen.

In other changes, a few new things and people show up. I gave Rose Rita a maternal grandfather, Mr. Galway, who's had a long and colorful past (though he lies about his age, making himself a decade *older* than he really is). A few previously unseen adults show up, and we learn a little about why New Zebedee is such a weirdness magnet. I also added a couple of new buildings to the town.

The book's New Zebedee Opera House is based on two different theaters: the one we explored, the Eagle Opera House, long closed, in Marshall, Michigan, and Pearce Auditorium, on the campus of Brenau University in Gainesville, Georgia, near my home town.

Pearce, which still is a functioning theater, is a delightful, old-fashioned theater in Victorian style, and it boasts its own theater ghost, Agnes. Once when I was doing a public reading of scenes from *The Ghost in the Mirror*, I stood on the Pearce Auditorium stage, reading into a microphone—and all the lights went out. In the darkness, I said, "Agnes, you should *like* this book. It's about a ghost!" Instantly the lights came back on. Honestly, I don't know for sure if Agnes was just fooling around with me.

The National House Hotel, mentioned in this novel, is based on the National House Inn Bed and Breakfast, where I stayed whenever I visited Marshall. It is a historic guesthouse, built in 1835, making it the oldest brick building in Calhoun County. Beginning as a hotel for stagecoach travelers halfway between Detroit and Chicago, it later became a railroad hotel (and legend has it, as a stop on the Underground Railroad as well, welcoming those who were escaping from slavery and traveling to make a new life in the free states). After a brief stint as a factory, it became an apartment house and then in 1976 an inn once again. It is a charming place to stay and is situated on Michigan Avenue, very close to the traffic circle with the pulsating fountain that John Bellairs described in his books.

In *Doom*, I purposely sprinkled in references to other works by John Bellairs. Lewis reprises something he did in *The House with a Clock in Its Walls*, improvising a goofy magic spell. At another time, the characters glimpse in a magic mirror a red-bearded wizard from medieval times: Roger Bacon—the one from John's book *The Face in the Frost*, not the historical one. And close to the climax, the characters wield one of Mrs. Zimmermann's amulets, an enchanted pearl marked with mystic signs from the Cabala by a medieval magician. Though the name is not stated, I'm sure that magician was Prospero, the hero of *The Face in the Frost*, who met an expert on the Cabala in that book.

The title of the opera that is in fact a disguised magic spell is *The Day of Doom*. I took it from a book-length poem by Michael Wigglesworth (no, really don't laugh), which was a best-seller in Puritan New England in the seventeenth century. It is the jolliest-sounding account of the end of the world you could ever hope to read, with terribly forced rhymes and a meter that would be more suited to something Lewis Carroll might write—something like "The Hunting of the Snark," perhaps.

Coming up with a suitably Bellairsian title took a little time. I suggested "Curse of the Haunted Opera," but the publisher thought the readership might not realize that "Opera" could mean a theater as well as a musical performance. "Curse of the Haunted Theater" didn't satisfy me, because the actual cursed object was the score and libretto for the opera, not the building. Then concerns arose that "curse" might offend some parents, who would think the book was talking about naughty words. I suggested "Bane of the Haunted Opera," but then the publisher decided "nobody knows what the word 'bane' means." Finally, I think more out of exhaustion than anything else, we settled on *Doom of the Haunted Opera* because, after all, the opera itself was titled *The Day of Doom.*

A misprint crept into Chapter 15. It isn't in my original manuscript, and and I don't recall it in the page proofs, but someone slipped up, probably thinking they were correcting a mistake. "The magicians" climb out of the orchestra pit in a theater. In my manuscript, "the musicians" are the climbers. That always bothered me, and it never got corrected, not even in later reprints. If you have the book, look in chapter 15, strike out "magicians," and pencil in "musicians." Thank you. And don't worry, I made my own mistakes, and I'll confess to them later.

I dedicated this novel to Ann and Tony La Pietra, in gratitude for their friendship and support and love for the works of John Bellairs. In addition, I put in an acknowledgement: "Thanks to Jeanne Sharp, reader and advisor." Jean was a teenager from Bellingham, WA, who had written to complain about an error I had made in describing Fergie in my first Johnny Dixon book. I sent her the next few manuscripts, and her commentary always helped. Unfortunately, she grew up, went to college, and became too busy to proofread. I value her advice anyway.

The reliable and talented Edward Gorey provided a delightfully atmospheric jacket and interior illustrations: the front shows a frightened Rose Rita and Lewis backing away from a serpentine horror in the cemetery, and the back the two of them surrounded and menaced by a flock of huge bats and a crowd of 1900-vintage opera-goers dressed in formal evening wear—but lacking their heads.

◆　◆　◆

## *The Doom of the Haunted Opera*:
## People, Places, and Things

**Amulet.** A pearl inscribed with magic symbols from the Cabala. Mrs. Zimmermann owns it as part of her collection. It is a bringer of blessed light, and though this is not explicit in the book, it was created in the Middle Ages by Prospero, the wizard from *The Face in the Frost*.

**Barnavelt House.** We learn that, to prevent being accidentally locked out, Jonathan hides a spare key behind the red reflecting number 1 in the house number, 100, bolted to the iron fence.

**Bessie.** Mrs. Zimmermann's automobile, a 1950 Plymouth Cranbrook. It was originally green, but thanks to Mrs. Zimmerman's recovery of her magical powers, it became a brilliant, bright purple at the end of *The Ghost in the Mirror*.

**Bombsight Factory.** Part of New Zebedee's war effort in World War II. It produced top-secret bomb sights for B-17 bombers.

**Capharnaum County Magicians Society.** Founded before 1850 by Lucius Mickleberry's father, this is a social organization of good magicians. Mrs. Zimmermann and Jonathan are prominent members. The membership roll is kept in a narrow, tall book bound in green cloth with the corners reinforced by leather triangles. The current president of the Society is Mrs. Zenobia Weatherly, who lives on West River Avenue. When Lewis seeks their help, though, he discovers that every member of the Society is weirdly missing—as are their houses.

**Caruso, Enrico (1873-1921).** A native of Italy, Caruso became the most famous operatic tenor of his era. He once performed in the New Zebedee Opera House.

**Chess.** Lewis and Rose Rita play a game with Uncle Jonathan's chessmen, carved from white and brown marble that can be found only in Lombardy, a region in Italy. Jonathan has cast a spell on the pieces that allows them to comment on the game, often complaining if the player makes a bad move.

**Comic strips.** Lewis reads several newspaper strips regularly. They include "Dick Tracy," "Li'l Abner," and "Little Orphan Annie."

**Commercial jingle.** Lewis picks out the catchy jingle for Pepsi-Cola on the piano in the opera house.

**Davis, Hugo.** The portly, dignified, white-haired mayor of New Zebedee. He is in the audience when Miss White first plays some music from the opera score. He has the idea of staging the opera and perhaps making New Zebedee a tourist attraction.

***Day of Doom, The.*** An Opera in English by Immanuel Vanderhelm. In reality a complex magical spell, the opera has never been performed when Lewis finds the score hidden inside a piano in the old theater. The music has power—and for that matter, so does the paper-and-ink score itself.

**Dreams**. Lewis has a nightmare of seeing the ghost of Vanderhelm playing a pipe organ in the old theater. A crowd of opera patrons comes in—but they are headless. As they pursue Lewis and Rose Rita, a flock of bats also menaces the two. Lewis wakes up as some creature grabs his head and threatens to wrench it off.

Rose Rita remembers she dreamed that a herd of whistling cats chased her into a tunnel, which then sealed itself at both ends.

**Farmers' Seed & Feed.** A downtown store on Main Street in the years when the countryside around New Zebedee was more rural. It adjoins the five-and-dime store, and above them both is the closed New Zebedee Opera House.

**Finster, Mordecai.** The manager of the New Zebedee Opera House. He vanished in 1919, when the theater closed, and people gossiped that he had skipped town with some of the theater's money. However, Lewis recognizes a photo of him because he saw Mr. Finster's ghost in the Opera House.

**Five-and-Dime Store.** One of the downtown stores on Main Street. Next to it is the Farmers' Seed & Feed, and above them is the old New Zebedee Opera House.

***Flash Gordon.*** The Bijou theater in New Zebedee occasionally shows the old Flash Gordon serials, movies that play out over the weeks in many thirty-minute episodes. The Flash Gordon series consists of tales about spaceman Flash Gordon, who becomes an interstellar hero fighting monstrous creatures all over the galaxy.

**Fog.** A magical one surrounds New Zebedee for a while. It does not permit anyone to leave the town.

**Fogarty, Mrs.** Lewis's and Rose Rita's English teacher. She is very finicky and picky and insists on her students' paying attention to every detail in an assignment.

**Friar Bacon.** The characters get a brief glimpse and exchange a few words with this medieval friar and magician. He is from John Bellairs's *The Face in the Frost* and is the deuteragonist to that novel's main character, Prospero. By the way, "deuteragonist" is a fancy-schmancy way of saying "sidekick."

**Fu-Manchu, Dr.** The insidious villain from a series of suspense-adventure novels by Sax Rohmer. Lewis has read at least some of the Fu-Manchu stories and has dreamed about the murderous doctor in nightmares.

**Fuse-Box Dwarf.** Like all of Jonathan Barnavelt's spells, the Fuse-Box Dwarf gradually faded away. Lewis misses him a little.

**Galway, Albert.** Rose Rita's maternal grandfather. Now about ninety (he claims), he has lived a colorful life, having been at different times a sailor, a surveyor, an architect, and a building contractor. He and his crew originally built the New Zebedee Opera House. Now a widower, he lives at 122 Sycamore Street, in a small cottage surrounded by things Mr. Galway has made: a fish pond, a stone terrace, and out back, a forest of whirligigs and windmills that perform animated tricks, like juggling. Mr. Galway is bald and wears spectacles. His eyes are a sparkling bright blue, and Lewis was very impressed to learn that when he was a young man, he once shook hands with Sir Arthur Conan Doyle, writer of the Sherlock Holmes stories.

**Galway, Coral.** Not Rose Rita's grandmother, but Mr. Galway's first wife, who died sometime around 1910.

**Ghosts.** Several appear in the book, including one that warns Lewis against the magic contained in the score of the opera. A group of them pursues Lewis when he is riding his bicycle around town, trying to investigate the mystery. Still more appear when the opera begins to be performed.

*Grand Ole Opry, The.* A long-running radio program out of Nashville. It featured country music and rural humor, and Uncle Jonathan sometimes listens to it. Lewis doesn't care for it.

**Hat stand.** Once again Lewis peers into the magic mirror in the front-hall hat stand. The first time he does, he gets a reassuring vision of his uncle in Florida. Then things get creepy.

**Holtz, Hannah.** A short, apple-cheeked, middle-aged woman who comes in twice a week to help with the housework in the Barnavelt house. She agrees to move in temporarily to watch after Lewis while Jonathan goes to Florida to deal with Lucius Mickleberry's estate.

**Houdini, Harry (1891-1926).** Houdini was the greatest magician and escape artist of the twentieth century. He once performed in the New Zebedee Opera House.

**Ipana toothpaste.** A commercial for this product is heard on the radio.

**Jaeger, Mildred Sherman.** A plump, gray-haired woman who lives in New Zebedee on Marshall Street. She drives a black 1939 Chevrolet and uses a wooden spoon as a magic wand. Lewis has heard that she is the most incompetent witch in town and can do a little magic, but it always seems to go wrong. Because of that, she has never been able to join the Capharnaum County Magicians Society. She remembers Immanuel Vanderhelm from when she was a girl, and Mr. Mickleberry once told her about the limits of his musical magic spell.

**Jailbird.** A black-and-white striped tomcat. He belongs to Miss Geer, the town librarian. The previous spring, Jonathan cast a magic spell on him just for fun, and Jailbird developed the ability to whistle, though he has problems staying on pitch for a song like "Goodnight Ladies." Miss Geer entered him in a radio talent contest, but he was disqualified because the radio station manager said (A) nobody in the radio audience would believe that a cat could whistle, and (B) Jailbird wasn't very good at carrying a tune. He tends to annoy people with songs like "On Top of Old Smokey" until they feed him.

*Lights Out.* A radio program specializing in horror and suspense stories. Lewis listens to it, though it can give him nightmares.

**Magic mirrors.** Several appear in the story, most prominently the one in Uncle Jonathan's hat stand. Rose Rita also remembers the one from *The Ghost in the Mirror.*

**Margate, Jimmy.** A flying-ace war hero from World War I. He was from New Zebedee.

**McGillis, Mr.** A barber in New Zebedee who knows Lewis well and who is one of the townsfolk trapped by the opera's enchantment.

**Mickleberry, Lucius.** A much older man than his good friends Jonathan and Mrs. Zimmermann, Mickleberry was a powerful good sorcerer and the son of the man who founded the Capharnaum County Magicians Society sometime before 1850. Lucius left

New Zebedee and retired to Florida in 1947. His death prompts Jonathan and Mrs. Zimmermann's visit to St. Petersburg, Florida, to administer his estate and dispose of his potentially dangerous magical paraphernalia.

Lewis finds in a book the story of how Immanuel Vanderhelm came to New Zebedee in 1918 and how the next spring he was going to direct a production of the opera he had written. The person recording the story is Mr. Mickleberry, and he summarizes, without much detail, a life-and-death struggle between the good magicians of New Zebedee and the evil outsider Immanuel Vanderhelm.

**Monopoly.** Two of the characters claim to have fallen asleep while playing a game. That is just a cover story.

**Moriarty, Professor.** Sherlock Holmes's evil nemesis. Lewis has dreamed about him while having nightmares.

**Mr. Hyde.** The monstrous alter ego of the kindly, mild Dr. Jekyll in Robert Louis Stevenson's horror novel *Dr. Jekyll and Mr. Hyde.* The hideous Hyde has troubled Lewis's dreams before.

**National House Hotel.** A hotel in New Zebedee, modeled on the real National House Inn, a historic bed-and-breakfast in Marshall, Michigan.

**New Zebedee and Magic**. Mrs. Zimmermann explains that earth magic resembles a magnetic field. Some locations have more of it than others, and New Zebedee has a very strong magical flow — which explains why magicians both good and evil are attracted to it. Though they can perform magic anywhere, the natural magic field of New Zebedee makes the spells stronger and more enduring.

**New Zebedee** *Chronicle*. The local newspaper. A story in it covers Lewis's discovery of the sheet music for the opera.

**New Zebedee Eleemosynary and Cultural League.** This was an organization active from the 1890s until 1919. It sponsored the building of the Opera House, and when the theater had to close in 1919, the league failed and disbanded, though a few members are still around at the time of the novel.

**New Zebedee Junior High School.** Both Lewis and Rose Rita attend this school. The building is made of black stone and is next to the high school, separated from it by a narrow alley.

**New Zebedee Opera House.** On the second floor above two downtown stores, the theater has been abandoned and closed for thirty years or so and lies under a layer of gray dust and cobwebs. The seats are upholstered in red velvet, with room for 480 people in the orchestra and another 120 in a horseshoe-shaped balcony. There is an orchestra pit for musicians, a stage, dressing rooms, and mementos of the days when the theater was open. A rickety piano is in the orchestra pit, and when he tries to play it and finds some keys don't work, Lewis looks inside and finds the script and score for *The Day of Doom,* an opera that was never performed.

Rose Rita's maternal grandfather, Mr. Galway, was the architect and contractor who designed and built the theater about the year 1900, with the support of the New Zebedee Eleemosynary and Cultural League. It was in operation from 1902 until 1919, when it closed because of poor business, combined with the horrendous influenza epidemic of that year.

**Oak Ridge Cemetery.** While trying to find a way out of town when a magic spell imprisons them, Lewis and Rose Rita revisit this place that Lewis avoids, since he was so traumatized by raising Mrs. Selenna Izard from the dead there. As they try unsuccessfully to get away, Rose Rita notices that the monumental sculptures are . . . moving.

**Paulson, Mr. and Mrs.** They own and publish the New Zebedee *Chronicle,* the local newspaper. They are a middle-aged couple who look a lot alike—chubby and short. They come to hear Miss White play some of the music from the opera.

**Pfeiffer, Mr.** A New Zebedee businessman who owns the Farmers' Seed & Feed and the five-and-dime next door. He is portly, bald on top with a fringe of salt-and-pepper gray hair, and a big red nose that he's in the habit of squeezing, as though to test it for ripeness.

**Phantasm.** In the context of the book, a phantasm is a ghostly duplicate of a sorcerer, conjured up by the magician and given a bit of his or her soul. It preserves the sorcerer's life even if the original dies or is killed. It is an exception to the general rule that a sorcerer's spells break when he or she dies.

*Pirates of Penzance.* A popular operetta by the British team of Gilbert and Sullivan, it was once performed in the New Zebedee Opera House.

*Popular Mechanics.* A magazine, just what the title says: It publishes stories about machines and mechanical devices and inventions and offers do-it-yourself advice.

**Potter, Mr.** The fussy principal of the junior high school in New Zebedee. He was not named after any British boy wizards.

**Pottinger, George and Louise.** Rose Rita's father and mother. Louise, like many of the townsfolk, falls under the spell of the opera and plans to sing a role in it. George is annoyed because she neglects everything else, but he decides it will be good to stir up a little life in New Zebedee. George was a Varsity letterman at the University of Michigan, and sometimes Rose Rita wears his old Navy blue and gold letterman's jacket.

**Pottinger, Rose Rita.** Still about a head taller than Lewis, though he's had a bit of a growth spurt. In *Doom,* she spins one of her tall tales, telling a stranger that the theater closed because after Houdini performed an underwater escape, two town boys tried to duplicate it and drowned, and the sad townsfolk closed the Opera House as a result. None of that is true, and the tale shocks Lewis a little.

**Radios.** Mrs. Holtz has a Motorola table-top model, and Jonathan owns a large floor model that picks up regular radio stations as well as fire department, police, and airplane bands, along with amateur and short-wave bands.

**Reese's Peanut Butter Cups**. Lewis makes a snack of two of them and a glass of milk.

**"Row, Row, Row Your Boat."** Becomes part of an improvised magical spell and functions as a chant.

*Saturday Evening Post.* A popular magazine, offering both factual stories and fiction, and illustrated by talented artists and photographers. It had a long history, claiming descent from an earlier publication begun by Benjamin Franklin in Colonial days.

**Scrying ball.** This is the term for a crystal ball that shows the user visions of things happening far away. Mrs. Zimmermann can use the crystal globe in her umbrella (she got it in *The Ghost in the Mirror)* as one, or a sorcerer can even use a plain glass of water. A clumsy sorcerer may wind up with a confused goldfish, though.

**St. Petersburg, Florida**. Uncle Jonathan and Mrs. Zimmermann stay here in the house of Lucius Mickleberry while they settle the old man's estate.

**Stained-glass window.** We glimpse the one in the back stairs of the south wing in the Barnavelt house, which is animated and which shows a different scene every time you look at it.

**Telephone number**. The Barnavelts' telephone in New Zebedee is 865.

*Transactions of the Capharnaum County Magicians Society.* A set of six books that contain the minutes of the meetings of the Society, along with record of their accomplishments and adventures. One of them records Mrs. Zimmermann's return to the USA from Europe, together with her husband, Honus. In another is the account of how Jonathan proved himself worthy of membership by eclipsing the moon.

**Vanderhelm, Henry.** Introduces himself as the grandson of Immanuel Vanderhelm. He, too, is a singer—a baritone. He comes to New Zebedee when he hears his father's opera has been discovered and offers to pay for staging the performance.

**Vanderhelm, Immanuel.** An opera singer who was said to be world-famous. He composed the opera *The Day of Doom* and rehearsed the cast, but for some reason he did not show up on the night planned for the opera's premiere. Lewis later learns that Vanderhelm was not only a musician, but a magician—and a very evil one.

**Wallpaper.** We learn that following the events of *House with a Clock in Its Walls,* Jonathan replaced the old wallpaper with Isaac Izard's initials worked into it with a more cheerful pattern.

**Wand breaking**. A ceremony performed by the friends of a deceased witch or wizard. If a sorcerer of either gender dies because of magic, his or her wand automatically breaks. If he or she dies a natural death, then the sorcerers who were the dead person's friends gather, remember the departed one, wish their friend well in the afterlife, and solemnly break the wand. That allows the soul of the magician to separate from Earthly cares and go on to its reward.

**White, Miss Ophelia.** The music teacher at the junior high school. She has only contempt for modern music, calling it jitterbug and bebop. She knows all about the late Mr. Vanderhelm, a world-famous tenor, and is a moving force in staging his previously unperformed opera.

*WLS National Barn Dance, The.* A radio program out of Chicago that Uncle Jonathan occasionally listens to. It's all country music, and Lewis is not a fan.

**WNZB.** New Zebedee's local radio station.

**Yuggoth.** Lewis once caught a glimpse of this accursed planet on the fringes of the Solar System. It comes from the writings of H.P. Lovecraft (probably inspired by the then-recent discovery of Pluto) and is mentioned several times in his horror stories about Cthulhu and other Great Old Ones, monstrous beings from prehistory and from outer space.

◆ ◆ ◆

## Chapter 5: John Bellairs's Lewis Barnavelt in
### *The Specter from the Magician's Museum*
### By Brad Strickland
### Dial Books for Young Readers, 1998

*The Specter from the Magician's Museum* is the seventh book in the New Zebedee series and is the first that does not have the "completed by Brad Strickland" byline. We had run out of John's ideas, and neither the editor nor I thought it was fair to continue to put that by-line on books not even inspired by one of John's suggestions. That clearly would be unfair, and in a way, false advertising. Yet I was playing in John's back yard and certainly wanted his name on the book. After all, he was the originator, the Prime Mover, the creator of the whole Lewis Barnavelt series, as well as of the characters, setting, and tone.

I recall several phone conversations with the editor about the problem. Nothing that we could think of sounded exactly right, and some were awkward and clunky. We puzzled about it probably longer than was necessary. Then one day when editor Toby Sherry and I were on the phone making another stab at brainstorming a solution, I asked, "Why don't we take the James Bond approach?"

After Ian Fleming, the original writer of the James Bond novels, passed away, other writers took up the character and created new adventures for the famous spy. Those books were almost all billed as "Ian Fleming's James Bond in *Title of Book* by Name of Author." That sounded all right to the Toby, so the cover of this and subsequent novels would read "John Bellairs's Lewis Barnavelt in *Title of Book*." Then I received the author's by-line.

Though Lewis does make a significant appearance, this story is very much Rose Rita's book. She is the one endangered and the one to launch the investigation of a spooky mystery. The character relationships and dynamics may remind readers a bit of *The Ghost in the Mirror*, but Lewis, Jonathan, and Mrs. Zimmermann all play bigger roles this time around, and the unraveling of the supernatural mystery becomes a team effort. One of John's recurring themes was the power of friendship. Here it shows up again.

◆ ◆ ◆

*Summary:*

On a warm fall day in the 1950s, we find Lewis terrified—not by a ghost or evil magician, but by the prospect of having to perform on stage in the school talent show. And Rose Rita is in the same boat. Both feel shy in front of an audience, and neither is confident about having any real talents. They decide to work together and put on a magic show— not using real magic, or even illusions like Uncle Jonathan's, but an ordinary conjuring show, the type stage magicians perform with glib patter, misdirection, and sleight of hand.

Uncle Jonathan advises the two to consult Mr. Robert Hardwick, a retired newspaperman and amateur conjuror whose fantastic collection of conjuring memorabilia is the heart of the National Museum of Magic, a recent addition to New Zebedee. Mr. Hardwick and some friends, fellow amateur conjurors, lend the two teens some books and suggest a few sure-fire tricks they can learn.

But when Rose Rita finds a scroll written by someone named Madame Frisson and gets a paper cut, the drop of blood from it falls on some powder wrapped up with the scroll . . . and turns into a live spider that scuttles away.

And that is only the beginning of Rose Rita's strange and terrifying encounter with Madame Frisson, who is reaching out to her from beyond the grave.

◆ ◆ ◆

*Behind the Scenes:*

There is a real magician's museum in Marshall, Michigan, with all sorts of magical paraphernalia collected by the Lunds, Bob and Elaine. In addition, the great national convention of North American magicians takes place annually in Colon, Michigan, only about 45 minutes away from Marshall by car. We planned our visit for early August, 1997, so we would be able to visit the Festival of Magic as well as Marshall.

Bob Lund had passed away, but his widow, Elaine, permitted Barbara and me to tour and photograph the American Museum of Magic, at 107 E Michigan Ave. Magic props and posters and other memorabilia take a visitor back as far as the 19th Century. Visitors can even examine one of the milk cans used by Houdini himself in his act. Though bound with chains and shackled and sealed inside the oversized milk can, Houdini escaped every single time.

The museum was, and is, a fascinating place, and many details in the fictional National Museum of Magic come straight from the real-life model. Because of Elaine's helpfulness and her late husband's enjoyment of all things magical, I dedicated this novel *"For Bob and Elaine Lund, whose museum shows that the secret of magic is people."* Although Elaine, too, passed away a few years ago, the Museum is still there. If you find yourself in Marshall, drop in.

At the Museum, in addition to getting a grounding in the history of American magicians, I also learned about conjuror Clarence "Clare" Cummings, who for many years baffled and delighted children with a TV show out of Detroit. It was sponsored by Twin Pines Dairy and played the role of the magical Milky the Clown. You may recognize a character in this novel who is loosely based on him. The name of the dairy, "Twin Pines" also coincidentally reminds me of a TV show that is extremely Bellairsian in its blend of humor, terror, and mystery: *Gravity Falls,* whose main characters are siblings, a boy and a girl who are twins—and whose name is Pines. Though I am grown up and then some, I became an enthusiastic fan, because when it debuted I felt as if the creators were channeling John Bellairs's storytelling style! Maybe more on that later.

My wife Barbara and I had advance notice of the Colon Magic Festival, sponsored by Abbott's Magic, which sells tricks, props, and instruction books to professional, amateur, and aspiring magicians everywhere. By timing our visit just right, Barbara and I were able to attend the conference, courtesy of Elaine Lund's giving us an introduction as a couple researching a book. We discovered that it was delightful being "civilians"—non-magicians—at the big magicians' conference. We were the audience they all wanted, and all day the conjurors kept coming over to show us one baffling close-up magic trick after another. It was great fun, and I can still do a neat illusion with two rubber bands that I learned in Colon.

Later in the visit, I also spoke at a school assembly in Marshall, talking about the books I had written and the one I was working on. One of the students asked if he could be a character in the next book. On the spur of the moment I said, "You'll have to earn it." I made up a trivia quiz of fifty questions, the school administered it as if it were a test, and Ann La Pietra of the Kids Place book store agreed to judge the contest. In the end, it was a three-way tie, so I got in touch with the three winners and gave them roles in the book: Chad Britton, Chris Walsh, and James Gensterblum.

The editor at Dial quickly approved the outline. Then at the end of August, I set to work writing it. The book flowed well, and writing it uncommonly fast, I had turned it in by October.

As in real life, things gradually change in New Zebedee. Uncle Jonathan and Mrs. Zimmermann have now officially given up smoking—though Jonathan keeps a pipe or two and now and then chews on one, unlighted, when he wants to think. Mrs. Zimmermann quit snapping her cigars out of thin air because Jonathan wanted to stop smoking, and she'd given him an I-will-if-you-will challenge. In town, the National Museum of Magic has opened within the last year or so on Main Street and is a new town attraction. Other New Zebedee details are different now and then, too.

In one part of the book, Rose Rita needs a fake name, and she makes up one: Rowena Potter. Readers have asked me if this was a tribute to J.K. Rowling, who wrote books that included a character named Rowena Ravenclaw and a boy, what was his name, Harry Potter.

No, it is not. The first Harry Potter novel was published in America the same month and year as *Specter:* September 1998. Rowling and I weren't copying each other—this is just one of those coincidences that sometimes happen. A few years later I met J.K. Rowling and in a brief conversation with her I found out that she had read and liked the Bellairs novels. She also complimented the tie I was wearing that day.

Re-reading the book now, I find the extremely gloomy and terrifying scenes toward the end rather surprise me. Oh, the story has humor, but this one also has an exceedingly grim overall tone—not that John's books never had that kind of feeling. I still think *The Figure in the*

*Shadows* is the scariest book in the New Zebedee series, but this one just might give a few readers nightmares, too.

Edward Gorey's cover features a mysterious tombstone with a stone sphere, inspired by the Charles Merchant monument in Marion, Ohio. A five-ton globe on the Merchant tomb marker mysteriously revolves on its own, and no one knows why. I put a similar thing in the book. From Gorey's sphere, enigmatic eyes peer as if gazing into your soul. The back includes one of Gorey's splendidly spooky haunted houses, and hovering above it the form of a gigantic spider.

*Specter* is one of the darker novels in the series, and re-reading it gives me the shivers. I would *not* recommend it as light reading just before bedtime. Spiders, moldy corpses, tombs reeking of rot, and a hateful evil sorceress laughing at the sufferings of our friends—ugh!

However, as always, there are counterbalances to the gloom and doom. Though reading the book is, to me, a spooky experience, it also brings back warm memories of that summer and the magic that we found up in Michigan.

Oddly, my memory of writing this scary tale ranks among the most pleasant. With the experiences of our visit and with the research under my belt, I once again, began writing while in Marshall. I worked up an outline and knew roughly what I wanted the climax to be. I remember writing the opening sentence on my yellow legal pad in my hotel room, late at night.

I still like it a lot: "Lewis Barnavelt had been frightened before in his life; but this time he was terrified."

◆　◆　◆

### *The Specter from the Magician's Museum:* People, Places, and Things

**Abbott Magic Company.** Uncle Jonathan refers to the (real) annual convention of magicians in Colon, Michigan and says he might take Lewis there next August if he wants to pick up some magic tricks.

**Al-Majah, the Mystic Sheik.** Lewis considers using this as his stage name for the magic show he plans with Rose Rita.

**Amulets.** Mrs. Zimmermann takes three from her collection when they go to confront the villain: an Egyptian scarab, symbolic of life; a tiny gold cross that bears the blessing of a saint; and a purple gemstone that glows with a spark of magic.

**Anansi.** A character from West African folklore, also well known in the Caribbean. Anansi is a spider, shape-shifter, and a trickster whose pranks range from merely mischievous to deadly.

**Anubis.** An ancient Egyptian god, who has the head of a jackal. He is the god of embalming and mummification and guards the gate between Life and Death.

**Arachne.** A character in Greek mythology. She won a weaving contest against the goddess Athena, who in a fit of anger changed Arachne to a spider. This, by the way, is why spiders belong to the class called arachnids.

**Astronomy.** Lewis considers this as a career—because he'd get to watch stars and planets every night and be all alone instead of being laughed at on stage. As a matter of fact, according to John Bellairs, he later did become a distinguished astronomer at Mt. Palomar Observatory in California.

**Barnavelt, Jonathan van Olden.** We learn that he has stopped smoking and has gained weight as a result. Mrs. Zimmermann advises him to diet, beginning tomorrow. He knows some ordinary conjuring tricks in addition to his skill at creating magical illusions, especially card tricks.

**Battle of Lepanto.** The last great naval battle between Christians and the Ottoman Turks, 1571. Uncle Jonathan created an illusion of it to amuse Lewis and Rose Rita.

**Blackstone.** Harry Blackstone, Sr. A real magician. Rose Rita remembers seeing him perform on TV, and one of the books in the museum was written by him. He owned an island in a lake near Colon, Michigan and created many fantastic magic tricks, including "The Floating Light Bulb," which convinced audiences that a lighted bulb was levitating over their heads. After he passed away in 1965, his son, Harry Blackstone, Jr., replicated his act for many years.

**Books of magic.** Rose Rita and Lewis borrow some from Mr. Hardwick's library in the National Museum of Magic. They are all about conjuring tricks and include such titles as *Chemical Magic with Everyday Ingredients; Close-Up Tricks with Matches,*

*Coins, and String; How to Amaze Your Friends;* and others. Though these titles are fictitious, they are modeled on actual books in Marshall's American Museum of Magic and on titles sold by the Abbott Magic Company.

**Britton, Chad.** A schoolmate of Lewis's. He wants to be a detective when he grows up, and he practices by following random people around town. He is pretty good at it. Chad is based on a real person from Marshall, one of the winners of the trivia contest.

**Bud Abbott and Lou Costello.** A real comedy team, popular in the movies and on TV during the 1940s and 1950s. Dave Shellenberger and Tom Lutz, Lewis's classmates, plan to perform Abbott and Costello's "Who's on First?" comedy baseball routine at the talent show.

**Camp Itchi-Kitti-Kippi.** A summer camp for girls. Rose Rita went to it the previous summer, but she did not enjoy her stay there. Based on a real camp, now closed, near Marshall.

**Candelini, the Great.** Stage name of Frederick Jeremy McCandles, a (fictional) magician who did magic with lighted candles. He died in 1943 and is buried in the cemetery near Cristobal, MI.

**Costumes.** Mrs. Zimmermann runs up costumes for Lewis and Rose Rita to wear in their magic act. Lewis wears a silvery turban with a peacock plume, a short black-velvet cape, lined in purple, a loose purple tunic, and loose scarlet pants, along with coverings that make his shoes look like Persian slippers with curly toes. Rose Rita wears a purple top, baggy purple harem pants, and golden slippers, plus a headdress made of imitation pearls and a gauzy purple veil. Mrs. Zimmermann tells them they look like something out of the Arabian Nights.

**Cracker Jack.** A sweet snack made with popcorn, peanuts, and a molasses coating. Each box contained a prize—in the 1950s, these might have been miniature harmonicas, small yo-yos, and similar toys.

**Creamy the Magical Clown.** Host of a TV show that features cartoons and magic tricks by Creamy, the host, a clown in whiteface makeup. Lewis gets inspiration from seeing this show to team with Rose Rita and do a magic act for the talent show. He is based on Milky the Clown, a popular kids' entertainer working out of a Detroit TV station in the 1950s.

**Cristobal.** Fictional town in Michigan, twenty miles from New Zebedee. It's hardly even a town, just a crossroads with a few stores and a gas station. A cemetery near the town, surrounded by a white-washed wooden picket fence, is the final resting place for many famous magicians—but the most prominent monument is the ominous sphere on a pillar that memorializes Belle Frisson. The inscription on her stone reads, "Belle Frisson (Born Elizabeth Proctor) 1822-1878. She Wants to Live Again."

Lewis and Rose Rita learn that she died in the nearby town after a train wreck, though she survived for several painful months before the end, and weeks before she died, she bought a farm and donated it to the county as a cemetery, provided she was the first one buried there. She even designed her tombstone and wrote out the scroll that Rose Rita discovered. After nearly two months of lingering after receiving her injuries, she died during a thunderstorm on Halloween night, 1878. After she passed away, strangers came to town, buried her, and erected the monument. According to the will, anyone who had a dead loved one but could not afford to bury him or her could have a plot in the cemetery, and any stage magician could also have a plot for free.

**Death Spider.** A phantom-like creature, a magical spider that is the familiar and companion of the Egyptian goddess Neith. That is fiction, by the way; mythology does not connect spiders with Neith.

**Detroit Tigers.** Rose Rita's dad, George, is a fan of the team and during baseball season, he listens to every Tigers game broadcast on radio.

**Dreams.** When the magic spell cast on her by the scroll begins to work, Rose Rita has a nightmare in which she is flying, and she passes above some girls on the ground making fun of her, not suspecting that she can hear them. A ghostly voice urges her to attack one of the girls, and Rose Rita is tempted, but then she discovers that she is dangling from a web, not flying, and she has eight legs and fangs drooling venom. She has been transformed into a spider.

Later she sees in a dream the tombstone of Elizabeth Proctor, also known as Belle Frisson. It is unusual—a stone globe atop a pillar—and Rose Rita feels compelled to go and find it.

**Drueke chessmen.** Produced by the Wm. F. Drueke Company of Grand Rapids, MI, these chess sets were classics and set the pattern for U.S. chessmen for many years. The earliest popular sets were carved from wood (Rose Rita has one of these sets), and later the company produced plastic ones. Their chessmen ranged from tiny ones meant to be used on a folding pocket chessboard which had holes for the pegs on the bottom of the pieces to majestic, handsome, large ones, with pieces more than three inches tall. Rose Rita's is in the middle, and the chessmen are made of dark brown and light tan wood.

**Egyptian Book of the Dead.** A real ancient book created by the Egyptians, full of incantations and prayers to help the souls of the dead find their place in the afterlife.

**Fantastic Fatima.** This is Rose Rita's stage name for her and Lewis's magic act.

**Fetch.** A supernatural apparition that goes from the realm of the spirits into the world to take away the soul of a doomed person. In England and Ireland, they may be doubles of the doomed person—Doppelgängers. In other countries, they might be animals, birds, insects—or spiders.

**Fogarty, Mrs.** Lewis and Rose Rita's English teacher. She is also the one in charge of keeping order at the talent show.

**Forrester, C.S.** British novelist, popular in the 1940s and 1950s. Rose Rita reads one of his novels about the fictional British naval hero Horatio Hornblower.

***Forty Years among the Magicians,* by Joseph W. Winston.** A fictitious book, published in Chicago in 1885, one of several that Rose Rita and Lewis borrow from the National Museum of Magic. In it, Rose Rita reads a brief biography of "Belle Frisson," which includes an engraved picture of her, a woman with piercing, dark eyes, jet-black hair, wearing an Egyptian headdress and a round medallion with an image of a spider on it. The biography also includes a photograph of her grave, with the notation that the stone ball atop the pillar slowly revolves as seasons go by.

**Fox Sisters.** These real-life girls started a craze for "table tipping" and trying to communicate with the dead. Maggie, Kate, and Leah Fox would hold séances and pretend to speak to the dead, who most often would answer by rapping on the table where they sat—one rap for "no," two for "yes." This began in Hydesville, NY, in 1848. Later the sisters confessed that the poltergeist activity at their performances was all faked, but many people still believed it was possible to speak to dead spirits following their procedure.

**Frisson, Belle.** Stage name of Elizabeth Proctor, an early and rare woman magician. Born in Savannah, Georgia, Elizabeth grew up to be an unsuccessful actress, but when she saw the Fox sisters perform their fake spirit-medium act around 1850, she saw through their tricks. Instead of exposing them, though, she went home to Savannah and put together an act in which she became Belle Frisson, a sorceress, seer, and mentalist who supposedly could call on spirits to aid her. She became quite successful as a magician and toured the country from 1855 to 1878 (except for the Civil War years, 1861-1865). She died in Michigan in 1878, and she is buried in a cemetery near Cristobal, Michigan, that is the final resting place of half a dozen famous stage magicians.

**Gensterblum, James.** Based on a real person from Marshall—one of the trivia contest winners—James plans to play his guitar as part of the talent show.

**Gottschalk, Sue.** One of Rose Rita's classmates. In her nightmare, Rose Rita thinks Sue is gossiping about her in a mean way.

**Hardwick, Robert and Ellen.** The couple recently moved to New Zebedee. Robert, a retired newspaperman and an avid amateur magician and collector, owned the collection of conjuring paraphernalia that makes up the heart of the museum's collection. He often plays cards upstairs in the museum with his friends, all of whom are professional magicians themselves. His wife Ellen is lovingly tolerant of his expansive hobby. Robert's younger brother is a gym teacher in *The Figure in the Shadows*.

**Henrietta.** Lewis's friend Timmy brings a full-grown hen to the magic show, when Lewis had asked for a baby chicken. Things do not go well.

**Hootchie-kootchie.** See "Little Egypt." This is a dance, usually done by a solo, underdressed lady. It apparently originated in Chicago in 1893 at the World's Fair by one of the three "Little Egypt" dancers. It is a belly dance, with many alternate spellings: "Coochy-Coochy," "Hoochy-Koochy," and others. The original tune was called "The Streets of Cairo; or, The Poor Little Country Maid." It is also called "The Snake Charmer's Song." In the movie *Meet Me in St. Louis,* the title song says that the singer and her boyfriend will "dance the hoochy-coochy" at the St. Louis World's Fair, though the dance is not intended for couples.

Oh, dear, my dear reader. If you are an adult, go out and close the door. We will wait. Are they gone? Very well, you have probably heard the song on the playground or at summer camp. The lyrics usually sung are a parody of the original ones and begin "There's a place in France where the ladies . . . ." From there on it gets rather naughty, I'm afraid, but your parents or grandparents probably remember the song. However, I won't reveal anything naughty in this book, so please don't ask me; not when the Internet is so handy.

**Houdini.** Probably the most famous American magician of his day, this was the stage name of Erik Weisz, born in Hungary in 1874. When he was only four years old, his family emigrated to America, where they changed the spelling of their last name to "Weiss," which is the German version, and the spelling of Erik's first name to "Erich." The family lived in Appleton, WI, and as a young fellow, Erich became a champion track star. At the age of sixteen, he read a biography of a famous French magician, Robert-Houdin, and decided to become a stage performer. He took the name "Harry Houdini" in tribute to his idol. By 1899, he had become famous, especially as an escape artist. He performed his act all over the world, baffling audiences everywhere.

He had some close calls. Once in a "buried alive" stunt, he nearly suffocated when the grave collapsed into the box he was sealed in. At another time, he claimed that he did an underwater escape in the middle of winter in a river—and when he got to the surface, he found himself trapped under inches of ice and had to swim for a long way on his back, breathing the little layer of air trapped between the ice and water. That may have been an exaggerated story, though.

Houdini emphatically did *not* believe in ghosts, spirit mediums, or real magic. He spent a lot of time debunking paranormal claims—that is, showing that trickery and fraud was a better explanation than magic for the supposed wonders that the paranormalists claimed.

Houdini died on Halloween night in 1926 of a ruptured appendix. Lewis sees some of his old equipment at the National Museum of Magic and hears of some of his flops as Mr. Hardwick and his friends comfort him for the failure of his magic act at the talent show.

**Lamp of Osiris.** A (fictional) magic spell from ancient Egypt that prepares for a human sacrifice. It is so called because it produces a dismally glowing green vapor. The glow is also called a "corpse candle" or a "will o' the wisp."

*Last Testament of Belle Frisson, the Greatest Sorceress of Her Age, The.* The full title handwritten on the scroll Rose Rita takes, by mistake, from the Museum of Magic.

**Lindholm, Timmy.** Classmate of Lewis's who lives on a farm. He promises to lend Lewis a young chicken for his magic act. Timmy himself plans to juggle.

**Little Duke playing cards.** Rose Rita owns a deck of these miniature cards. They measure only about 1 x 1 ½ inches and are more like toys than cards you'd play games with.

**Little Egypt.** The stage name of three exotic dancers from the late 19th and early 20th Centuries. They wore abbreviated costumes and did the kind of dance that Mrs. Zimmermann calls the "hootchie-cootchie." Mrs. Zimmermann's friends called her "Little Egypt" after an accident on the dance floor made Mrs. Zimmermann's skirt fall down to her ankles.

**Lutz, Tom.** A classmate of Lewis and Rose Rita. He is a popular student at New Zebedee Junior High, athletic, good-looking, and a snappy dresser. Lewis is envious and a little afraid of him. With Dave Shellenberger, he dominates the other kids in their class.

**Lyon Lake.** Mrs. Zimmermann invites Lewis, Rose Rita, and Jonathan down to her lake cottage for an afternoon, but Rose Rita refuses to come along.

*Macbeth.* Mrs. Zimmermann refers to this Shakespeare play and the line, "By the pricking of my thumbs, / Something wicked this way comes!" She's right—it's a magical attack against Rose Rita. By the way, Ray Bradbury titled one of his best books *Something Wicked This Way Comes.* I highly recommend it.

*Madame Frisson: Her Testament from Beyond the Grave.* A hand-written scroll that Rose Rita finds in the library of the National Museum of Magic. Unlike the books about conjuring, the scroll is magical—and evil. With it is a cursed gray powder that, when exposed to blood, becomes a live spider . . . and begins a dire spell. The scroll is aged parchment, wound on a wooden rod, and it has a cloth cover that looks as if it were once purple velvet, but it has faded to a dull maroon. The gold letters of the title on it have become a faded greenish yellow. Rose Rita finally discovers that some markings on the scroll line up with markings on Frisson's tombstone to create a dangerous magical incantation.

**Magic act.** Lewis and Rose Rita plan four tricks: Producing a live chicken from a simple sheet of newsprint; levitating Rose Rita so she floats in the air; magically transporting Rose Rita from one mystifying cabinet (a large, painted cardboard box) to another one; and making Rose Rita's severed head float in mid-air. They don't get through the whole act because things happen.

**Model farmhouse and barn.** Rose Rita has a hand-carved wooden miniature farm, a souvenir from the trip to Pennsylvania she and Mrs. Zimmermann took in *Ghost in the Mirror.*

**Muggins Simoon.** Uncle Jonathan is still driving his antique 1935 car. It is fictitious; no such car was ever made.

**Muller, Lauren.** In Rose Rita's nightmare, she is one of the girls from the junior high school who gossip about Rose Rita and make nasty comments on her looks.

**Mussenberger, Clarence "Clare."** One of Bob Hardwick's poker buddies. He is the actor who plays Creamy the Clown on TV five days a week.

**"Mystical Production of a Rabbit."** One of the magic tricks that Lewis learns, except since he has no rabbit, he plans to use a young chicken a classmate promises to bring to the talent show. The instructions for the trick are in Chapter 4.

**Mystifying Mysto, Master of Illusion.** This is the stage name that Lewis finally selects for his and Rose Rita's magic act.

*National Geographic.* Lewis likes this magazine a lot and sometimes thinks it would be fun when he grows up to work for it, roaming the world and photographing landscapes, animals, and people as subjects of his photographs.

**National Museum of Magic, The.** Recently opened in the old Eugster's Brewery building on Main Street in New Zebedee. The building is red brick, with round, high windows on one wall. It was built in 1842, according to the cornerstone. The brewery went out of business long before Lewis arrived in town, and the building stood empty until the museum opened.

The owner and operator of the museum is Mr. Robert W. Hardwick. It contains props, mementos, and posters from the 19th and 20th centuries: mummy cases, trunks thrust through with swords, a padlocked steel milk canister, top hats, canes, and wands. The posters on the wall advertise such magic acts of the past as the Great Rapiri, the Hindoo Fakir; Long Chi, the Chinese Wonder; and the Mystic Marquis, among many others.

On the second floor of the museum are the offices and the library, which contains more than seven thousand books about stage magic. Rose Rita and Lewis borrow some of these.

**Neith.** An ancient Egyptian goddess, whose symbol is the spider. She leads souls to the afterlife, and some of her followers believed that if they gave her a human sacrifice, a dead person might be reborn.

**New Zebedee Opera House.** Now an auditorium for the area schools, it is the site of the talent show in October. The story of how it was reopened is in *The Doom of the Haunted Opera.*

**Old Dutch Cleanser.** A real product, a scouring powder. When Rose Rita hides in the school janitor's closet she notices stacks of cans containing this product.

**Perkins, Thomas.** One of Bob Hardwick's poker buddies. In his magic act, he is Lord Puzzlewit, specializing in close-up magic and card tricks.

**Phantom spider.** One begins to follow Rose Rita and gradually grows larger and larger until it is gigantic.

**"Pink Pajama" song.** Rose Rita learned it at camp, and normally it makes her smile. It is sung to the tune of "Battle Hymn of the Republic." The lyrics are in Chapter 6. This is a real song, often sung at scout camps or summer camps around a campfire, and I've even seen versions of it performed on the internet. Like all such folk and playground songs, it has many different versions, some more polite than others. However, in every version I've read or seen performed, the singer inevitably "sometimes jumps right in between the sheets with nothing on at all."

**Potter, Rowena.** The fake name that Rose Rita makes up when she hitchhikes a ride to Cristobal from Mrs. Susanna Seidler.

**Pottinger, Rose Rita.** Still gawky, tall, and self-conscious about her looks. Rose Rita wears a blouse and skirt to school, but once home she changes into casual clothes. In Chapter 1, the outfit consists of a ratty old Notre Dame sweatshirt (her mom got it from one of her college boyfriends, and Mr. Pottinger doesn't like it because of that, so Rose Rita inherited it), jeans, and black P.F. Flyers tennis shoes. Rose Rita also occasionally wears a Notre Dame jacket, but her father doesn't mind that because it used to belong to his brother, who also went to Notre Dame.

Rose Rita still tells convoluted tall tales. When a classmate, Bill Mackey, irritates her, she makes up a story about how he was kidnapped by Martians as a baby and raised in low gravity on Mars—that's why he grew up to be such a gangly beanpole of a boy. That's not a fib, just a tale to help her and Lewis feel a little better. Later, though, she spins a very strange yarn while hitchhiking from New Zebedee to Cristobal, a neighboring town, claiming that she came to New Zebedee with her uncle, who had to have an emergency operation, and she couldn't call her parents to come and get her because they had no phone to begin with, and furthermore were both deaf.

**Prayer.** Worried about Rose Rita, Lewis murmurs the Latin prayer that begins *Omnipotens sempiterne Deus*, which asks for protection against adversity.

**Quackenbush, Ben.** When Rose Rita is publicly embarrassed, Mrs. Zimmermann tells about when she was in school and danced with Ben. He was handsome and rugged but clumsy, and as the two danced, he stepped on the hem of her long skirt and tugged it right down to her ankles. After her first embarrassment, Mrs. Zimmermann began to laugh at how ridiculous it all was, and she tells Rose Rita that one day she'll be able to laugh at what now she sees as a humiliating experience.

**"Saber Dance."** An instrumental musical number composed by Aram Khachaturian in 1942 as part of the score of his ballet *Gayane*. It is a fast, furious piece of music, with wild, careening music and is often used in stage shows for magic acts and the like. Lewis has a recording of it for his and Rose Rita's act. It is perhaps more frequently seen with the British spelling "Sabre Dance."

**Seidler, Susanna.** A plump, middle-aged woman who gives Rose Rita a lift in her red Ford pickup truck. She likes to talk about her family, Hiram, Ernst, Clara, and Velma, whom everyone calls "Snookums."

**Shellenberger, Dave.** A classmate of Lewis and Rose Rita and, like his friend Dave Lutz, a big wheel in school, popular, handsome and a good dresser.

**Stone, Johnny.** One of Bob Hardwick's poker buddies. His state name is Bondini, and like Houdini, he specializes in escaping from handcuffs, strait jackets, and jail cells.

**Television set.** TV has just come to the Barnavelt house in the form of a Zenith Stratosphere, which had a perfectly circular screen, like a porthole. The screen is small, about the size of a dinner plate, and with a rooftop antenna, the set can pick up three channels, though the black-and-white images tend to be staticky and full of snow.

**Twin Oaks Dairy.** The sponsor of *Creamy, the Magical Clown* on TV. Based on the actual Twin Pines Dairy in Detroit.

**Walsh, Chris.** Ten years old, with short brown hair, he is the son of the famous archaeologist David Walsh. He loans Lewis and Jonathan some of his dad's books on Ancient Egypt. Chris is based on a real person from Marshall, one of the boys who won the trivia contest.

**Walsh, David.** A local celebrity in New Zebedee, an archaeologist whose specialty is Egyptology. He is away on an expedition in the Nile Valley, but his son Chris goes to Lewis's school.

**White, Miss.** The school music teacher. She accompanies some of the acts at the talent show on the piano. She is modeled on my favorite elementary-school teacher, Miss Elise Walpole.

**Zimmermann, Florence.** In a climactic battle between Good and Evil, we see proof that her powers have fully returned. She transforms into her sorceress form as she performs a powerful magic spell.

◆ ◆ ◆

**Chapter 6: John Bellairs's Lewis Barnavelt in**
*The Beast Under the Wizard's Bridge*
**By Brad Strickland**
**Dial Books for Young Readers, 2000**

Jeanne Sharp, the fellow Bellairs fan who read and advised me on some of the earlier manuscripts, once reminded me that John often used works of classic horror writers as inspirations for his stories. However, she said, he had overlooked one. I thought about her suggestion as I began to work on the eighty novel in the Lewis Barnavelt series. Maybe it was time for an H.P. Lovecraft turn.

Though John clearly was aware of H.P. Lovecraft's works, he had never overtly ventured into what is called the Cthulhu Mythos, a sort of artificial mythology that Lovecraft created and used in his own weird fiction, and which he generously invited other writers to share. Thinking about that, I began to mull over some elements.

Howard Phillips Lovecraft (1890-1937) was not a particularly admirable fellow. He had many prejudices and biases against foreigners and people of races different from his own. His writing could be difficult to follow, digressive, and drily pedantic. He loved prose that read as if it had been written in the Eighteenth Century. His narrators tend to be rather bloodless and uninvolving. And yet . . ..

Some of his stories create what he called "cosmic horror," horror not grounded in ghosts and goblins and ghouls, but in the uneasy feeling that humans are not alone in the universe, and were not even the first to claim Earth as their home. The Great Old Ones, as Lovecraft calls them, were here first, according to his Mythos, and they are straining to destroy humankind and reclaim the planet as their own. The Universe did not hinder or help humans because the terrifying fact was—it just didn't care about us. Later writers who wrote stories set in the same milieu—especially August Derleth, a devout Catholic—added the overtones of conventional good and evil.

When I was twelve, Lovecraft was my favorite writer of weird fiction. Later I began to see some of his limitations and the problems with his world view, and to some extent I outgrew my preference for his writing. Yet the stories themselves lingered, horrific and disturbing. That was what I wanted to get at in this tale of something alien lurking near New Zebedee.

Also, as I read Sir James George Frazer's monumental *The Golden Bough* (1922), a kind of multivolume compendium of human mythology and folklore, I latched onto the concept of the separable soul—a way that a shaman or sorcerer could become virtually immortal by hiding his or her soul in some unlikely object. I did a little more research into the folklore legends about the concept, including the Russian folk tale about Koshchie the Deathless. He was either a demon or a sorcerer who took his soul from his body and placed it inside a needle, which he placed inside an egg, which he placed inside a duck, which he placed inside a rabbit, which he locked in a chest and buried. He could only be killed when someone dug up the chest, freed the rabbit, took the duck from inside it, took the egg from the duck, broke the egg, and then destroyed the needle.

In the book I refer to a variant of this legend, but it is only one of a host of similar tales familiar to folklorists. The Arabian Nights and Grimm's fairy tales contain other stories of separable souls. J.K. Rowling later independently used the same idea for the horcruxes in the Harry Potter books.

With these elements in mind—Lovecraftian horror and the separable soul—I began to plot the book.

◆　◆　◆

*Summary:*

The story begins in February, when Jonathan Barnavelt becomes disgruntled and upset as he reads a news story that reveals the county has plans to tear down and replace the old iron bridge over Wilder Creek, which has stood there for about sixty years. Lewis remembers that once Mrs. Zimmermann told him that the bridge had been built by a wizard, old Elihu Clabbernong, in 1892, and he had put something in the iron to keep the ghost of his uncle from crossing the river and getting him.

Lewis later learns that both his uncle and Mrs. Zimmermann fear that when the old bridge is demolished, something evil will be released from the waters. Rose Rita agrees to help Lewis learn more when both Mrs. Zimmermann and his uncle turn reticent and refuse to share their worries and concerns with Lewis—a fact that only makes him more anxious. In the early summer, they all visit the construction site, and Lewis picks up a loose rivet that has fallen from one of the girders of the iron bridge. That becomes important later. Meanwhile, readers—but not the characters—become aware that a sinister, unpleasant, quarreling elderly couple are sneaking around New Zebedee, hard at work trying to summon . . . something terrible.

Before the adventure is over, Lewis and Rose Rita must face a monstrous enemy who comes from beyond the time and space that humans know.

◆ ◆ ◆

***Behind the Scenes:***

I went back to the very first book in the series, *The House with a Clock in Its Walls,* for the inspiration. One of my favorite scenes in that novel is the moment in Chapter 6 when Jonathan, Mrs. Zimmermann, and Lewis are out for a late-night drive . . . and something monstrous, maybe a car, maybe not, follows them, forcing Uncle Jonathan to push the old Muggins Simoon to its limits as they speed down a dark and twisting highway. Mrs. Zimmermann advises Jonathan to make for the bridge over Wilder Creek, and the old car crosses it just in time. The pursuer screeches to a halt. Evil things cannot cross that bridge.

So . . . what happens when the bridge is eventually replaced, as all bridges are? That was the launching pad for the plot. The quarreling elderly couple, Mephistopheles and Ermine Moote, seize on the news to free the ancient monstrous thing that lies under the water of Wilder Creek. It is an alien creature with the power to absorb and twist magic, and it will be a real problem for Jonathan and Mrs. Zimmermann. From there on, it became a battle of wits and wills between the representatives of Good and the minions of Evil.

Mrs. Jaeger, now a member of the Capharnaum County Magicians Society, makes another appearance, as do some other familiar figures. We also see a bit of Capharnaum County and visit a few places in New

Zebedee. Uncle Jonathan gets to cast another of his entertaining illusions, though this one goes badly wrong. And Lewis must summon up courage that he's not sure he even has—this one will be a close-run race, for sure.

For a change, the title was set early. I thought about a Lovecraftian approach. Lovecraft's short-story titles tend to be distinctive: "The Call of Cthulhu"; "The Whisperer in Darkness"; "The Colour out of Space"; and "The Dunwich Horror." They didn't quite mesh with Bellairs, though. The working notes show that the title was first "The Beast Under the Bridge," and that soon changed to "The Beast Under the Wizard's Bridge," and that was it.

I drew on Lovecraft's Cthulhu Mythos for the monster. The Great Cthulhu, as the creature is often called, is a monstrous octopoid/humanoid abomination that slumbers in the depths of the sea. He is one of the Great Old Ones who constantly dream of sweeping humanity off the face of the Earth and reclaiming the planet as their own. Cthulhu and his kind are not of the Earth, nor do they consist of any Earthly matter—their bodies, their chemistry, are quite different from any ordinary biology. For that matter, the region of the universe from which they come even has physical laws at odds with the ones we know. Geometry is different there. Gravity and other physical forces that we know act in bizarre ways. A few hints of this appear. However, the Beast is not Cthulhu, but maybe a cousin of his.

The Lovecraft story that this novel echoes most is "The Colour out of Space," a tale of a meteor that sizzles into the atmosphere and bears the seeds of some monster so alien that we cannot see it because its body reflects only light in wavelengths the human eye cannot perceive. It absorbs the life force of Earthly creatures . . . and of humans. And it rests beneath water until its time comes around again.

Another, incidental, inspiration came from the legend of Jim Bowie and the knife made for him by the blacksmith James Black. Bowie, a frontiersman who was one of the ill-fated defenders of the Alamo during the Texas Revolution, designed a special dagger, and the blacksmith James Black forged it for him, using a secret process that produced an unusually strong, flexible steel. The story sprang up that he had added to the ordinary iron a meteorite, and the meteoric iron mysteriously toughened the steel he smelted for the Bowie knife. That is a myth, but an interesting one, and I used it as an explanation for the mysterious something that Elihu Clabbernong put in the iron for the Wilder Creek Bridge.

I dedicated this novel to my wife, Barbara, who over the years has put up with a lot from me and who is always loving and supportive when I disappear into my downstairs office for weeks or months to write a novel. Edward Gorey's cover features on the front a hideously deformed creature—maybe a gopher or groundhog—that has been corrupted by the strange visitor from outer space. The back cover shows the octopus-like Beast itself, beneath the baleful light of a red comet. The two are linked in the book's climax.

This is one of the more unusual entries in that it blends science fiction—the alien creature, the comet—with suspense and horror. In that sense it is a little like the Johnny Dixon novel *The Trolley to Yesterday,* which includes the science-fiction device of a time machine.

◆ ◆ ◆

### *The Beast Under the Wizard's Bridge:* **People, Places, and Things**

**Andrews, James.** In 1885, the town constable of New Zebedee. His account of the red meteor is quoted in a local newspaper story.

**Autry, Gene** (1907-1998). A singing cowboy whose full name was Orvon Grover Autry ("Gene" was his nickname). He made nearly a hundred movies and starred as a version of himself, an honest good-guy cowboy who was also a singer. Autry was also a country-western musician and songwriter and had many hit recordings, including "Back in the Saddle Again," but his biggest success was "Rudolph, the Red-Nosed Reindeer." Uncle Jonathan tries to persuade Lewis and Rose Rita to go see one of his movies in town, but Lewis prefers the non-singing type of cowboy.

**Badminton.** Lewis and Rose Rita play a game on the lawn of Mrs. Zimmermann's lake cottage, though they don't really keep score. They just enjoy batting the birdie back and forth.

**Barnavelt, Lewis.** Lewis's timidity and his insecurity both work against him in this story. With Rose Rita's help, he must overcome both of these—especially his fear that Uncle Jonathan may resent him and view him as an interfering annoyance—to deal with the monstrous danger that has come to New Zebedee.

**Battle of the Nile, The.** Uncle Jonathan casts one of his grand illusion spells on the evening of July 4th to celebrate the holiday. The spell makes it seem like Jonathan, Mrs. Zimmermann, Lewis, and Rose Rita are on the deck of a British ship in Nelson's squadron on the night of August 1, 1798.

However, everything goes horribly wrong when it seems the ship tilts and dumps everyone into the ocean, where a bloodthirsty monster attacks them.

**Beast.** The tentacled monster that lurks in the water of Wilder Creek is part human, but mostly an alien being, a Great Old One or its descendant. It absorbed the human, but since the man's body was cremated before that happened, the human part of the monstrosity cannot remember its old identity.

**Boyd, Ernest.** One of Mephistopheles Moote's law partners in Kalamazoo, MI.

**Capharnaum County Magicians Society.** When Rose Rita and Lewis turn over the diary of an evil magician to Uncle Jonathan, he and Mrs. Zimmermann call an emergency meeting of the Society. Rose Rita and Lewis hide in the secret passage and eavesdrop, learning some dreadful secrets about old Jebediah Clabbernong.

**Captain Midnight Secret Decoder Ring.** These were generally pins or badges, not rings. They were given as advertising premiums by the sponsors of *Captain Midnight*, first a radio show and then later a TV show about a pilot who had a private jet and who fought bad guys. The show would end with a secret code (not a true code but a letter-replacement cipher) that was a clue to the next week's program. Those who had the decoder could decipher the message. I compounded John's misremembering the decoder as a ring here; he had made the same mistake in *Figure*. I have found out this is a common failing among people who remember the device—they forget it was a badge and almost always call it a ring.

**Clabbernong Farm.** An expanse of many hundred acres on the Twelve-Mile Road. It belonged first to Jebediah Clabbernong, and on his death, his nephew Elihu inherited it. At the time the story takes place, the roof of the farmhouse has collapsed, and all around the building a strange, ghastly blight has broken out: all the plants and trees have died, and they are so brittle they crumble to powder if anyone touches them. Jonathan recalls something that happened twenty years earlier, when he explored the farm and found what he thought was the mummified body of a woodchuck, caught in the act of climbing out of its burrow. He supposes it has been dead since the night the meteorite struck nearby decades before. Yet, the horrible, crumbling, dead-looking thing feebly moved. Somehow, though it was flaking to pieces, it was still alive.

**Clabbernong, Elihu.** A wealthy farmer who owned hundreds of acres of farm and pasture land outside of New Zebedee, he built the original iron bridge over Wilder Creek in 1892 and gave it to the county, supposedly to help farmers get their crops to market. Mrs. Zimmermann says he built it to protect himself from the spirit of his vengeful uncle Jebediah. Both were practitioners of magic, Jebediah a particularly evil one. When Jebediah died on the night that a brilliant meteorite crashed to earth on their farm, Elihu inherited everything. He sold everything he owned except the uncanny meteorite, which made people nervous because it just looked weird. With part of the money, he built the iron bridge. Then he moved to town and lived there almost like a hermit for the rest of his life, getting richer and richer until he passed peacefully away in 1947.

**Clabbernong, Jebediah.** The great-uncle of Elihu Clabbernong. When his nephew Elihu's parents died, Jebediah took the boy in, raised him, and taught him magic. In December 1885, an uncanny red meteorite plunged to earth on the Clabbernong farm, and the same night, old Jebediah died. However, his evil influence seems to have remained behind.

**Comet.** A long-period comet with an extraordinarily extended orbit makes an appearance in the book. Its orbit is so elongated it has a period of 14,000 years (Halley's Comet, by contrast, returns to our neighborhood once every 75 years). Its light is a baleful red, and it is hurtling toward the Earth at the time of the novel.

***Cyclopaedic Dictionary of Magic and the Magical Arts.*** An imaginary reference book in Uncle Jonathan's library, this is by someone named van Schull. It is as big as an unabridged dictionary, and in it Lewis finds an article on separable souls.

**D'Erlette, Comte.** A fictional scholar of magic. H.P. Lovecraft coined the name and used it in some of his fiction. It was a tribute to Lovecraft's friend August Derleth, later a writer himself

**Dill pickles.** Mrs. Zimmermann makes delicious ones. She won a blue ribbon for them at the 1938 County Fair.

**Donner Party.** Jonathan refers to this historical tragedy. In the fall of 1846, the Donner Party of pioneers, 87 in all, tried to cross the Sierra Nevada in covered wagons. It was November, and a blizzard stranded them in the mountains. With their oxen dying of cold and starvation, the members of the party built temporary shelters and tried to ride out the storm. The weather got even worse, and as weeks passed, the people began to die of starvation. At last the living resorted to cannibalism of their dead friends and relatives to survive. When finally they were rescued in the spring of 1847, only 48 were left alive out of the initial 87 in the party.

**Dreams.** Lewis has a nightmare about a trip to a horrific zoo, a ride on a miniature train being driven by a skeletal engineer, and a monstrous creature in cage that falls apart. It may have been caused by his fretting and worrying about the destruction of Wilder Creek Bridge.

**Enchanted Heart.** Not an actual heart, but a large ruby carved as an accurate model of a human heart. It pulses with its own eerie inner light—like a heartbeat.

**Feather bed.** One of Lewis's aunts had a superstition that in a thunderstorm, the only place in a house safe from lightning was a feather bed.

**Field Street.** Street in New Zebedee. On it is the house where Mr. and Mrs. Moote have moved.

**Flashback.** Chapter 1 includes a close re-telling of the exciting late-night chase from Chapter 6 of *House*, as Lewis tells the story to Rose Rita.

**Flavius.** One of the members of the Magicians Society mentions him. Probably this is Flavius Josephus, a first-century scholar who wrote a history of the Jewish people.

**Great Old Ones.** *The Mystic Journal of Jedediah Clabbernong* mentions these demonic alien creatures. They come from the Cthulhu Mythos created by American writer H.P. Lovecraft.

**Hawaii House.** Not very far from the Barnavelt house in New Zebedee, it was built by a townsman who in the 1800s had been a U.S. government representative to the Sandwich Islands, as Hawaii was then called. It is built on an eccentric plan, like a house intended to be in tropical Hawaii instead of cold Michigan. It is based on the real Honolulu House in Marshall, MI, and reappears in a later story, *The House Where Nobody Lived.*

**Heemsoth's Rexall Drug Store.** Patterned after the real Hemmingsen Rexall Drug Store on Michigan Avenue in downtown Marshall, this is a fixture on Main Street. It features an old-fashioned soda fountain, and Lewis, Rose Rita, and other town kids frequently drop in for a frosty treat.

**Hopalong Cassidy.** A movie cowboy played by William Boyd. The original magazine stories about the fictional cowboy were written by Clarence E. Mulford in the early 1900s. That version of Cassidy portrayed him as a gruff, grouchy cowpoke with an artificial leg. The movie version shows him much kinder and gentler, an older Western hero with silver-white hair. Boyd made more than sixty movies, bought the rights to the films and the character in the 1940s, and in the early 1950s the movies went to TV and made the actor rich and famous. Lewis watches a Hopalong Cassidy western on the Barnavelts' TV, a Zenith Stratosphere (see *The Specter from the Magician's* Museum for a description).

**Horseshoes.** Lewis and Rose Rita play this on the lawn of Mrs. Zimmermann's lake cottage. Rose Rita easily wins. Her aim is much more accurate than Lewis's.

**Humphries, Dr**. The local physician, a big, hearty, comfortable-looking man with a voice like a bass viol. Lewis likes him, and Dr. Humphries examines him after Lewis takes a bad spill on his bike.

**Jaeger, Mildred.** The most untalented witch in the Capharnaum County Magicians Society (see *Doom of the Haunted Opera)* returns to help Lewis and Rose Rita find something vital in the last chapters of the book.

**Kabbala.** An alternate spelling of *Cabala,* a system of mystical philosophy and knowledge developed by Jewish scholars. One of the members of the Magicians Society says it mentions the "red star," really a comet.

**Lovecraft, H.P.** (189—1937). A native of Providence, Rhode Island, Lovecraft became a cult favorite when he began to write weird stories that mingled mystery, science fiction, and horror. He became the center of a writers' group and encouraged the others to use his settings, ideas, and characters in their own stories. These included August Derleth, Clark Ashton Smith, Robert Bloch, Hart Crane, artist Virgil Finlay, author/editor Hugo Gernsback, Edmund Hamilton, magician/writer Harry Houdini, Henry Kuttner, C.L. Moore, Vincent Starrett, and many more. Sadly, Lovecraft couldn't make a good living just as a writer and was usually poor. Rose Rita checks out some of his books from the library, and she notices that the name ahead of hers on the card—the last person to read the books before her—was Mrs. E. Moote.

**Lyon Lake.** At her lake cottage, Mrs. Zimmerman hosts an end-of-school party for Lewis and Rose Rita the day summer vacation begins.

*Macbeth.* Once again, Mrs. Zimmermann quotes the line spoken by the Witches in William Shakespeare's tragedy: "By the pricking of my thumbs, something wicked this way comes!"

**Meteorite.** The great, blazing-red meteorite of 1885 streaked to Earth the same night that Jebediah Clabbernong died. Elihu found and retrieved it. It is described as about the size of a baseball, and it shimmered with colors that looked like no other hues on Earth. Just looking at it made people shiver with fear. Elihu melted it down and added it to the steel he used to make the trusses of Wilder Creek Bridge.

**Moote, Ermine.** The eighty-year-old wife of Mephistopheles Moote. She drives the couple's car, an old black Buick. She and her husband are both adept in sorcery and both as wicked as they come.

**Moote, Mephistopheles P. ("Mephisto").** The eighty-year-old husband of Ermine. He is a lawyer who worked for Elihu Clabbernong. Like Ermine, he is a student of dark magic and a sorcerer. The couple is quarrelsome and unpleasant, even to each other. They look forward to the day that they can seize control of the Earth. The name "Mephistopheles" comes from literature. It is the name of the demon who tempts and ensnares Dr. Faust in the early legends of the man who sold his soul to the Devil, and the major antagonist in Goethe's epic *Faust* (1829, 1382). No parents in their right mind would name a child that.

Mephisto's magical incantation in Chapter 14 is taken from the works of H.P. Lovecraft, by the way. I have acted in a radio play that used some of these chants. You wouldn't believe how hard they are to pronounce.

**Moote, Mull, and Boyd.** The law firm in Kalamazoo, MI, that were Elihu Clabbernong's attorneys. The name of the firm is a pun on "moot, null, and void," indicating that they were perhaps not the best at their job.

**Movies.** Jonathan, Lewis, Mrs. Zimmermann, and Rose Rita see a pirate movie, probably in the Bijou Theater in New Zebedee. Lewis also watches a Hopalong Cassidy movie on TV.

**Mrs. Zimmermann's folder.** After Mrs. Zimmermann spends a day researching the Clabbernong mystery, Rose Rita sneaks a look at a folder of evidence her elderly friend has collected. It contains a newspaper item from the 1920s saying that since Elihu sold the farm, no one has been able to live there for more than a few weeks because of a strange blight that killed all the plants. Then there is an obituary for Elihu, who died at the age of 84 in 1947 of pneumonia. There is a note of the Kalamazoo address for the law firm of Moote, Mull, and Boyd. Since Lewis and Rose Rita have overheard Lewis's uncle and Mrs. Zimmermann complaining about two irritating know-it-alls who are sticking their noses in where they don't belong—and think that means them—they decide to investigate without asking Uncle Jonathan's permission.

***Mystic Journal of Jedediah Clabbernong.*** A handwritten book that Rose Rita discovers in a red cedar box hidden on the old Clabbernong farm. It reveals a terrifying secret: in a dark magic ritual, Jedediah killed his own brother and sister-in-law to gain an extension of his life so he would be able to witness the coming of the "red star" (a long-period comet).

***Necronomicon.*** An imaginary book of magic lore, the most famous one dreamed up by H.P. Lovecraft. The title means something like "A Classification of the Dead." It lists the Great Old Ones and describes their powers. It was supposed to have been written by a man named Abdul Alhazred (or possibly Abd-al-Hazred) in the 8th century A.D. The knowledge of the terrifying Great Old Ones drove the author insane. The book, in various translations, is always said to be terribly rare, and yet in the fiction of the Cthulhu Mythos, copies turn up everywhere.

*New Zebedee Chronicle.* The local newspaper. Rose Rita and Lewis find a bound issue of the paper from December 22, 1885, that gives an account of the unusual meteorite that struck the Clabbernong farm on the previous midnight.

*Philip Marlowe.* The full title was *The Adventures of Philip Marlowe.* This is a radio show that Rose Rita likes. It is based on a private detective character, Philip Marlowe, created by writer Raymond Chandler. Marlowe is a tough guy, played at different times by actors Van Heflin, Gerald Mohr, and William Conrad. Rose Rita knows a tricky way to disguise one's handwriting, and she says she learned it from an episode of this show.

**Poker.** Just for fun, Jonathan, Mrs. Zimmermann, Lewis, and Rose Rita play several hands of oddball varieties of poker, including Johnny's Nightshirt, Shifty Jack, Grocery Store, and Seven-Toed Pete. These are all real games, but Jonathan prefers straight five-card draw.

**Pottinger, Rose Rita.** She still has a phobia about closed-in spaces, and she still makes up stories on the spot. When Lewis has a minor bike accident, to get away from the adults who want to help them Rose Rita spins a yarn that they're brother and sister and her brother cracks up on his bike all the time because when he was four he saw a circus bear doing tricks on a bike and he's always trying to imitate the bear. At that point Lewis drags her away.

**Riddle.** Elihu Clabbernong left a puzzling one in his will. If solved, it can lead to something that just might defeat the monster threatening the town.

**Rivet**. At the site where workmen are dismantling the old iron Wilder Creek Bridge, Lewis picks up a loose rivet, three inches long, and made of the same steel as the bride Elihu Clabbernong built. It seems to have special properties.

**Roy G. Biv.** A mnemonic device, used to help one remember all the colors of the rainbow in sequence: Red, Orange, Yellow, Green, Blue, Indigo, and Violet. Lewis remembers this when, during the night, he sees the rivet he picked up at the site of the Wilder Creek Bridge flickering with all these colors—and other, stranger hues that he can't even name.

**Separable Soul**. An old trope in myth and folklore: a magical creature, demon, or human sorcerer can become immortal if it removes the soul from its body and hides it where it can never be found. If the object containing the soul is destroyed, though, the soul passes and the owner of it dies.

**Spruce Creek Park.** A small city park with a playground, near the waterworks. The creek flows out of the town reservoir and winds through the park. A footbridge built with three barrel arches leads over the widest and deepest part of the creek in the park.

**St. George's.** Catholic church that Jonathan and Lewis attend.

**Stained-glass window.** The one in the back stairway of the Barnavelt house changes because it's been enchanted. When Lewis first arrived, it showed a sun as red as a tomato setting in a sea the color of old medicine bottles. In Chapter 3, it has turned scarlet, except for an enigmatic word in bright yellow: CAVE. Lewis can't think of any nearby caves . . . but then he doesn't at first realize that the window speaks Latin.

**Storm cellar.** These were shelters from tornadoes. An ancient brick-walled one on the Clabbernong farm had a wooden roof level with the ground, but the wood has rotted and first Rose Rita and then a horrific half-alive horse that is literally falling to pieces tumble into it. Only one of them gets out alive.

**Telescope.** Jonathan buys one, supposedly because he wants to take up astronomy as a hobby, but really to look for the "red star," a comet that passes by the Earth about once every 14,000 years. It's an eight-inch reflector with a motor drive and eyepieces that range from thirty to five hundred magnification.

***Thaumaturgy.*** An imaginary grimoire, or book of magic spells, by Livius the Younger. "Thaumaturgy" is just a fancy way of saying "creating magic."

**Twelve-Mile Road**. A country road outside of New Zebedee that intersects with Wilder Creek Road. The old, ruined Clabbernong farmhouse is on this road, at the center of an expanse of dead, decaying vegetation.

**Twin Oaks Dairy.** Milkmen from this dairy deliver milk in New Zebedee.

***Unnameable Cults.*** An English translation of a German book title, *Von unaussprechlichen Kulten*. This fictional volume is used in H.P. Lovecraft's writing and in the stories by his friends. It is supposed to be a study of strange pagan cults and their lore.

**Waterworks.** The New Zebedee waterworks is beside the reservoir off Spruce Street, a huge brick building that hums with machinery used to pump water up into the water towers to serve the town.

**Wilder Creek Bridge, New.** A concrete span that replaces the old iron bridge. Several hundred yards of Wilder Creek Road have been diverted and re-paved with asphalt to take the road over the bridge.

**Wilder Creek Bridge.** The original one was built privately by Elihu Clabbernong in the 1890s and given to the county. An iron truss bridge, it is floored with heavy planking. Though it was fine for horse-and-wagon traffic, in the 1950s it's a bit too narrow for automobiles and trucks, and the county intends to tear it down and replace it.

See Chapter 6 of *The House with a Clock in Its Walls* for a description of how and why Clabbernong built the bridge. Mrs. Zimmermann says he deliberately put something in the iron to prevent the ghost of his uncle from crossing Wilder Creek to "get him." Elihu, it seems, was a part-time wizard. His uncle was a full-bore evil sorcerer.

◆ ◆ ◆

# Chapter 7: John Bellairs's Lewis Barnavelt in
## *The Tower at the End of the World*
### By Brad Strickland
### Dial Books for Young Readers, 2001

The ninth novel in the New Zebedee series appeared in that dreary year 2001, the year of the 9-11 terror attacks, the year after Edward Gorey and Frank Bellairs both passed away.

In my own life, it was a hard year, too, marked by family illness and a death, overwork in my teaching job because of added responsibilities (but no added pay), and other stresses and strains.

The title of the book was *The Tower at the End of the World,* and in the year that was taken up with my writing it and seeing it through the press, some things felt as if they really were ending. However, life goes on, and the New Zebedee series was continuing, but with changes.

◆ ◆ ◆

*Summary:*

On a warm June day in the 1950s, Lewis Barnavelt sits in a lawn chair under the chestnut tree in the front yard of the Barnavelt house at 100 High Street, New Zebedee, eating creamy chocolate-covered mints and feeling unhappy. He has just finished reading the very last book in a series that he likes a lot, and he hates the idea that there will be no more adventures involving Dr. Fu-Manchu, the notorious international criminal and spy. But then Rose Rita comes over with a tempting offer: her Grampa Galway is going to be house-sitting all summer for an old Navy buddy of his who has a house right on Lake Superior in the Upper Peninsula, and he's invited them all to come up and stay with him. But when Uncle Jonathan takes a bad spill on the basement stairs and they discover an intruder has come into the basement, our heroes begin to worry.

As well they should. Up north, in the town of Porcupine Bay on Lake Superior, Lewis is surprised to find a letter waiting for him in the Post Office. However, it turns out to be mystifying: a steel engraving on a page apparently torn from an old book, plus a slip of parchment with runic writing on it. The engraving will give him nightmares.

The little slip of parchment may cost him his life.

◆　◆　◆

*Behind the Scenes:*

My editor and I had talked for some time about a direct sequel to *The House with a Clock in Its Walls*. I had worked up a proposal outline for a different novel, *The Whistle, the Grave, and the Ghost,* but she kept saying she wanted a return to the feeling of that first novel—something that is hard to accomplish because, well, you know, things do change. Anyway, I put the "Nobody Lived" outline on the back burner and decided I would try to find a way of writing the sequel that Toby wanted.

It must have been in the early winter of 2000 that I started fooling around with ideas. What if Isaac Izard came back? No, John had dispatched him and Selenna for good—literally for good.

Too bad they'd never had children.

Or wait . . . had they?

*House* didn't mention any, but it didn't say much about their lives before they came to New Zebedee from . . . wherever. It was possible they might have had a son.

The name came first: Ishmael Izard. I envisioned a son who took after both his abominable parents, and who wanted to complete his fanatical father's work of creating a doomsday clock to end it all. But it couldn't be the same kind of clock, could it? Maybe it would be a completely different type . . . but one that could serve the same fatal purpose as the original one.

I took the name Ishmael from Herman Melville's narrator in *Moby-Dick* (don't leave out the hyphen. You don't want to make a whale mad at you. Trust me on this). Melville, in turn, took it from the Bible, specifically from Genesis, where Ishmael was a son of Abraham not by his wife Sarah, but by his bondservant or slave, Hagar. Abraham exiled

Ishmael and his mother, sending them away into the wilderness, so "Ishmael" sounded like a good name for someone whose family sent him away and whom they did not mention to others.

As for the setting, what about returning to the Upper Peninsula for this one? It had been a long time since *The Figure in the Shadows.* Maybe this was a good opportunity for Lewis and Jonathan to get away from it all. See how the upper half lives. And as I mulled this over, the notion for the type of clock came to me.

I hitched the magic in the story to a classic English horror tale, "Casting the Runes," by M.R. James, published in 1911. The gimmick of the cursed parchment came from that story, which, by the way, later was adapted into a British horror movie, *Night of the Demon* (1957; released in the U.S. as *Curse of the Demon*), which is not a very close adaptation, though atmospheric and spooky.

*The Key of Solomon,* a real grimoire, or book of magic, figures in the story, too, though I will admit to fictionalizing it freely. Two books share that title, one known just as *The Key of Solomon* and the other as *The Lesser Key of Solomon.* The first, in Latin called *Clavicula Salomonis,* a translation from the Hebrew *Mafteah Shelomoh.* It purports to be a work by the biblical King Solomon himself, enumerating various spirits and containing magical glyphs and designs that allowed Solomon to summon and control these spirits. In fact, the book apparently comes from Italy, ca. 1350-1450, and has no biblical roots. Still, such a book of spells seems like something an evil magician might own.

I decided that the villain in the book was a world traveler who had learned about various nasty-type spirits and spells from all over. Therefore, he summons a Japanese ghost and an Irish one, just to terrify Lewis and to intimidate his friends. He is also, of course, someone who has made a long and careful study of different types of clocks and time-keeping apparatuses. That will come in handy for someone trying to complete the work of the late, unlamented Isaac Izard.

As I mentioned, the year of its composition was a sad one, with not much good news in it for me personally or for the country. The dedication of the book still rings with sadness: "In memory of three who will be forever missed, John Bellairs, Frank Bellairs, Edward Gorey."

The new artist was a talented one, S.D. Schindler, whose style is very reminiscent of Gorey's (whom Schindler much admired, by the way). The cover designs became a bit more modern in graphics, with a different approach to typefaces and the way the titles appeared on the cover, and we lost the back-of-the-jacket illustrations to ads for the other Bellairs books. However, good old New Zebedee is there between the covers, along with all the friends I had learned to love, fictional though they might be.

Schindler's front cover pictures Lewis and Rose Rita standing in the shadow of the mysterious dark tower on Gnomon Island, in Lake Superior off the Upper Peninsula of Michigan. In the bottom left foreground, something evil lurks in the shadows and stretches forth a dreadful, skeletal hand, unnoticed by our heroes.

We had the usual discussions about a suitable title. I would have gone for *The Dark Tower,* or some variant of it, had not Stephen King beaten me to the punch. It's a reference to a cryptic poem by Robert Browning, "Childe Roland to the Dark Tower Came." It's a poem without a beginning or end, but it's a mysterious and intriguing middle.

Looking at my notes, I see the possibilities that ran through my mind: *The Warlock's Revenge. When Time Runs Out. The Return of the Doomsday Clock.* None seemed right, but when I was thinking about Bellairsian titles, something made *The Mansion in the Mist* pop into my mind. From the editorial work I had done on it, I knew that one of his unused titles for that work was *The Mansion at the End of the World.* Just by substituting one word, I had an authentically Bellairsian title, and the editor liked it and told me to go with that.

Although I didn't know it at the time, something else was coming to an end. My editor, Toby Sherry, had decided to retire from Dial Books for Young Readers. This was to be the last of the Strickland/Bellairs novels that she would see all the way through from outline to first draft to editing to published book. She is still a good friend of my wife and me. I will have to say, though, that no one else quite understood John Bellairs or got the books the way Toby did. She had worked with both John and me for many years, and she knew in her bones what a John Bellairs novel needed so it would be true to the writer's original vision and intent. When she did retire, I missed her terribly.

As to the process of writing *Tower,* complicated as it was by my full-time job and by my father's final, lingering illness, it proceeded more or less in the usual way. Once the initial idea passed muster with my editor, I buckled down to the task of seeing what the people in the book were going to do. I started by writing short biographies of the new characters, describing them and exploring their histories (we didn't call them "backstories" at that point). The characters came into focus, and over one weekend of many hours at the computer, I plotted out the book.

Forgive me now for a personal digression about how I write:

In those days I was still teaching college English full-time. I had learned that even so, I could write books and keep my job, but only if I stuck to a strict routine. In order to finish a novel and keep it reasonably consistent, I would write seven days a week, for at least a full hour per day.

The hour was 5:00 AM-6:00 AM. Each weekday I got up before my wife or kids, parked myself at the computer, and started banging away at the keyboard (I'm rough on keyboards, going through about three a year). In the early days, I wrote my books on a second-hand office-model typewriter, one of the mechanical kind on which you had to slap a lever to move to the next line. The typewriter, an Underwood, only cost about ten dollars at a used-typewriter store near the University of Georgia in Athens, Georgia, where I was a graduate student.

But after my first book came out, my wife Barbara told me I needed an electric one, so we bought a brand-new IBM Selectric. It was faster and smoother, and I didn't have to swat the lever every fifteen seconds. Then after three more novels, computers beckoned. My first was an Apple II-E, which had a klunky word-processing program and which recorded files on 5 ¼ inch floppy disks—about half a chapter to a disk.

The display was a black screen with green letters made up of dots. What you saw on the screen was *not* what you got. The printer was a buzzing dot-matrix thing with punch-hole tractor-fed paper. You had one choice of font: whatever the printer was programmed with.

Those were the days, and I'm glad I'm out of them. There was no way to create an entire file for one book, because neither the computer memory nor floppy disks had space enough for that, so you had to assemble the book piece by piece before printing.

However, by January 2000, things had again changed considerably. I'd swapped my old Apple II-E for a PC with—gasp—a color screen. Now I had a dozen fonts from which to choose. Floppy disks had become plastic-encased and had shrunk down to 3 ½ inches. One of them could hold a whole novel (as opposed to ten to twenty of the 5 ¼ inch ones). Best of all, the screen accurately showed what the page would look like, and you didn't have to start a new paragraph by typing in .p or end a chapter by typing in .ff. You could do things like that by hitting "tab" or holding down the CTRL key and hitting "return."

Now, as a writer my trouble had always been that my brain outran my fingers. Typing was a tedious chore, even with a nifty electric typewriter. The Apple II-e was better, but constantly interrupting my thoughts to put in the code characters slowed me down and caused me to make frequent mistakes. By the time I graduated to a PC and WordPerfect, most of those obstacles had vanished. I became a fast keyboardist just by dint of writing so much and so often. Practice might not make me perfect, but it did make me fast.

What that means—and this is the point, you can sigh with relief now because the digression's almost over—is that in an hour, on a good day when the story is flowing, I can write from eight to ten pages. A New Zebedee manuscript, in finished form, ran to about 180-200 pages. I could type that in three weeks max, easy. Usually less.

*Type* it. I couldn't *write* it. The difference, of course, is that just typing is a mechanical process. Writing is a lot more than that. It calls for researching, pondering, putting the words down, reading them critically, and correcting and changing them. I grew to love rewriting and revisions—that part of the process let me shape the book more to the ideal form of it I had in mind. That makes me different from almost every other writer in the world. Even different from John, who dreaded revising and rewriting, because he'd lost that on-fire enthusiasm he always got when creating a story from nothing.

Anyway, for an hour every day Monday-Friday equaled perhaps 45 pages of manuscript. On weekends I could write for three or four hours at a stretch, depending on what my wife and children wanted to do with the days. When I had a solid weekend of writing, I might add another 45 pages. Ninety pages in a week; in two weeks, 180 pages, or a full draft (except I'd always get hung up and go back and fix things, so it worked out to about three weeks for the rough draft).

At that point, I put it away for about a month, then printed it out, re-read it, marked it up with different colored inks, and rewrote it. Generally for the rewrite I started a whole new computer file, because there were always so many changes that retyping the whole thing was easier and faster than hunting, changing, and replacing. It normally took me three drafts and about four or five months to produce the submission version of a novel.

This one took about six months. I had research to do, and that year my father passed away in March. I spent a lot of time with him, days and nights, over the three-month-period when he was under hospice care. But somehow or other, between that concern, my school schedule, and my spending some time with my wife and children, the book my editor wanted was written.

We had our official sequel to *The House with a Clock in Its Walls*.

◆ ◆ ◆

## *The Tower at the End of the World:* People, Places and Things

**Ainu.** The Ainu are a minority indigenous people in Japan, with customs and traditions that differ markedly from the Japanese mainstream. They are somewhat mysterious, and Mrs. Zimmermann learns that Ishmael Izard studied Asian magic with an Ainu shaman in the 1930s.

**Athanasius, Hermann, D.Mag.A.** The elderly Dr. Athanasius is a professor at the University of Göttingen in Germany who was one of Mrs. Zimmermann's teachers. Like her, he holds a Doctorate of Magical Arts degree. He has retired and must be in his nineties, but in the novel, Mrs. Zimmermann enlists his aid to uncover some of Ishmael Izard's background and to help her understand the strange parchment marked with runes that an unknown person sent to Lewis. He deciphers the cryptic runes on the parchment, and they turn out to be a deadly curse.

**Athletic Fields.** New Zebedee's fourth-of-July fireworks shows take place there.

**Azrael.** The runic inscription on the parchment Lewis receives invokes the name of this being, an Angel of Death. Azrael is extra-biblical, existing in Judaic and Christian lore but not in scripture.

**Banshee.** An Irish ghostly apparition, taking the shape of a woman who wails and weeps. In Irish lore, she is attached to a particular family and appears to forewarn the family members of an approaching death. The villain summons one to torment Lewis.

**Barnavelt house**. At one point, Lewis comes home at night and to his horror discovers that the house has gone back to the way it looked before his uncle bought it—when the owner was the dreadful mad wizard Isaac Izard. Even the II wallpaper is back.

**Bessie**. Mrs. Zimmermann's purple Plymouth Cranbrook. At her insistence, they all crowd into it for the long drive to the ferry and then across the Upper Peninsula. She doesn't trust Jonathan's old Muggins Simoon to get them there.

***Boys' Life.*** The magazine of Scouting. Mrs. Zimmermann refers to it at one point. I was the one who fouled up the punctuation. My version was incorrectly written as *Boy's Life.*

**Brannigan, Jake.** Owner of the general store in Porcupine Bay, MI. He is also the postmaster and justice of the peace. And probably about five per cent of the population.

***Celtic Lands and Peoples.*** A fictitious book that Lewis finds while staying for a while in Mrs. Zimmermann's house. Its main importance is that inside it he finds a folded letter to Mrs. Zimmermann from Dr. Athanasius in which there is a full translation of the inscription on the parchment he received. It reveals that Lewis is cursed to die forty-eight days from his receiving the parchment.

**Chimera.** A mythological creature, a composite monster whose body is made up of parts from different animals. The original Chimera, in Greek myth, was a fire-breathing creature whose body combined a snake, a goat, and a lion.

***Chinese Orange Mystery, The,*** by Ellery Queen. Though not identified by title, this is the book that Lewis is reading in bed when he has a sudden dream that the candy box he has been eating from is swarming with roaches. Published in 1934, *The Chinese Orange Mystery* concerns a murder in which the victim's clothes have been replaced on his body—backwards. And not only that, every item in the room that can be moved has been turned backwards, too. There's a perfectly logical reason for this, making the novel one of Ellery Queen's best mysteries.

**Chippewa.** The Chippewa, also known as the Ojibwe, are the Native American group indigenous to the Upper Peninsula of Michigan. Mr. Galway guesses that the tower on Gnomon Island might have been built by them.

**Cloud formations.** Isaac Izard used to study them from his observatory in what later became Jonathan's house. Jonathan explains he was watching for a particular formation that would empower him to speak a spell that could end the world—but he saw such a formation only twice over a forty-year period, and by the time he knew for certain it was the one he wanted, it had changed (clouds do move) and the spell wouldn't work. That is why he built the Doomsday Clock.

**Clusko, Ladislav.** A short, unpleasant-looking man with wiry black hair and only one eyebrow that runs right across the bridge of his nose. He seems very nervous when first hearing that Jonathan Barnavelt has come to Porcupine Bay. He moves oddly, in jerks and twitches, and he has a habit of darting his head this way and that, as though looking for enemies. Mrs. Zimmermann remembers him from long ago: He came to New Zebedee a few months after Isaac Izard died and was asking questions about him. He is a failed wizard himself.

**Coal bin.** In the first chapters, someone breaks into the Barnavelt house and searches the coal bin in the cellar. That was the gateway to the Doomsday Clock in *House,* and Jonathan is afraid someone might have come to search the cellar thinking the clock—which Lewis destroyed—still exists.

**Crawley, Lem.** According to an old man named Samuel, he caught a fish in Lake Superior that began to talk. The fish predicted the end of the world on August 15th. However, as Jake Brannigan points out, Lem is known to drink while out fishing and sometimes has long conversations with his bait.

**Dreams.** Lewis has one of the most disgusting ones in the series. As he drifts off to sleep while eating chocolate-covered peanuts, he dreams that they have come to life and morphed into squirming cockroaches. And one is in his mouth . . ..

**Eclipse.** According to a prophecy, one is supposed to trigger great changes in the earth on August 15. However, no ordinary eclipse will take place on that day. Uncle Jonathan says if it happens, it will have to be produced by magic.

**Einstein, Albert** (1879-1955). A brilliant theoretical physicist, Einstein devised the equation $E=mc^2$, a deceptively simple mathematical statement that codifies the relationship of energy, matter, and space-time. At the time of the novel, Einstein was working at Princeton University on a unified field theory, a goal he was never able to reach. Jonathan references him in connection with the theory that there may be trillions of universes, and that sometimes one may touch another and, um, bleed into it.

**Farmers Seed and Feed.** This store, on the ground floor of the block where the New Zebedee Opera House occupies the second floor of all the businesses, is mentioned again.

**Feasal, Jute.** Still employed by the county Public Works Department, he comes with a dump truck to haul off junk when Jonathan does his spring cleaning in the middle of July. He still curses colorfully and smokes King Edward cigars (a rare instance of my sneaking a smoking reference in).

**Fishing dock.** A ramshackle, neglected one long stood next to Mrs. Zimmermann's property on Lyon Lake; she buys it and has it demolished in this novel.

**Fishing.** Uncle Jonathan likes fishing from a dock, and during their vacation on Mr. Marvin's private island, he catches some good ones, including lake trout, steelheads, and coho. Most of the time Jonathan, Lewis, and Rose Rita catch and release the fish, but they do have a big fish fry when he takes a haul of trout.

**Forester, C.S.** (1899-1966). Pen name of the British author Cecil Lewis Troughton Smith. Among many other books, Forester wrote the series of rousing sea adventures featuring the British Naval hero Horatio Hornblower. Lewis likes these books.

**Galway, Albert.** We learn in this novel that he has fibbed about his age, claiming to be about ten years older than he really is (82). He has agreed to house-sit in the Northern Peninsula for an old Navy buddy of his while his friend is off racing a yacht in Australia. Grampa Galway has invited Rose Rita, Mrs. Zimmermann, Jonathan, and Lewis all to come up and stay with him for a few days.

**General Delivery.** A letter or package may be sent to certain designated post offices to be held for thirty days. The addressee must come to the post office with identification to claim the letter. This is used sometimes when people are vacationing or otherwise on the road and away from their permanent address. Someone sends a letter to Lewis in Porcupine Bay with the address "Lewis Baravelt, General Delivery, Porcupine Bay, Mich." Lewis receives the mail, but wishes he had not.

**General Order for Emergencies**. Mr. Galway tells Lewis the US Navy has this. He even recites it: "When in danger or in doubt, run in circles, scream and shout!"

**General Store**. There is one in Porcupine Bay, a long, low building with a front door that faces a long wharf leading out into the lake. The owner is a man named Jake. It's a homey place where men gather to play checkers and one can buy everything from an outboard motor to cans of pork and beans.

**Gnomon Island.** Lewis, Rose Rita, Uncle Jonathan, Mrs. Zimmermann, and Grampa Galway picnic there and run into mysterious and threatening magic. The place is fictitious, but it is partly based on Manitou Island, off Keweenaw Point. The real island has an automated lighthouse and is open to the public for hiking, exploring, fishing, camping, and so on. The name of the fictitious island is a clue and a pun. I won't spoil the clue, but if someone asked, "What the heck is Gnomon, anyhow?" and someone else said, "Gnomon is an island," the pun would pop up. If the first person said, "Do you have more horrible puns?" and the second said, "No, I'm Donne," it would be perfect.

*Golden Hind.* Sir Francis Drake's flagship on his voyage around the world, 1577-1580, during which he captured a great treasure by taking a Spanish galleon. There is a replica of the ship in London today, a tourist attraction. Trivia: The name of the ship was originally *Pelican,* but Drake changed the name to honor one of his sponsors, Sir Christopher Hatton, whose family crest pictured a hind (female red deer). Rose Rita says that while they're on their trip to the Upper Peninsula they can pretend to be the crew of Sir Francis Drake.

**Gothic.** An ancient, dead Germanic language. Mrs. Zimmermann uses it in one of her most powerful spells.

**Greyhound Bus.** Alone, Rose Rita rides one up to Porcupine Bay in July when she returns to make sure her uncle and Lewis's Uncle

Jonathan (who is investigating the mysterious Gnomon Island) are safe.

**Grimoire.** A sorcerer's book of spells. Mrs. Zimmermann tells the villain that she can do great magic with hers, and a friend has it for safekeeping. This is a deception, but it works to her advantage.

*Guide to the Upper Peninsula, A.* A travel book that Lewis reads. Mundane though the book is, it somehow summons a monstrous apparition.

**Hawaii House.** This is mentioned, though not by name, and is said to have been built in the 1850s. A later novel, *The House Where Nobody Lived,* tells its story in full.

**Hörbiger, Hans** (1860-1931). A real person, Hanns or Hans Hörbiger was an Austrian engineer and inventor who patented a type of valve still used today. He also dabbled in magic and astronomy and was a bit of a crackpot. In 1913, he co-authored a book on cosmology (the structure of the universe), titled *Wirbelstürme, Wetterstürze, Hagel Katastrophen und Marskanal Verdoppelungen* (*Hurricanes, Weather Calamities, Hail Disasters, and the Doubling of Martian Canals*). In this book he described his *Welteislehre* (World Ice Theory) that supposed the moon and all the planets were made of ice.

He further said that Earth gets a new moon every few million years, and the present one is only the latest of many. Each moon, he said, spirals in and crashes to Earth, the ice melting in the process. That was how oceans were formed. When scientists said that mathematically orbits don't work that way, Hörbiger yelled, "Then ignore the numbers!" When astronomers said telescopes proved the Milky Way was not, as he claimed, a swarm of ice blocks surrounding the Earth, but stars trillions of miles away, he accused scientists of lying to make him look bad. After his death, the Nazi government of Germany adopted the World Ice Theory as official doctrine, though even then scientists knew it was wrong.

In the novel, Ishmael Izard spends some time as one of Hörbiger's apprentices. I'm not sure what he would have learned, though.

**Hull, USS**. A US navy destroyer in World War I. Albert Galway and his friend Jim Marvin both served on her, and Galway saved Marvin's life when, as a German U-boat torpedoed the American ship, Marvin fell overboard and Galway jumped in and rescued him. The ship was able to return to port for repairs. This action happened in real life in June, 1918, by the way.

**Humphries, Dr.** When Uncle Jonathan takes a fall going down the cellar stairs—because someone has loosened the lightbulb in the cellar—Dr. Humphries makes a house call and treats him. Trying to make sure he hasn't suffered a concussion, Dr. Humphries holds up three fingers, asking Jonathan to count them. Jonathan says, "Eleven!" He then explains that is in binomial notation, but in base 10 math, it's three. Dr. Humprhies says he doesn't have a concussion but is suffering from orneriness.

**Ivarhaven**. An island in Lake Superior, not far off the coast of Michigan. That is where Jim Marvin's house, which the gang will house-sit during most of the summer, is located.

**Izard, Isaac**. Lewis sees an apparition of the long-dead magician in the Barnavelt house.

**Izard, Ishmael**. Mrs. Zimmermann learns that the Izards had a son, probably born early in the 20th century. They put out the word that he had died, but apparently they shipped him off to school as soon as they could. He studied dark magic in England, Austria, and elsewhere. He is a naturally cruel individual and one who holds a grudge. Physically, he is tall and thin, with very long iron-gray hair that falls to his shoulders. He has a craggy face dominated by a prominent nose like a hawk's bill. His name is familiar as that of the narrator of Melville's *Moby-Dick* (which is a book worth reading, though most people turn green at the prospect) but is ultimately from a biblical character.

**Izard, Selenna**. Isaac Izard's wife, she is identified by Mrs. Zimmerman as the real sorcerer in the family.

**Karswell**. A wizard who, in the early years of the 20th century, lived in Cornwall, England. Young Ishmael Izard studied magic with him for some time. In fact, Karswell is the evil magician in M.R. James's short story "Casting the Runes," and my using the character name was a nod to my source for the parchment covered with runic writing.

**Kebsmayer, Marta.** A 12 ½ year old girl whose father is a fishing guide in Porcupine Bay and whose mother is a teacher. Marty is chunky, with short, dark-blond hair. Like Rose Rita, she has a fondness for baseball. As they play catch, Rose Rita questions Marta about events in Porcupine Bay and learns some interesting facts about Ishmael Izard.

**Kuchisake Onna.** This is a Japanese ghost. She appears as a distressed young woman, concealing her face with a handkerchief or fan or keeping her eyes turned down toward the earth as she approaches someone. She always asks the same question: "Do you think I'm pretty?" When the victim looks at her, she reveals that her mouth literally is a slit from ear to ear and stuffed with sharp teeth.

If you answer "Yes," she will slit your cheeks so your mouth is like hers. If you answer "No," she vanishes, but will come back later and kill you. It's better to answer "Yes," I suppose, since the result isn't fatal and might get you a job in a Batman movie.

The ghost in the story transforms into the skeletal figure that Lewis saw in the engraving someone sent him before fading away. It's more an illusion than a real ghost, but it's scary.

I put the Japanese ghost in because I saw one. She didn't ask me the question, though. I was in my car, at night, in Athens, Georgia, waiting to make a right turn. A car came up beside me in the left-turn lane. In the passenger seat, only a few feet from me, was a woman with long, dark, hair. She looked toward me and grinned with that sharp-toothed, ear-to-ear smile. The teeth looked like small shark teeth, all pointed and curved. Scared me.

I told a friend about the experience, and in return, he told me he had lived in Japan for five years and knew about such things: I had seen a *Kuchisake Onna*. I then put her in the book, as one of the international spooks the villain could conjure up.

***La Vega's Tagalog/English Maritime Phrasebook.*** A small book, not much larger than a deck of cards. Tagalog is a language spoken in the Philippine Islands. With mixtures from Spanish and

English, it is the basis for the national language, Filipino. This booklet gives English-speaking sailors a means of communicating with Tagalog speakers to ask such questions as "When is the next spring tide?" or "What is this animal that is chewing on my foot?" Grampa Galway has this book, which he bought years and years before, when he was a sailor. He lends it to Lewis for a special purpose.

*Lux et veritas.* A spell that Jonathan Barnavelt can use in dark emergencies. The Latin words command, "Light and Truth."

**Macy's Thanksgiving Day Parade.** Rose Rita has watched it on TV, and when she's cloud-watching and sees a peculiarly shaped cloud, she thinks of the helium balloons in the parade.

**Marquette.** A larger town in the Upper Peninsula in Michigan. At the time of the story, it had a military surplus store.

**Mars.** Uncle Jonathan conjures up an illusion of Mars as it might look hundreds or thousands of years in the future, when it has been made habitable and colonized by humans. He and his friends have a snowball fight there.

**Marvin, Jim**. An old Navy buddy of Grampa Galway's. Lieutenant Marvin fell overboard when, during World War I, their ship, the destroyer *USS Hull*, was torpedoed by a German submarine. Albert Galway, then a Seaman First Class, leaped into the water with a life ring and rescued Marvin, and they became friends. After the war, Marvin made a fortune in oil and steel and eventually bought the island of Ivarhaven for his estate.

**Marvin's Mansion**. Jim Marvin had his house built on Ivarhaven Island in a modernistic style. It is a white-marble building terraced and stacked on a hillside on the island. It has lots of picture windows and glass doors to give spectacular views of Lake Superior. The top of the hill has been flattened and holds a croquet court and a tennis court, as well as a flagpole. Lewis and Rose Rita agree to hoist the U.S. flag every morning and take it down with the proper respect every evening. Mrs. Zimmermann doesn't particularly care for the angular, blocky style, and has the opinion that Frank Lloyd Wright (the famous architect) "has a lot to answer for."

**Michigander.** This is one of the terms that means a native of Michigan. Uncle Jonathan thinks it sounds silly and says "Michiganders" should be used only for men, because women from Michigan would have to be "Michigeese."

***Mineralogical Field Guide to the Upper Midwest, A.*** One of the books that Lewis finds in Mr. Marvin's library. Marvin is in the oil business.

**Moxie.** Originally the name of a soft drink (it's still around) that was among the earliest bottled sodas sold in the United States as a tonic, the word has come to mean "courage, determination, pluck, nerve." Mrs. Zimmermann uses it in that way.

**Mr. Wizard.** When Jonathan offers a scientific reason for why the cellar light might have loosened in the socket on its own, Mrs. Zimmermann tells him to cut out the "Mr. Wizard" stuff. *Watch Mr. Wizard* was a TV science show for kids, starring Don Herbert, a World War II bomber pilot who had studied general science in college. In each episode of the show, Mr. Wizard invited the neighborhood kids to join him as he showed them how to do science experiments with everyday items. *Watch Mr. Wizard* began broadcasting in 1951 and was very popular. It ran on network TV for 14 years.

**Osee Five Hills.** Town where Uncle Jonathan's sister lives. Its name comes from an alternate spelling of the prophet Hosea in the Old Testament. There is no real town of that name in Michigan.

**Painted Cliffs.** A fictional landscape in the novel, patterned on the real Pictured Rocks National Seashore, where visitors can see sandstone cliffs with streaks of color formed by minerals that leach out of the stone and evaporate, leaving iron (red), copper (green), limonite (yellow) and other vivid tints on the cliff surface.

**Porcupine Bay.** A fictional small town in the Upper Peninsula, near the island where Grampa Galway is house-sitting for the summer. It is loosely based on Copper Harbor on Lake Superior.

**Psalms.** When he is badly frightened, Lewis recites Psalms 23 in Latin as a prayer.

**Queen, Ellery.** Lewis discovers this classic American mystery writer on his trip to the Upper Peninsula and seeks out more Ellery Queen novels. In real life, "Ellery Queen" was the pen name of two cousins, Manfred B. Lee and Frederic Dannay. They began as writers in 1928, entering their first novel, *The Roman Hat Mystery,* in a magazine contest and won. Unfortunately, the magazine went bankrupt and didn't publish the work, but the cousins found a book publisher who was glad to take them on.

The cousins named their young, brilliant, bookish amateur detective "Ellery Queen," too, and gave him a father who was an Inspector with the New York City Police. A writer (of mystery stories) as well as an amateur sleuth, Ellery solved crimes by piecing together incredibly difficult and seemingly unrelated clues. The writers played fair with their readers, always giving them every clue as Ellery discovered it, and sometimes offering a Challenge to the Reader at a point when an alert reader should be able to solve the case. The novels and short stories about Ellery Queen appeared for nearly forty years, and they spawned movies, radio and TV shows, and a popular mystery fiction magazine, *Ellery Queen's Mystery Magazine* (of course). Special to me because (1) for many years I corresponded with Dannay, who offered advice to a college kid who wanted to be a writer, and (2) my first-ever published story appeared in Queen's magazine.

**Runes**. A primitive alphabet. Because the letters were carved in wood or stone, they consist mostly of straight lines. Some common runes were *futhark,* so-called because the first letters of its alphabet were f-u-th-a-r-k; the Old English variant is called futhorc, because the sounds were a little different. These were known in Scandinavian and Germanic countries, and Old English was at heart a Germanic language. Futhorc runes, by the way, appear in inscriptions in J.R.R. Tolkien's *The Hobbit* and *The Lord of the Rings.* Futhark was only one variant, and there were several other runic alphabets around in the Middle Ages.

Lewis receives a "gift" of a small slip of parchment with an inscription in runic writing. Mrs. Zimmermann determines that this is a particularly nasty curse. The device is patterned after a plot point in the story "Casting the Runes," by M.R. James, a well-known British writer of ghost stories.

**Samuel.** An old man in the general store in Porcupine Bay. He tells a tale of a fisherman who recently caught a talking, prophetic fish.

***Shadow of Fu-Manchu, The*** (1948). Novel by Sax Rohmer, the eleventh in his series of books about the international criminal and genius, Dr. Fu-Manchu, and his nemesis, the stalwart British investigator Nayland Smith. Lewis reads it in Chapter 1 and is upset because it is the last book in the series. *Tower* therefore takes place before 1957, when Rohmer published *Re-Enter Fu-Manchu.* Two more books, one a novel and one a collection of short stories, later added to the fiction about the mysterious Chinese criminal.

**"Star-Spangled Banner, The."** Rose Rita mentions the song on the evening of July Fourth, wondering if someday Uncle Jonathan might create an illusion of the British Navy's bombardment of Fort McHenry. She knows history well enough to tell Lewis that Francis Scott Key, who composed the lyrics to "The Star-Spangled Banner," was detained aboard the British 80-gun ship *H.M.S. Tonnant* and witnessed the action, which inspired him to write the poem that became the national anthem of the USA.

The *Tonnant* was originally a French ship, but the British captured her and took her into their service. She was a ship of the line, a powerful 80-gun vessel, and fought in many battles, including Trafalgar (in which Lord Nelson was victorious but died from a sniper's bullet), and in the War of 1812, the ship bombarded Washington DC and Baltimore. This was the occasion for the attack on Fort McHenry.

**Stereopticon.** More properly, a stereoscope, this was an early device that let you view photographs in three dimensions. They were popular in the late 1800s and required photos taken with a special kind of camera. Uncle Jonathan has an antique one and hundreds of photos to go with it. I made the very common mistake of confusing the handheld viewer with a primitive sort of slide projector.

*Sunfish.* The sailboat that goes with the house where Grampa Galway is staying. The house, and the sailboat's dock, is on Iverhaven Island, out in Lake Superior. It is loosely based on Porter's Island. *The Sunfish* is a single-masted sloop, just about big enough for five people—any more would be crowding it. Grampa Galway gets enormous joy from sailing the sloop, and Lewis loves to act as the crew. He learns the rudiments of sailing and can at least raise and lower a sail and perform such standard moves as jibing, luffing, and tacking, and he can trim sail. Grampa Galway tells him he qualifies as an able-bodied sailor, which pleases Lewis greatly.

**Temple of Thalestris, The.** Fictitious magical cult created by the magician Karswell in the early 20th century (modeled on Thelema, founded by Aleister Crowley). The cult of Thalestris is probably devoted to goddess worship, because in a myth about Alexander the Great, Thalestris was Queen of the Amazons.

*The Tempest.* Shakespeare play about a magician, his daughter, and a magical island. Mrs. Zimmermann quotes a line from it.

*Topographic Indicators of Oil-Bearing Strata.* One of the books that Lewis finds in Mr. Marvin's library. Marvin is in the oil business. Hey, didn't you just read that? *Déjà vu!*

**Walpurgis Night.** This begins at sunset on April 30. According to German folklore, all the witches in Europe meet on the Brocken, the tallest mountain in the Harz Mountain Range, for an evil celebration. In the novel, Mrs. Zimmermann says there are rumors that around the end of World War II, a terrible wizards' duel broke out during the Walpurgis Night gathering. Ladislav Clusko was somehow involved, because whatever happened ended in his coven being broken up and scattered.

**Witch of Endor.** Rose Rita erroneously supposes that the picture sent to Lewis shows "King Solomon delivering judgment on the Witch of Endor." The story of the Witch of Endor is in the Old Testament book of 1 Samuel, and it involves not Solomon, but King Saul, who in a moment of despair asks the woman of Endor (supposedly a witch) to call up the spirit of the prophet Samuel, who gives Saul a dire prophecy of doom at the hands of the Philistines.

I really thought I'd get at least one letter on this, but none showed up. And yes, this was deliberate, and I knew Rose Rita was making the mistake—my brother is a Methodist minister, and at the time of this novel, one of my beta readers—friends whom I talked into proofreading the manuscript—was a nun. None of my readers caught Rose Rita's error.

**Zenith Stratosphere.** The Barnavelt TV is mentioned again, though I absent-mindedly called it a Stratocaster and no one caught the error. A Stratocaster is a guitar. Lewis notices an afternoon show, *House Party,* is on. That was a variety and talk show hosted by Art Linkletter, and it was popular in the 1950s. It first came on the air in 1952, which might give an indication of the year—though Lewis is still "about thirteen."

◆ ◆ ◆

## Chapter 8: John Bellairs's Lewis Barnavelt in
### *The Whistle, the Grave, and the Ghost*
### By Brad Strickland
### Dial Books for Young Readers, 2003

Back in 1999-2000 I had begun plotting out a Lewis Barnavelt book that would show something of Lewis's Boy Scouting experiences. As Chapter 7 explains, my editor interrupted that process to ask me to write a direct sequel to *The House with a Clock in Its Walls.* She believed that John had left enough potential plot lines in that novel for me to pick up and continue the story, somehow involving the Izard family, though as far as I, or Lewis, knew Selenna and Isaac were gone for good, and good and gone.

But I've told the story of how I did manage to extend the basic notion of *House.* I'm still not entirely satisfied with it—bringing back the offspring of a character is, after all, something of a narrative cliché. However, the editor liked it, and so was born *The Tower at the End of the World.*

Once I had turned in that book, I had more work to do on some non-Bellairs writing, and then I got back to the Scouting story. Some time earlier, a fan had asked me to write a book that paid homage to M.R. James, and I had already selected one of James's stories, "Oh, Whistle and I'll Come to You, My Lad," as the inspiration for the Scouting novel.

When *Tower* intervened, I switched to another story, "Casting the Runes" by the same author, because the threat in that book was an evil sorcerer who would use some threatening spell like the one in the James story. However, since I had the set-up in mind for the (as yet untitled) Boy Scout book and in fact had already jotted down a very rough preliminary outline, I kept the inspiration and returned to the Scouting story in 2002. This novel, the first one written without the editorial supervision of Toby Sherry, became the tenth New Zebedee book, *The Whistle, the Grave, and the Ghost.*

◆ ◆ ◆

*Summary:*

It's summer again, and Lewis Barnavelt is on a weekend hike and camping trip with his Boy Scout troop. Though the Scout leader, Mr. Halvers, tries his best to instill a positive and helpful attitude in the dozen boys he's leading, there are a couple of bad apples in the group, Stan Peters and Billy Fox. Both of them are big, strong guys, and for no reason, they have it in for kids like Lewis and the similarly hefty and clumsy Barney Bajorski. When Lewis does a good job pitching his tent, Mr. Halvers praises him and mildly scolds the others for not being as fast as he is. Later he sends Billy and Stan for firewood and Lewis for flat stones so they can make a firepit for their campfire. While doing this chore, Lewis finds two things: One is a strange silver whistle, like a dog whistle, untarnished though it has lain under a stone for perhaps hundreds of years. The second is an enormous boulder with words carved on it indicating it is a grave. And that night when the bullies ruin his tent, something very mysterious and dangerous begins when . . . *something* stirs that will offer a deadly kind of revenge. Something that is called by the sound of the silver whistle.

◆ ◆ ◆

*Behind the Scenes:*

After Toby Sherry retired, leaving Dial when this novel was still in early manuscript stages, I had no regular editor—indeed, four different ones edited the last three New Zebedee books. None were very familiar with the Bellairs canon, and sometimes I had to explain to them that a few of their editorial suggestions just could not be done without violating the spirit and the characters of the series.

That wasn't much of a problem this time around. My second editor had worked closely with Toby, though she had not read any of the Bellairs novels, and she knew that I had a pretty good handle on New Zebedee and its inhabitants. I did, however, have to explain a couple of times that things she thought were irrelevant were really references to earlier books in the series and belonged in *Whistle* because they gave the story a kind of resonance with the earlier works.

Lewis had been established as a member of the Boy Scouts, but we really hadn't seen him in any kind of Scouting activity—it was mostly offstage, with references in *Letter* to his being away at Boy Scout Camp for a couple of weeks. This time around, I opened with Lewis being on a weekend camp-out and created his Scoutmaster, Mr. Fred Halvers, as a leader.

Though he's not as tubby as he was in *House,* Lewis is still overweight, and he's still a bit clumsy, so I thought he would struggle a bit and might be the target of bullies. Side note: I think the Boy Scouts are a wonderful organization, but my couple of years of experience in Scouting showed me that bullies are everywhere, and some of them wear Scout uniforms. I didn't get pushed around as much as a friend of mine did, but both of us got sick of suffering from the attentions of the two mean kids—who had a real genius for harassing others when the Scoutmaster wasn't around and who never got caught. My friend and I both dropped out of Scouting because of that.

Anyway, the M.R. James story supplied the whistle, and a poem by John Keats supplied the idea for the Lamia, a monster going back to ancient Greece. She preyed on children, and she was bloodthirsty. Keats's poem takes its inspiration primarily from this myth and from Robert Burton's book *The Anatomy of Melancholy*[4] (1651), which purports to be a medical treatise but actually is a discursive consideration of moods, reality, illusion, spirituality, mental states, and many other subjects. There is in the Keats poem a little hint of vampirism that I also borrowed, though it's not exactly of the bite-their-necks variety.

Lewis also gets a kind of secondary antagonist this time around: Father Foley, the new priest of St. George's. He is Irish, sour-tempered, and he is harsh, too quick to give Lewis penances for his sins. Lewis misses the former priests, who would assign him penances like saying fifty Hail Marys, which he always carried out faithfully. Father Foley is more inclined to make him mow the church lawn, wash the stained-glass windows, or spend an afternoon reading a hundred and fifty pages of the *Confessions* of St. Augustine of Hippo. The edition I had in

---

4 This is one of the Renaissance books that John Bellairs loved. Another is Sir Thomas Browne's *Hydrotaphia, or Urn-Burial* (1658), a similar rambling, introspective, philosophical work.

mind is chock-full of commentary and footnotes and runs to about six hundred pages. It is tough going for a student still in junior high school.

All in all, Lewis is feeling more than usually put-upon in the novel, especially when Stan and Billy, who destroy Lewis's pup tent on the camping trip, decide they'll beat Lewis up because the Scoutmaster praised him and—after they had cut his tent in the middle of the night and Lewis hadn't told on them, nor had any of the other boys—the Scoutmaster had refused to award any of the boys credit for the trip, except for Lewis. The whistle that he found figures in the story. It seems to have the power of appearing when Lewis is afraid or threatened, but what it calls up is a force of pure evil that threatens to corrupt Lewis, making him the kind of person he dislikes—someone more powerful than others who pushes people around.

If you read the M.R. James story, you'll see a few parallels between his whistle and Lewis's, but they're really two distinct things. The plots are also very different from each other. *Whistle* is more of a tip of the hat to James than an imitation.

Many familiar places and figures come into play during the plot: the New Zebedee hospital, the library with the librarian, kindly Mrs. Geer, as helpful as ever. Heemsoth's Rexall Drug store is there, of course, and the junior high, with its narrow alley separating it from the high school—one scene takes place in that alley as the bullies jump Lewis one evening after a Scout meeting.

A reader of the series will see mentions of events and people from several of the earlier books, including *House, Letter, Ghost in the Mirror,* and even *Tower*. The website tvtropes.com says that I provide lots of "continuity porn," which is a rude term, but it really means that I like making connections to other books in the series.

Occasionally I had to explain these to my new editor, who didn't always understand because she had not read the previous novels. It just seems to me that this kind of reference reinforces a reader's sense of entering a real world, where people have lots of experiences that they are likely to remember in times of stress.

Some of these are subtle. In the very first book, in a flash-forward, I guess you'd call it, John Bellairs established that when Lewis grows up, he is destined to become a professional astronomer at Mount Palomar Observatory, in California not too far from San Diego. In later books, as

Lewis gets, well, not older but more experienced, he becomes interested in books about planets and stars, and then Uncle Jonathan buys a nifty and powerful backyard telescope.

In *Whistle*, we find Lewis reading a book on astronomy by Sir Patrick Moore, one of my favorite writers when I was a kid, and dabbling with astrophotography, using the backyard telescope and a specially adapted camera. It all points to his eventually becoming an astronomer and landing a prestigious position at one of the major observatories in the country.

I've always liked to invent imaginary books, and this novel gave me the chance to indulge in that pastime. I like inventing passages that sound as if they were written in bygone times and trying to make them sound as authentic as I possibly can. The index that follows will alert you to a good many non-existent but—to me, anyway—intriguing volumes of forgotten lore, as Poe puts it. I mingle my imaginary library of books on magic, history, and so forth with references to actual works by real writers.

The Patrick Moore book is an example of one of the real works. Other real writers referenced range from Montague Rhodes James (better known as M.R. James), whose *Ghost Stories of an Antiquary* (1904) contains the short story that inspired the whistle, and authors whose work Lewis enjoys, ranging from Ellery Queen and Sir Arthur Conan Doyle to Robert Louis Stevenson. Both Lewis and Rose Rita started out as avid readers, and I have kept them that way. I identify with Lewis—as a kid, I loved nothing better than settling down with an interesting book and a snack.

The writing took a little longer than usual partly because I had been given more responsibility at Gainesville State College (as it then was; later it became the University of North Georgia), coordinating the Study Abroad program and becoming the creator of the teaching schedules every term. Then, too, I was writing for other publishers as well and had to adjust my writing schedule. Finally, it took a while and several drafts before I seemed to hit the tone that I aimed for—I wanted to give hints that even good people, like Lewis, could be sorely tempted to do things that they know to be wrong. Tempted—but they can also resist.

I think the book went through four different drafts and an additional polish-and-edit draft, not an excessive number, but more than I normally did.

For a little bit, I'd like to write about the process of revision. Many beginning writers are too quick to be satisfied and too defensive of their words. Very, very few of us can get it right the first time. The novelist Truman Capote is credited with the saying, "All good writing is rewriting." I'm not sure he was the first to make that observation, but I agree with the idea; many writers don't.

Writers write in different ways. John would hurry through a rough draft and then ask for editorial help—What needs changing? What should I add? What should I cut out? He would then revise according to editorial direction. Other writers are perfectionists who agonize over each word and each punctuation mark, trying to produce a flawless first draft. None of them ever succeeds but they sure try.

In my case, the first draft is by far the hardest work. I do tend to write fast, or at least steadily, so the pages mount up almost before I realize it. However, never have I turned in a first draft as a submission to a publisher.[5]

On the other hand, I don't revise until I have a whole, complete manuscript. The trouble is that if I've done, say, Chapter 1, and I want to revise that before I get to Chapter 2, it takes me far too long and I keep fussing with details that don't need to be changed.

What's more, even though I outline, as the book develops, it takes on a life of its own. Characters will have conversations that I never planned or will surprise me by doing things I had never thought of. That's fine. That means that the book is vital, that it seems real to me and, I hope, will feel real to the reader, too. But—you see where this is going—since the story is changeable all the way to the end, I really need a finished first draft before revising.

I've met writers who act as if they carve their words in stone, and changing them is just beyond their talents. Not me. My dreadful secret— and once a writer I'd met slapped me when I said this on a panel—is that *I like rewriting much better than writing a first draft.*

A few writers I've met agree with me. The majority want to punch me. They hate rewriting and find it a terrible chore.

However, to me it's a matter of shaping the story so it's more like the ideal that I carry in my mind. That ideal story is beyond my reach, and I will never manage to put it on paper, but still—my goal is to get

---

5 Informal writing for the internet is another matter. That's almost all first-draft.

as close to it as I can. You get there by rewriting. And that's where you make the language better, the descriptions sharper, the actions more interesting, the conversations wittier, and so on. It's a pleasure to see the novel gradually emerge from the primordial ooze of the first draft.

Typically, my submission draft is either the third or fourth revision. There's the first, rough draft; the first revision, which cuts unnecessary undergrowth (that's the hardest part, cutting) and adds and expands as necessary; the second revision, which cleans up and polishes and shapes the story; and the final edit, which mainly corrects typos, misspellings, and other errors. In the first and second revisions, I really try to look for scenes of narrative (summary) that can be changed to action and dialogue.

Say it with me: For a fiction writer, the golden rule is *Show, don't tell.* As often as you can, instead of writing, "Lewis was terrified," show him being terrified:

> Lewis's heart pounded hard. He couldn't stop shaking, and he felt a cold sweat bead on his forehead and crawl down his cheeks. His legs twitched, wanting to run—but feeling frozen in place.

That kind of revision does a book good.

Some trivia: At least four of the character names in the book came from fans of the series: Abucejo, Richardson, Engels, and Kemp. It was just a friendly nod to readers who had offered commentary and advice on previous books. In science-fiction circles, this is called "Tuckerization," after Wilson (Bob) Tucker, a genial writer who loved to put the names of friends and fans in his work. I don't do it often, or very much, but after having written the previous book for my editor, this time around I wanted to write one that was clearly for the fans.

At that time, the main internet site for anyone interested in John Bellairs and his work was thecompleatbelllairs.com, created and maintained by Jonathan Abucejo, a staunch supporter and good friend. When he became too busy to keep up with it (little things like getting married, having a family, and getting a demanding job took up too much of his time), another group of fans took over the name and created a John Bellairs wiki that is still going strong.

Not only do I deeply appreciate all the Bellairs fans, I am one. Accordingly, the dedication for *The Whistle, the Grave, and the Ghost* reads, "This one is for the fans I've met at compleatbellairs.com. Keep the faith, all!"

Now a word about fans and writers, if you'll permit. I have been fortunate to meet, or correspond with, or speak to on the phone, a whole host of writers whose work I admire: Frederic Dannay (half of the Ellery Queen writing team and the founder and editor-in-chief of *Ellery Queen's Mystery Magazine*); Ross Macdonald (mysteries); Ray Bradbury (fantasy); Isaac Asimov (science fiction); Jane Yolen (YA); Terry Pratchett (humorous fantasy/sf); Neil Gaiman (graphic novels, YA, lots of other stuff); Madeleine L'Engel (YA fantasy); Stephen King (horror); Ursula K. LeGuin (SF, fantasy)—oh, many, many, many more. Here's what I have learned: Writers are some of the nicest people in the world.

There are exceptions, but they are few. Once or twice I've been disappointed to learn that a writer whose works I like are, in person, unpleasant, crabby, and argumentative. But most of the time, writers are friendly and welcoming. They are quick to give fans attention and encouragement. Most of them love to get fan mail or fan email, and almost all the time they will respond. Granted, sometimes that's difficult. Dial would save up fan letters and send them all to me in a bundle maybe once a year—so sometimes my replies were a year late. But I did always try to respond.

This is a long-winded way of encouraging you to write to your favorite writers. Well, make sure they're alive first, of course. But if you read a book that you love, write and let the author know that. Don't ask for an autographed photo, though—writers aren't movie stars, and we don't have them in stock. But chances are the writer will reply to your letter with at least a brief note. Time and again I have heard from fans of John Bellairs who wrote to him and received a response. I've seen a couple of them, when John returned the original letter to a fan with his reply written on the bottom, continuing onto the back.

Writing is a lonely business. For that reason, writers do value hearing from readers. In fact, most of them probably wouldn't mind getting critical remarks. Once a young reader wrote something like

> Our teacher made us read your book and I thought it was stupid. Why do you write about such losers and nerds?

I replied,

> I'm sorry you were forced to read a book you didn't like. I write about these characters because while the cool kids are going to the movies and hanging out in the arcade or texting their friends, my losers and nerds are saving the world.

Did the student's note offend me? Hmm. No, not really. I understand that my writing won't please everyone. Sometimes it doesn't even please me. Fortunately, most Bellairs fans are suave, cultured, intelligent people of discriminating taste. Oh, and polite. Come on, you know you are.

S.C. Schindler again supplied the cover and interior illustrations for this book. The same format for the book jacket that had begun with *Tower* continues, with no back illustration, but a list of some of the other books in the series. The front of the jacket shows Lewis atop the big flat boulder that is in reality a tombstone, grasping a rather oversized whistle as he leans away from the menacing, snake-like form of the lamia, looming over him like a cobra. It is an atmospheric and properly menacing picture. Once more, Schindler's style recalls Edward Gorey's. This was to be the last book in the series, though, that had a Gorey-esque cover.

◆ ◆ ◆

## *The Whistle, the Grave, and the Ghost:*
## People, Places and Things

**"99 Bottles of Beer on the Wall."** This well-known song has the power to annoy listeners after only about forty verses. It's compared to Lewis's Boy Scout marching song because of that.

***Ad Altare Dei* Incense.** The incense in the censers the altar boys and priest use in the church. It has a resiny, balsamic, rather citrus-like, faintly sweet aroma and signifies purity and the prayers of the faithful rising like smoke in the air and up to heaven. One of the ingredients is likely frankincense. Lewis finds the aroma comforting.

*Amulets.* Mrs. Zimmermann's bound doctoral dissertation. We first saw it in *House with a Clock in Its Walls.* Rose Rita looks through it to try to find information about the silver whistle.

**Anemia**. A medical condition in which the victim suffers from not having enough red blood cells or hemoglobin. It causes the victim to become pale, listless, and increasingly weaker and in extreme forms can be fatal. Two cases break out in New Zebedee in the novel, causing deep public concern. This is a parallel to the 1957 Asian flu epidemic, which made millions of Americans very sick and dominated the news for weeks. Unlike the epidemic, the anemia outbreak remains limited.

**Bajorksi, Barney.** An overweight, timid boy about Lewis's age. He is pale and has coppery red hair. Like Lewis, Barney is a bully magnet. At one point, the bullies terrify him into yelling for Lewis to come and help him—just so they can lure Lewis into an alley and jump him. Barney is apologetic and ashamed.

**Barnavelt, Jonathan.** He explains to Lewis why his grandfather left almost all of his money to him and not to Lewis's dad Charlie or his two aunts. Charlie was energetic and a go-getter, and everyone knew he would be a success. Both aunts had left the Catholic Church to marry Baptists, irritating the old man, and besides both were bossy and nosy. By contrast, Jonathan says, his grandfather admired him because they were both so much alike: "fat, lazy, and too easygoing to worry about making money."

**Barnavelt, Lewis.** We get to see Lewis interacting with the other members of his Scout troop for the first time. Though still overweight and not athletic, Lewis is good at Scouting. He puts up his pup tent before any of the other guys manage to finish theirs, and his is taut and neat. Mr. Halvers praises his ability—which makes Billy Fox and Stan Peters angry.

**Bfstplk, Joe**. Mrs. Zimmermann says at one point that Lewis, who is afraid that just being around him causes his friends to have trouble, is like this cartoon character. Joe Bfstplk was a character in Al Capp's comic strip Li'l Abner. He was a raggedy, woebegone-looking figure who always had a dark rain cloud hovering over his head and who, though good-hearted and well-meaning, always jinxed anyone who came near him so they had bad luck. According to the strip's creator, the only way to pronounce Joe's last name was to blow a raspberry.

**Boy Scout Marching Song.** The boys of Troop 133 have an unofficial marching song, very repetitive, that begins, "We are the true Scouts, true blue are we. . . ." It's a song I made up, not a real one. The tune I imagine is sort of a cross between "Victory March," the Notre Dame fight song, and "John Jacob Jingleheimer Schmidt." It's the kind of song that quickly gets on an adult's nerves, and so it's lots of fun for boys singing it.

**Boy Scout Troop 133.** New Zebedee's troop. It has a dozen members, plus the Scoutmaster, and it generally meets Tuesday evenings at seven in the high-school cafeteria.

**Campfire stories.** The Boy Scouts in the novel amuse themselves by telling spooky stories around their campfire at night. They tell the one about the escaped homicidal maniac who has a hook instead of a hand, and the Bluebeard story (or an American variant). Billy Fox tells a story about a hermit named Crazy Jake who lives "in these very woods" and who murders people for their hair. That's a lead-in to his buddy Stan's sneaking up and pulling Barney Bajorski's hair, causing him to shriek in fear as the other Scouts laugh at him.

**Capharnaum County Magicians' Society.** The group is still holding its monthly meetings. During one of these—not at the Barnavelt or Zimmermann house this time—Lewis and Rose Rita take advantage of the adults' absence to look in Uncle Jonathan's study for books that might help them deal with the Lamia.

*City of Escanaba, The.* A ferryboat that crosses between Escanaba, MI, on the Upper Peninsula, and Charlevoix, MI on the Lower Peninsula. It really doesn't exist except in the novel. Louis has a souvenir pencil with a picture of the ferry on it.

*Compendium of Myths and Legends of All Nations, A.* A fictional reference book that Lewis reads in the New Zebedee Public Library. It briefly tells the story of Lamia, identifying her as a half-serpent, half-human female vampire and referring to Greek myths about her.

*Confessions of St. Augustine of Hippo.* A book by one of the early fathers of the Catholic Church, Aurelius Augustus (354-430). Augustine was born in Numidia, a province of Rome in North

Africa. Though his mother, Monica, was a devout Christian, his father, Patricius, was a pagan. Augustine was well-educated and ambitious, and as a young man he yearned to become a famous teacher and philosopher. He became a Manichean, following a religion that saw the universe in dualistic terms as a realm ruled over by equal forces of light and darkness. While working as a teacher in Milan, Italy, Augustine had an intense religious experience and converted to Christianity. He became a priest and, rapidly, the Archbishop of Hippo, in his native North Africa. He wrote two important works: *The City of God*, a theological work examining some of the toughest problems of religious philosophy, and *Confessions*, an autobiography in which he describes his life and his religion. In the novel, Father Foley has Lewis read 150 pages of the *Confessions*, a difficult assignment for a middle schooler, because Lewis dozed off during Mass.

**Cream pitcher.** Jonathan has one in the shape of a friendly-looking cow. He has enchanted it so when someone wants cream in their coffee, it walks over and pours the cream in from the spout, which is its open mouth. Mrs. Zimmermann isn't crazy about it.

**Crockett, Davy** (1786-1836). A frontiersman and politician from the early years of the 19th century. He became a folk hero even prior to his death defending the Alamo in Texas from the Mexican army. In the 1950s, kids were spellbound by a TV series and two movies about him, leading to the success of a popular song and the popularity of raccoon-skin caps. Rose Rita references Crockett and another legendary frontiersman, Daniel Boone (1734-1820).

**D'Anjou, Pierre Michel.** A fictional occultist, mystic, and priest who lived in France in the 16th century and who in 1587 had an encounter with a lamia. Some magic spell gave him an incredibly extended life span. In 1611, when he was about seventy, he emigrated to North America, where he vanished. Mrs. Zimmermann turns up a very rare book, *Of the Lamia*, which includes his story.

**Deep Magic.** Unlike human magic—the kind that Mrs. Zimmermann and, to a lesser degree, Uncle Jonathan both have—deep magic is magic that comes from *outside*, from the realms of ancient myths or other dimensions where the laws of science don't operate as they do on Earth. Deep magic almost always has ancient roots and often is attached to magical items, like amulets or talismans. Because it is not subject to human control, deep magic is sometimes known as wild magic, and it can be very dangerous.

*Directory of Magical Creatures.* A fictional reference book. Lewis reads through it to see if it has anything to say about the Lamia. It lists a number of vampiric spirits from around the world, including the penang-galen, the lou-garou, the wurdalak, the strigoi, and the m'rani. Finally he finds an informative short article about lamiae, which connects the myth of the lamia to Lilith from Hebrew folklore.

**Dreams.** One of Lewis's nightmares is the scene on the front jacket cover: He returns to the gravestone at night, and in the moonlight a spectral, eyeless serpent comes from under the stone and rears up like a cobra, ready to attack him. Then he wakes up. He has another one about midway through the book in which the two bullies are dead, but their bodies move and grab Lewis and try to throw him in a tomb already full of human bones. Uncle Jonathan has one about an ivory-colored cobra slithering around his bedroom. Lewis's Aunt Helen has a similar bad dream, but in hers, the curtain in her bedroom take the shape of a ghost without eyes and threaten her.

**Engels, Doris.** A young, dark-haired nurse who wears round spectacles and works at the New Zebedee Hospital. She is named for Sara Engels, a Bellairs fan.

**Foley, Father.** St. George's Catholic Church in New Zebedee has had a rapid turnover of priests, and Father Foley is the third one in a year to take the pulpit there. He is an older priest, Irish, with a permanent scowl and a sour disposition. Lewis thinks that Father Foley believes all boys his age are evil. He makes confessions difficult, and he gives hard penances, usually involving putting the boys to work cleaning the church or the church grounds. He also scolds Lewis publicly. Stan Peters also goes to the same church, but Lewis notices that Father Foley is much easier on Stan (who's a popular kid) and never gives him the kind of harsh penance he doles out to Lewis routinely.

Jonathan gets upset over how his nephew is being treated, but Mrs. Zimmermann urges Lewis to consider that Father Foley might have had a bad childhood or might have suffered in some way to make them short-tempered. She essentially says that Lewis should try to understand troublesome people before getting angry at them. Late in the novel, though, we learn that Father Foley isn't what he appears to be.

**Fountain.** At the west end of Main Street is a traffic circle, and the circular space is used as a small park. The main feature at the center of the park is a circle of white marble columns surrounding a fountain that sends up a plume of water like a liquid willow tree.

**Fox, Billy.** A Scout in Lewis's troop. A stubby, heavy-set, muscular boy with a round face and brownish-blond hair cut in a flattop style, he is a football player and a pretty strong kid. Unfortunately, he likes to use his muscles to push other kids around, and together with Stan Peters, he bullies Lewis (among other victims) and makes him start to regret even being in the Scouts.

**Fox, Phil.** Father of Billy Fox, one of the bullies.

***From the Vasty Deep, by Girardus Abucejo.*** A fictitious book written in 1888. The title comes from Shakespeare's *1 Henry IV*, in which the Welsh magician Owen Glendower boasts, "I can call spirits from the vasty deep." Uncle Jonathan has a copy of this book in his library, and in it Lewis reads a horrifying description of the evil that a spirit like the Lamia can cause to befall humans. The author's name is inspired by Jonathan Abucejo, a long-time Bellairs fan and the creator of the first website devoted to Bellairs, compleatbellairs.com.

***Gangbusters.*** An old-time police-procedural radio show. Its opening wasn't a theme song, but the sounds of sirens and machine guns blasting. "To come on like *Gangbusters*" meant to make a noisy commotion, or to charge into a situation. Rose Rita uses the phrase like this in the novel.

**Glaciers.** At times in the past, glaciers covered most or all of what is today Michigan. Glacial moraines—sediments left behind as glaciers melted and retreated—are common there, and much of the state is fairly flat with rich soil. However, glaciers also push or haul rocks along, and in the middle of Richardson's Woods in the story are heaps of boulders, ranging from small to huge, left behind in one of the Ice Age glaciations. The mysterious flat stone tomb that Lewis finds is part of this mass of stones.

***Great Poems of the English-Speaking World.*** A fictitious anthology of poetry. In it Rose Rita finds and reads "Lamia," by John Keats, which offers one interpretation of what a lamia might be. Keats's version is about a beautiful woman transformed into a serpent. She offers to help the god Hermes if he will restore her humanity. She helps him, and he does make her fully human again. Later, she falls in love with a young man named Lycius. At their wedding feast, a philosopher, Apollonius, sees through her outward appearance and identifies her as a serpent. She vanishes, and that night Lycius dies of grief.

***Guide to the Planets, A.*** Book by Sir Patrick Moore (1923-2012). A teacher and a brilliant amateur astronomer, Moore eventually became President of the British Astronomical Society, a television personality hosting a show about professional and amateur astronomy, and author of more than seventy books. This one was written in the 1950s and is essentially a guide for amateurs who want to observe the planets through binoculars or backyard telescopes. Moore later revised the book to reflect later discoveries about the planets that made some of the information in the first edition obsolete. In one chapter of *Whistle,* Lewis tries to calm his nerves by reading this book.

**Halvers, Fred.** He is the Scoutmaster of Lewis's troop and also a teacher at the high school. He's patient and normally a kind man, but sometimes the hijinks of his Scouts just get on his nerves. He's in his forties, tall and athletic-looking, with a round bulbous nose, close-clipped gray hair that looks almost white in the light (it was blond before he went gray), and he wears glasses with heavy black rims.

**Hardwick, Robert.** The owner and operator of the National Museum of Magic in New Zebedee (he features in *The Specter from the Magician's Museum*). When they need to look up information on magic and its history, Lewis and Rose Rita consider borrowing some books from his collection.

**Heemsoth's Rexall Drug Store.** Lewis visits it for supplies after his uncle is injured.

**Helen, Aunt**. No last name given. Uncle Jonathan's sister, who has the personality of a leaky inner tube. She has no patience with kids. Jonathan and Lewis visit her and her husband Jimmy, who live near Osee Five Hills, and get stranded there overnight when the Muggins Simoon won't start for the return trip.

**HIC IACET LAMIA.** Lewis finds an automobile-sized boulder, worn flat, in the woods while on his Boy Scout camping trip, and carved into it are these worn and weathered letters. In Latin, the inscription means "Here Lies Lamia." Lewis immediately realizes the stone covers a tomb, and of course that knowledge makes him nervous.

**Holyrood Abbey**. A ruined monastery near Edinburgh in Scotland. The enchanted stained-glass window shows Lewis an image of the stone tombs there.

**Humphries, Doc.** The Barnavelt's family doctor from earlier books. Rose Rita mentions him.

**Indian-head pennies.** Lewis has five of these, dating back to the 1880s.

**James, M.R.** (1862-1936). While researching the significance of the whistle, Rose Rita reads a short story by this British writer. The story is about an elderly academic who discovers an ancient, cursed silver whistle that summons a ghost. Though she doesn't mention the title, it is "Oh, Whistle and I'll Come to You, My Lad," the ghost tale that inspired the whistle in this novel.

**Jimmy, Uncle**. No last name given. Lewis's uncle by marriage (to Jonathan's sister Helen). Jonathan and Lewis visit Uncle Jimmy and Aunt Helen in their home near Osee Five Hills.

**Lamia Brand Super-Sudsy Washday Detergent.** Does not actually exist. When Lewis is trying to figure out who the "Lamia" mentioned on the stone inscription might have been, Rose Rita teasingly suggests that the inscription might only be an ad for this imaginary detergent.

**Lilith.** Sometimes the story of Lilith becomes conflated with that of Lamia. The word Lilith appears only once in the Bible, in the Old Testament, Isaiah 34, where, spelled "lilit," it seems to refer to a demonic spirit, one among many. The Latin translation of the Hebrew scripture renders the word as "lamia." In biblical folklore, Lilith was Adam's first wife, created at the same time as he was. However, she refused to be subservient to him and subsequently was cast out and became a demonic spirit, often said to steal children in the depth of the night. She was also a vampire, and her legend blends with the Greek lamia to make her a serpent-woman hybrid. This lore is referenced in the novel. By the way, other biblical translations use "night hag," not "lamia," for the word in Isaiah 34:14.

**Mansion Street.** The book explains that it has no mansions on it, but was named "Mansion Street" because back in the 19th century New Zebedee hoped to be chosen as the state capital, and they planned to build a fine governor's mansion on that street. Unfortunately, New Zebedee lost out to Lansing, but they were left with a street named for a mansion that was never built. The Pottingers live at 39 Mansion Street.

**Mystery stories.** Lewis has been on a mystery-novel reading spree. His favorite authors include Sir Arthur Conan Doyle, H. Rider Haggard, Ellery Queen, and Robert Louis Stevenson. Some of these wrote detective mysteries, like Doyle and Queen; others wrote novels that had no detective as such, but offered puzzles and mysteries to explore.

**New Zebedee Hospital.** In a renovated old mansion not far from the library. Two characters are hospitalized there with a strange form of anemia.

**New Zebedee Public Library.** As before, it is a big gray stone-fronted building not too far from the Civil War memorial. Mrs. Geer is the head librarian there.

**Newspaper Ghost.** When the bullies attack Lewis for the second time, at night and during a thunderstorm, the Lamia manifests by whipping up a scatter of old newspapers and forming a body from them.

***Of the Lamia, Together with the Memoirs of Fr. Pierre Michel d'Anjou.*** A fictitious book, published in France in 1656, and written by a priest named St. Francis Xavier Kemp. Kemp was mentored by Pierre d'Anjou and came with him in 1611 when d'Anjou traveled to North America. The book claims that d'Anjou had a silver whistle which summoned, but could not control, a deadly spirit. The book itself is a magical artifact, with a hand-made cover that includes protective symbols. Kemp is named for Margaret Kemp, a Bellairs fan.

**Old English furniture polish.** A real product, Lewis has to use this to polish up the pews in the church as part of his ongoing penance.

**Peters, Stan.** One of the Boy Scouts in Lewis's troop. He is tall and lanky, with red hair, a big nose, and jug ears, and his cheeks are splattered with about a thousand pale orange freckles. He is not evil, exactly, but he's one of those kids who will fall in with some little plot to annoy or bully another weaker kid, if someone else starts it. He's one of two boys in the troop who make Lewis's life fairly miserable.

**Pottinger, Rose Rita.** She wears a Detroit Tigers baseball cap in this book. She continues to spin tall tales, and when Lewis calls her on the habit, she shoots back, "I'll be a famous writer one of these days." In my biography of Rose Rita, prepared as background to the series, she does just that, rising to great prominence just after graduating from college when she begins to publish thrillers. She becomes a best-selling writer whose fame rivals that of Stephen King.

***Quantum materiae materietur marmota monax si marmota monax materiam possit meteriari?*** At one point, Father Foley demands that Lewis translate this Latin question into English. It has to do with woodchucks.

**Richardson's Woods.** A stretch of forest in Capharnaum County, some miles northwest of New Zebedee. In the middle of the woods Lewis finds the clearings where the carved stone lies. The place is named for Matthew Richardson, a long-time fan of John Bellairs.

**Roman ships.** Rose Rita knows about at least two different types: a *galley* was a ship mostly propelled by rowers at long-handled oars, not by the sails. The word "galley" itself is Greek and came into use late, in Europe during the Middle Ages. It derives from a Greek word, *galea,* which identified a warship with only one deck of oars. The Roman warships had one, two, or three decks of oars and were called respectively monoremes, biremes, and triremes. These were the types of Roman war galleys. The second type of ship that Rose Rita mentions is the *quinquireme,* which, like the trireme, has three decks but is extra-large. Each oar in a quinquireme had five men rowing it, and that's how it got its name—it means "Five-ship." The quinquireme was the battleship of its day, for many years the largest type of vessel used in the Roman Navy.

**Rosary.** Lewis still has his mother's rosary, which he keeps as a memento of her.

**Salk, Jonas** (1914-1995). Mrs. Zimmermann mentions him. Dr. Salk devoted seven years to devising and testing a successful vaccine for the prevention of polio, previously an incurable disease that regularly every year caused panic when it broke out, usually in the summer. The introduction of the Salk vaccine in 1955 is one of the indications that *Whistle* takes place in that year, though Lewis is still "about thirteen."

*Sibila et veniam.* A Latin phrase etched on the silver whistle that Lewis finds. It is not Classical Latin, but medieval Church Latin and can be translated as "Whistle and I will come."

*Spiritum nolite extinguere.* Father Foley rather unfairly springs this biblical quotation on Lewis and demands that he identify where it comes from and what the translation is. Lewis guesses (correctly) that it is from the New Testament and from the Epistles of Paul, but Father Foley is dissatisfied and tells him it's from First Thessalonians (1 Thessalonians 5:19). Lewis's halting translation is "Do not extinguish the spirit," which the priest refuses to accept as correct, insisting it should be rendered as "Quench not the spirit," an older way of translating the sentence. He calls Lewis a little heathen and instructs him to read First Thessalonians to prepare for a quiz on it the next day.

There's a little significance to this. Paul's first Letter to the Thessalonians is more personal and less theological than his other epistles. In it he comforts the members of the Christian Church in Thessalonica, who were becoming discouraged with Roman opposition to their faith. Crucially, a bit earlier Paul counsels the congregation, *Videte ne quis malum pro malo alicui reddat : sed semper quod bonum est sectamini in invicem, et in omnes* ("See that no one returns evil for evil to anyone: but always do good to one another, and to every person"—1 Thessalonians 5:15). This is precisely Lewis's moral dilemma. He acquires the power to punish the bullies by bullying them. The temptation will be difficult to resist.

**St. Anthony's Medal.** Lewis has one as a memento of his first Communion. St. Anthony of Padua (1195-1231) was a Franciscan priest noted for his knowledge and his charity toward the poor and the sick. He is also considered the saint of lost things—a prayer to him is thought to help people find things they've lost. When Lewis is searching for the whistle, which has vanished, it seemed appropriate that he would find his old St. Anthony's medal instead.

**Stone arrowhead.** Louis has one that he found in a creek bed near the Waterworks.

**Swazzle.** Louis has one of these, a small device containing a reed and meant to be held in the mouth. It produces a raspy "voice," and is sometimes used by puppeteers and ventriloquists. Louis, however, was never able to master it.

**Telephone numbers.** We learn that New Zebedee has changed to a more modern system of phone numbers, superseding the old three-digit system. The new system uses five numbers. Billy Fox's family's number is 2-3432.

**The Game of Authors.** Louis has an Authors deck. This is a card game, still available in the U.S. It requires a deck of 44 cards with pictures of 11 authors on them, each author represented by four cards. The individual cards for an author will name one of his or her works. The game is played like Go Fish, with players asking others for specific cards—"Do you have Mark Twain, *Huckleberry Finn*?" If the challenged player does, he or she must give up the card to the challenger. The goal is for each player to collect as many four-card sets of authors as possible. The winner is the one with the most complete sets. In addition to Twain, in the 1950s the cards represented Louisa May Alcott, James Fenimore Cooper, Charles Dickens, Nathaniel Hawthorne, William Shakespeare, Washington Irving, Henry Wadsworth Longfellow, Sir Walter Scott, Robert Louis Stevenson, and Alfred, Lord Tennyson.

**Tithonus.** A character in ancient Greek mythology, misprinted in the book as Tithonis. His lover, the goddess of the dawn, Eos, asked Zeus to make him immortal, but did not ask for him to be kept forever young. He could not die, but continually and horribly withered with age.

**Whistle, Silver.** While gathering stones to make a fire pit on the Boy Scout trip, Lewis uncovers a silver whistle, one of the kind that looks like a British policeman's whistle or a large dog whistle — a straight barrel with a mouthpiece at one end. Though obviously very old and crammed and packed with dirt, the whistle is strangely untarnished. This one is engraved, though the figures and decorations are worn and hard to make out. Lewis also reads an inscription on the whistle: *"Sibila et veniam."* It takes some time for him to translate this difficult Latin phrase.

Lewis soon notices that the whistle is uncanny. He finds a chain to thread through its loop so he can hang it around his neck, but somehow the whistle keeps vanishing from his pocket or from where it dangles on the chain, only to reappear when Lewis is feeling frightened and angry. He discovers fairly early on that when he blows the whistle, the sound produces fear in those who hear it.

**Willow Creek Road.** A rural road in Capharnaum County. At one point it winds close to Richardson's Woods.

**Zimmermann, Florence.** When Lewis's pup tent is slashed in three places, Uncle Jonathan says he will buy a new one, since it's too far gone even to patch. He observes that Mrs. Zimmermann could easily mend the tent by magic, but they won't ask her because she insists that magic must be used only for things that are important. In a scene at the mysterious inscribed stone, Mrs. Zimmermann casts a spell to let everyone see all the deaths that have occurred in that spot. The only ones they see are animal deaths — no human perished there. Jonathan comes up with a new nickname for her in this novel: Witch Hazel.

◆ ◆ ◆

## Chapter 9: A John Bellairs Mystery:
### *The House where Nobody Lived*
### By Brad Strickland
### Dial Books for Young Readers, 2006

The eleventh New Zebedee novel had its seeds planted years earlier, on an occasion when Barbara and I visited the Honolulu House in Marshall. In a town of eclectic and eccentric architecture, it stands out, which is quite a feat.

If you stroll any of the old established streets of Marshall, you'll pass houses that range in style from stately Georgian to austere Federal to elaborate Victorian to practical modernistic, all companionably existing together side by side. Once when I was speaking to a group of Marshall school children, I remarked they were lucky to live in a town that had such an interesting variety of architecture, such fine, historic old houses because my home town didn't.

One of the students asked me why, and I said, "Well, because your ancestors marched through and burned them all."

That was a bit of a stretch, but basically the point holds true—one of Marshall's great charms is the scenic hodge-podge of its houses and buildings. The Honolulu House, though, stands unique, and I remembered it long after our tour.

Later, when I heard from our friends Eddie and Carolyn Carroll a story of the baffling bad luck their family had when they returned from a vacation in Hawaii and then discovered that their children had brought home bits of lava as souvenirs—and how they had learned that the volcano goddess Pele would bring bad luck to them until the stones were returned to Hawaii (they mailed them back)—the wheels started turning. I'd mentioned New Zebedee's Hawaii House before. This time it was to be the scene of the most exciting action.

For a change, there was no back-and-forth about the title. It came to me at once, and it stuck. This title, of course, is equivocal. Possibly it's a little of a Harry Potter influence, though I really wasn't thinking of "The

Boy who Lived" when I came up with it. "The house where nobody lived" can mean either a vacant house, one where nobody resides; or, (more darkly)  it can name a house in which none of the inhabitants manage to survive.

◆ ◆ ◆

*Summary:*

On a hot early-summer day when Lewis is eleven and his new friend Rose Rita is twelve, the two of them walk along a highway leading out of town—but not far beyond the town limits, certainly less than a mile, though they are exploring territory unknown to them.

While investigating a grassy lane that leads into a grove of trees, they discover the empty, spooky Hawaii House, abandoned and eerie, but not falling apart. As they step up on the porch, they hear an ominous warning drumbeat begin. They quickly retreat.

Mrs. Zimmermann and Jonathan tell them the history of the house— it was built by a sea captain who had brought a beautiful bride home from Hawaii in the 1860s—and people in town fear it. It seems that one night in the 1870s, everyone in the house—the husband, his wife, all the servants—died, all at once, of no evident cause. Since then the house has the reputation of being haunted.

Lewis wants nothing to do with it, and for years he seldom even thinks about it. But then when he's over thirteen, a family of newcomers to town finally buys the house, moves into it, and—sinister things begin to happen. Lewis and Rose Rita meet the family's son—David Keller, about their age, painfully shy and with a bad stutter—and  try to get to the bottom of the strange occurrences.

They don't know it, but they are risking their own sanity, and their lives.

◆ ◆ ◆

*Behind the Scenes:*

I'd thought about writing a book featuring a fictional version of Marshall's Honolulu House for a while. In 2004 I started doing the research. Barbara and I had already toured the real, original Honolulu House, a true oddity among its eclectic neighbors.

The house came about when Abner Pratt (1801-1863), former Consul to the Sandwich Islands (Hawaii today) under President James Buchanan, built it as his home. Pratt, a native of Springfield, New York, had lived in Marshall since 1832. He practiced law and, over the years, became a state legislator and a Michigan Supreme Court justice before President Buchanan appointed him as the U.S. Consul to the Kingdom of Hawaii. He spent seven years there, and on his return to Marshall, he had his house built in the style of Hawaii's Iolanai Palace, the official residence of the King and Queen of the islands.

Alas, Pratt didn't live to enjoy the mansion for long. He died in 1863—the legend in Marshall is that he decided to sleep outside in the open front tower of the house, as he had done in Hawaii on muggy nights. Unfortunately, it was a bitter winter night in Michigan, and, the story says, Pratt fell ill and died of pneumonia.

The house he left behind is a fabulous tribute to his fascination with Hawaii. Pratt furnished it with mementoes and furniture from the islands, had tropical murals painted on the walls, and made sure the architects included a wide wrap-around porch, just like the ones he had seen while living in Hawaii. It was expensive and difficult to keep up, and it fell into disrepair until in 1951 a new owner renovated it. In 1961 it became the property of the Marshall Historical Society. The Society transformed it into a marvelous museum commemorating the town's colorful past resident.

I'd mentioned the fictional Hawaii House once or twice in my novels, but when I decided to set this novel there, I relocated it a bit. Previously I'd written that it wasn't far from the Barnavelt House, but that wasn't very specific. To kick off the action in *The House where Nobody Lived,* I did something unusual for a New Zebedee book: I opened with a flashback to when Lewis was only eleven, school was recently out, and on a hot day in early summer, he and Rose Rita went exploring alongside a highway leading outside of town. Lewis had never been that far on foot, though it was only a mile or so from the Barnavelt house.

They didn't go very far before Rose Rita notices an overgrown lane leading off through a thick grove of trees. At the end of the lane is the derelict Hawaii House—where the two receive a fright. After establishing the location as spooky, the novel jumps ahead—to when

Lewis was "older than thirteen," a first in his glacial aging after *The Vengeance of the Witch-Finder.*

He's also more confident—he and Rose Rita have been through some amazing adventures together. Because he was himself a victim of bullies, he feels empathy when David begins to be pushed around. We see a new side of Lewis, protective and encouraging to a boy weaker than he is.

One other note: David Keller's horrific dream, coupled with sleep paralysis, one that my college roommate suffered as a recurring nightmare. In it, some shadowy thing crouches over him, with a clawed hand spread out inches from his face. It never hurt him, but he would wake up sweating with dread when he had it.

Finally, I really do try to be modest, but re-reading the book, I like the climax a lot. It's fast, it's suspenseful, all our friends are there, and it just seems to me I got that one right. It's sweet when that happens.

The book went through two editors, neither of whom was familiar with the Bellairs canon. When I turned in the outline, the first one didn't like the 1950s setting and encouraged me to update it to the 1990s. I explained that Lewis would be in his fifties by then, and she said, "Nobody will know. Just change the date."

Sigh.

However, I carefully explained the background of the other books and pointed out this was only one in a long series that needed to stay internally consistent, and in the end, she didn't insist on the date change.

My writing on this one was slower than usual. A good part of that came from my increased workload at the college, but our children were also growing up and going to college. Homebodies, they both chose to do their first two years of study where I taught, and I had to tread very carefully to avoid butting in or hovering over them as they made their way through.

Then our son graduated from the University of Georgia, got his first job, and eventually met someone special and married her. Our daughter took a degree in theater, went to Utah for a while to work with the Utah Shakespeare Festival, and then spent some time in Orlando, working for Universal Studios and then Disney as a costumed character/wardrobe wiz/puppeteer (her true love). With a family suddenly extended over three states, I had less time in the summers.

At any rate, juggling school, family, and writing assignments, I completed the submission manuscript over about nine months of writing and revision. The new editor (number 2 on this book; my first one had taken a job offer with a different publisher and had moved on) signed off on it, and it went into production.

Dial decided to market the book as a YA mystery, and accordingly the billing on the cover and title page changed. It was now "A John Bellairs Mystery, featuring Lewis Barnavelt." It appeared under the Dial Sleuth imprint, a new line that concentrated on mystery stories. That rather misplaced a Bellairs book, but it was a corporate decision, not my own.

The publishing industry was going into a recession, and Penguin, the parent company of Dial, had pared down its work force. It took longer for the book to move through the press than the former ones had. It was published in 2006.

Jay Cooper designed the cover, which shows Rose Rita and Lewis staring through a window in horror as a tiki monster, gigantic, bares its teeth at them. It's a more colorful jacket than the Bellairs books had normally sported, and its style is reminiscent of 1950s illustrations. It is not in the mood of Edward Gorey, though. The back of the jacket is given over to a quotation from the novel.

This time I dedicated the novel "To my daughter Amy, who always sees the magic." That seemed appropriate for a young woman who had been a stage and TV actress and who currently was pulling strings in Florida as a puppeteer adept at everything from hand-and-rod puppets to marionettes to puppets she literally had to inhabit—climbing inside them to animate their expressions and gestures.

Some sidelights in general about publishing that many people have asked me about: Format, editing, and covers.

Some readers become distressed because all the books in the series are not quite of a uniform size. That is not under the control of the writer, but the book's layout and design team, and influenced by economics. When a publisher is facing economic hard times, one of the natural ways of responding is to cut costs: the work force is thinned out, with the employees left working harder to cover more responsibilities, for example. Acquisitions slow—fewer manuscripts are bought because the costs of production remain high—and manufacturing budgets are reduced. That means the book size may be shaved down a bit. The covers will be a little smaller, and perhaps not as sturdy as earlier covers have been. The jackets are printed on a thinner grade of paper, and so on.

Once upon a time, American publishers were independent businesses. The big imprints, like Random House, Alfred A. Knopf, Scribner's, and so on, were self-contained enterprises. Each had its own staff of editors, production experts, and accounting. In the 1960s, that began to change. Conglomerates began to buy up the publishing houses.

Now, a conglomerate may throw together a strange combination of enterprises. A German company, Bertlesmann, now owns both Random House and Penguin—as well as printing companies, investment-services companies, internet-service providing companies, and many other concerns. The chief concern of a conglomerate's accounting department is that each division of the conglomerate must show a profit.

More and more, under corporate pressure, publishers who must deliver to their owners want to publish only best-sellers. That's one reason for the explosion of celebrity books: the publishers hope that a celebrity's name on the cover will result in huge sales. It doesn't always happen, but they keep hoping. More, with the company's future on the line, publishers become wary about buying manuscripts that will do well—but not spectacularly. A book that a publisher would take a chance on in 1950 might be turned down by everyone in the 21$^{st}$ century as a "midlist book," and publishers really want only best-sellers.

And the accountants who overlook the bottom lines of the publisher keep insisting "Cut costs! Increase sales!"

It's a problem.

Some fans want to know how the editing process goes. First, understand the process that a traditionally-published book goes through just to be accepted. Virtually all commercial publishers these days won't consider a novel unless it comes in from an agent. Most aspiring novelists don't have agents. Most agents don't want to consider writers as clients unless they have a track record. Writers can't get a track record until they've published a novel, so round and round it goes.

However, assuming a writer finds a publisher that will look at unagented submissions, traditionally the writer sends a copy of the manuscript to the publisher. No editor will look at it initially. Instead, a cadre of first readers will go through what is called the "slush pile" (unsolicited manuscripts) and will read to see if any are interesting enough to be taken to an editor.

Honestly, I suspect most of the unsolicited manuscripts are never read through. Sometimes ten or twenty pages will tell a reader that the novel is not publishable, and those are rejected. Some are good enough to read through, but not yet close to being ready, and those are rejected. A few will strike a spark with a first reader, and the reader will take those to an editor with a recommendation to acquire the book

Next, the editor herself will read the manuscript and decide whether to accept or reject it. Or, more often, the editor will take the novel to a meeting with other editors—an editorial board—and will make a case for publishing it. But every editor has novels to recommend. If the publisher has decreed that in that month the editors will acquire no more than one dozen novels, and if the editors have a total of twenty possibilities to present, then eight of the potential novels will be rejected—usually not with a form letter but with a friendly note from the editor who recommended them.

Ah, but let's look at one of the lucky ones. The editor who made the case is the acquisitions editor; she will lead the book through the revision and publishing process. This editor is looking for the big picture and will ask for changes on a story scale: "You need to make Chapter 8 more suspenseful. Chapters 12 and 13 are too long on description and way too short on action. Give me a rewrite in a month."

When your editor is finished, and you have made the revisions, next up to the plate is the copy editor, who will go through your manuscript with a blue pencil, making changes. If you have a British character who says, "I saw that man on the lift." The copy editor will change the line to "I saw that man in the elevator." If your favorite dialogue tag is "said Lewis," the copy editor will change it to "Lewis said."

This is sentence- and word-level stuff, much more focused and exacting than the concerns of the overall editor. Writers who argue with editors more often argue with copy editors than with any other type. Sometimes you win, sometimes you lose. When Lewis was feeling sick, I said he was "nauseated." The copy editor insisted the proper word was "nauseous."

I'm sensitive to the histories of words. "Nauseous" historically meant "sickening, revolting, disgusting." "The dog dragged in some nauseous lump of garbage." If Lewis is nauseous, he makes *other* people sick.

But the editor agreed with the copy editor, and I lost that one. It still bothers me. In one of the Johnny Dixon novels, I had Professor Childermass call something "insanitary." The copy editor insisted that was wrong and it had to be "unsanitary." However, I pointed out that with Childermass's education and age, he would be far more likely to use the old-fashioned term "insanitary," and that would help to characterize him. I got that one.

In general, I will say that editors are helpful and interested in bringing the best possible version of the novel to the public. Well, so are the writers. Really, if you think about it, the editor and the writer are teammates, not adversaries. In fact, over a long career of novel writing, I have always gotten along well with my editors, though I may complain and quibble from time to time.

Finally, I've been verbally abused by fans who blame me for "firing Edward Gorey!"

No, Edward Gorey passed away. Otherwise, if it were up to me, he would have done all the covers. However, writers have no control over who illustrates the book. In fact, at Dial there was a strict company policy that writers could not get in touch with the artists; the Art Department controlled artist relations. I truly wanted to send Edward Gorey a note saying that I admired his work on the Bellairs books and was grateful to be working on the books with him.

Dial refused even to forward the note and told me never to try to get in touch with Mr. Gorey in any way. They didn't want authors trying to decide what illustrations were done for their books—not suggesting scenes, or subjects, or compositions, nothing.

I wouldn't have done that, anyway. I really loved Edward Gorey's art, and I knew that he read every page of the novels before deciding what he would put on the covers. Far be it from me to try to tell such a professional what should be done.

More than once I have met unhappy writer/illustrator teams of children's books. The publisher accepted the story but turned down the artwork. Or the Art Department wants the artist to work for them, but Editorial turned down the story. If you're going with traditional publishing, don't count on being able to name an artist. You probably won't be allowed. Now, once the artist was working on the cover, the writer gets a peek, right? Or approval?

Nope. The first a writer sees of the jacket is after it is finished, probably after the printing process has begun (jackets are printed separately from the books) and after it's too late to make changes.

Once I got a proof of the cover, and to my shock, the little blurb about the book was completely wrong. It gave an incorrect summary and mentioned characters not in the book. I called my editor and told him, and he discovered that the blurb writer, an overworked fellow, had two back covers to write, and he got them mixed up. My plot and characters were on the back of someone else's book. They briefly considered having me rewrite my book to put in some characters with the names on the back—color printing is expensive—but finally managed to reunite the descriptions with the proper books.

Once someone asked me do how you keep from getting a bad cover? You don't, not always. I really don't like about half a dozen of the cover that my books have sported, but most of the time I've liked them. About seventy-five out of eighty are interesting or striking. That's a pretty good batting average, I think. And I've *really* liked almost all the covers for the books I did in the Bellairs series, and that's something to be thankful for.

◆ ◆ ◆

## *The House Where Nobody Lived:* People, Places and Things

**Angdale, Mrs**. Her subjects are history and social studies. She is the oldest teacher in the school, with white hair kept in a hard-looking tight bun on the back of her head. She always wears black dresses, and by the end of the day they're sprinkled and streaked with chalk dust. She is very farsighted and hard of hearing, and she wears thick spectacles that magnify her eyes and demands that the students speak loudly when she calls roll or asks a question.

**Ann Arbor.** A university town not too far from New Zebedee. They have an excellent facility for speech therapy.

**Arrowhead.** Rose Rita has a sharp eye for these and has collected a good many. She adds a small white-quartz one in Chapter 1.

**Barlow, Bishop.** We first met him in *The House with a Clock in Its Walls*, when he was a realtor who sold the Hanchett House. He's still in business, and he handled the sale of the Hawaii House.

**Barnavelt, Charlie.** Uncle Jonathan remembers a time when his younger brother, Lewis's deceased father, went to the rescue of a kid named Francis, who was picked on because he had a stutter. When two bullies were beating on him, Charlie Barnavelt, a baseball star and a strong guy, waded in and between them he and Francis chased the bullies away.

**Barnavelt, Jonathan.** We learn that Jonathan has a phobia about talking on the phone during a storm, because he is afraid the lightning might run in on the lines and fry him. He plays the harmonica and when they have a singalong, he asks David Keller if he can hit a high C, or even better a high W. Later in the book he shows an unexpected talent when he successfully turns on the water in the Hawaii House after it has been shut off for more than thirty years.

**Barnavelt, Lewis.** In the first chapters we revisit him as an eleven-year-old, not quite a year in New Zebedee, overweight, clumsy, and timid. Later in the book we go to the time when he's "more than thirteen." He has one awesome moment of pride in the novel, when he volunteers for a dangerous mission, although he is terrified, and Jonathan says softly, "Lewis, I am so proud of you."

We learn in Chapter 3 of some changes he has gone through since first coming to New Zebedee: Rose Rita has taught him to play a fair game of baseball—though he remains clumsy and knows he will never be as good a player as she is. He's no longer a complete scaredy-cat, but still is timid and doesn't play football because he's afraid of getting hurt in a contact sport. After Lewis's and Jonathan's European vacation in *Vengeance of the Witch-Finder*, when he lost some weight due to extensive walking tours and his distaste for strange foods, Lewis is no longer fat, just heavyset.

In other ways, he's just the same—an avid reader, getting good grades (so much that sometimes people tease him about being a teacher's pet), and still a worrier. However, his adventures with Rose Rita have given him a bit of courage.

Soon, somewhat to his own surprise, Lewis befriends David Keller, the new kid in town, who quickly becomes the victim of bullies. It's the first time that any other kid has looked up to Lewis in that way, and it gives him a feeling of maturity.

**Beemuth, Mr**. Lewis's home-room teacher and his teacher for general science.

**Betty Crocker**. She is an advertising trademark for a line of food items. The character was created in 1921 by an advertising man, Bruce Barton, for the General Mills Company. Pictures of her are on the boxes of products named for her, and several actors have portrayed her in commercials. Rose Rita, complaining about home economics, says she doesn't want to grow up to be Betty Crocker.

**Biggins, Brenda**. A stuck-up girl in Rose Rita's class at school.

**Borax Hand Soap.** A coarse-textured soap containing sodium borate or sodium tetraborate. Because of its texture and the mineral it contains, it is good for scrubbing oil and other stubborn stains off the skin. The most popular brand of it is Boraxo.

**Callandar, Mary**. A classmate of Lewis and Rose Rita.

**Capharnaum County Magicians Society.** When David Keller comes over for lunch, Lewis and Rose Rita promise not to mention this, or that Jonathan and Mrs. Zimmermann can perform magic. They don't want to spook the new kid.

**Chadwick, Captain Abadiah**. The builder and owner of the Hawaii House. He was a sea captain who spent three years in Hawaii and fell in love with a beautiful Hawaiian princess. He ran away with her, they got married aboard ship, and eventually they moved to Michigan—almost as far from the ocean as anyone could get in the USA. Chadwick hired a staff of many servants to help run the place, and on the night of January 19, 1876, every person in the house mysteriously died with no sign of a wound or poison. Chadwick was found on the open platform over the verandah. He had barricaded himself outside the house and had frozen to death. Since then, no one has stayed in the house for more than one night. Though a real-estate company bought the house and modernized it, they can't persuade anyone to buy it. For years it stands empty—until the Keller family moves in.

As Lewis comes to learn about Captain Chadwick, he begins to understand his motives and his courage. He concludes that even a vengeful goddess could not defeat this man—she could only kill him.

**Cheerios.** The breakfast staple in the Barnavelt house turns up again.

**Coat rack mirror.** This is the one that Jonathan enchanted years before. It picks up radio broadcasts from WGN in Chicago, and sometimes it doesn't reflect one's face, but shows scenes from history or even from outer space. In the novel, at one point it shows an erupting volcano. Another time it shows Lewis the face of an unearthly woman with eyes that literally blaze.

**Comic strips.** Two adventure-themed newspaper comic strips are mentioned: *Dick Tracy* and *The Phantom*.

**Corrigan's Hardware.** A store on Main Street. It is owned by Tarby Corrigan's father; we first met Tarby in *The House with a Clock in Its Walls.*

**Crow Corners.** Fictional rural village off the Homer Road near New Zebedee. A man Jonathan calls Old Pete has a seed-and-feed and hardware store there, and Jonathan buys some insulation for the Kellers so they won't find out he didn't have it all along.

**Crystal orb.** Mrs. Zimmermann gives Lewis a small one, half the size of a marble, to wear as a protective amulet. It dates back to 1050 and once decorated the hilt of a mystic sword owned by many good magicians over the centuries, finally coming into the hands of a man descended from the Knights Templar, who gave it to Mrs. Zimmermann when she was a University student. Although it is merely a sphere of quartz crystal, so many good sorcerers have cast spells on it over the years that Mrs. Zimmermann thinks it would protect Lewis against any magic.

**"Defying gravity."** The phrase occurs in Chapter 15, but is NOT a reference to *Wicked*. It's just coincidence.

*Dragnet.* The radio and TV police show, created by and starring Jack Webb as detective Joe Friday, is mentioned. Because of it, Rose Rita knows what a stake-out is.

**Dreams.** David Keller has a recurring nightmare about tiki drums pounding and another in which he feels frozen in bed, unable to move, but knows some person or creature is standing over him, holding a hand spread out in front of his face. Later Lewis has a nightmare in which he sees the sad ghost of the princess Makalani beckoning him from an upper window of the Hawaii House. But when he goes inside, the Night Marchers appear in fierce warrior regalia, threatening to run him through with a spear.

**Drum.** Lewis and Rose Rita hear a terribly loud, booming war drum when they first try to look through the windows of the derelict Hawaii House. It may be an illusion, but it frightens them.

**Dugan, Mike.** One of the eighth-grade bullies. Mike is quieter than the others, but quick to play mean tricks like tripping a victim. Later, he blames the Keller family when Skunky Stevenson has a fright so bad it lands him in a mental hospital.

**Elemental spirits.** Some belief systems, like that of the Rosicrucians, think that the natural world is controlled by spirits that are not ghosts, because they have never inhabited a body. They command the Four Elements of the ancient world: Earth, Air, Fire, and Water. Mrs. Zimmerman thinks it's barely possible that elementals are responsible for the trouble at the Hawaii House.

**Furling, Mr.** A math teacher at Lewis's school.

**Galway, Albert.** Rose Rita's grandfather makes an appearance. He has now filled his whole yard with fanciful miniature windmills which animate little figures when the wind blows: a cyclist on a bonebreaker-style two-wheeler, a farmer trying unsuccessfully to chop off a turkey's head, and two sailors desperately paddling a rowboat away from a sperm whale that "surfaces" and snaps at them, among others. He has visited Oahu and Maui and the big island of Hawaii and fondly recalls the beautiful landscape and the graceful hula dance.

He also knows a little about Hawaiian ghosts and curses. He is the one who tells them about Pele, the volcano goddess who is said to live in the crater of Kilauea. She's a trickster who sometimes randomly appears to strangers or sends a ghostly dog to chase interlopers. To be fair, though, if she appears near someone who is doing wrong, she never punishes that person without a warning first: "Mend your ways!" He recalls a Navy buddy of his who had an unnerving encounter with Pele, who was angry at him for buying souvenirs cheap from the poor islanders and reselling them for a profit.

**Gartener, Francis "Frank."** A childhood friend of Jonathan and Charlie Barnavelt. Like David Keller, Francis had a bad stutter, but learned that if he sang, his stutter vanished. Lewis, who's heard only that the kid's name was Francis until Charlie started calling him "Frank," mistakenly thinks he grew up to be Frank Sinatra. However, he was Frank Gartener, who grew up to own a great and famous restaurant in Chicago.

**Ghosts.** When David asks if Rose Rita and Lewis believe in them, Rose Rita remembers the events of *The Figure in the Shadows* and *The Doom of the Haunted Opera*.

**Gib-cat.** Mrs. Zimmermann tells Rose Rita that she looks as glum as one—she doesn't know what one is, but she recalls that in Shakespeare's *1 Henry IV*, one of the characters is said to be "as melancholy as a gib-cat." It's an elderly, neutered male cat, in fact.

**Halloween.** The novel reaches a climax during Halloween.

**Heemsoth's Rexall Drug Store.** Again, this is a landmark where people meet each other in New Zebedee.

**"It Ain't Gonna Rain No More."** A silly song, based on a folk poem that Carl Sandburg traced back to the 1870s. It became a popular tune in the 1920s, often accompanied by a ukulele. Uncle Jonathan plays it on the harmonica for a backyard singalong.

**Izard, Isaac.** Gets a mention from Mrs. Zimmermann.

**Jonah.** Uncle Jonathan mentions this biblical figure on a stormy day of flooding rains, but Jonathan correctly observes that he was swallowed not by a whale but by "a great fish."

**Kamehameha.** Historically, the first king to unite all the Hawaiian Islands under one government. Mrs. Zimmermann learns that Princess Makalani was a distant relative of Kamehameha, and she suspects that one of Makalani's relatives on the island, angry because she ran away with an American sailor, appealed to Pele to avenge her abduction. Moreover, Mrs. Zimmermann thinks the ghosts persist because they want to retrieve some physical object from the Hawaii House—but, being ghosts, they can't.

**Keller, David**. The new kid in town, whose parents have bought the Hawaii House. He is shy and easily frightened, and he has a persistent, terrible stutter that makes it hard for him to talk.

**Keller, Ernest.** David Keller's father. He has mild blue eyes behind rimless spectacles, is balding, and resembles his son. The sinister history of the Hawaii house meant it sold for a low value, but buying the house strained Mr. Keller's finances, so he does a lot of the fix-up and renovation work himself. He works for the Post Office.

**Keller, Evelyn.** David's mother and wife of Ernest. She is a tired-eyed, mousy-haired woman with dark circles under her eyes and a nervous disposition.

**Lemon, Lawrence**. A classmate of Lewis and Rose Rita. He is always upset because everyone constantly mispronounces his name. It's "Le-MON," and rhymes with "on," but people pronounce it like the fruit.

**Levitation spell.** Uncle Jonathan manages to pull one off at a crucial moment.

*Lights Out.* A spooky old-time radio show featuring suspenseful tales. Wyllis Cooper and Arch Oboler, two of the best writers of radio drama, were the brains behind the show. Though it went off the air in 1947, it inspired a television version that played into the 1950s. Rose Rita is a fan either of the TV or the radio version.

**Lowan, Patty.** A classmate of Lewis and Rose Rita.

**Makalani, Princess.** The Hawaiian woman whom Abadiah Chadwick married and for whom he built the Hawaii House.

**Mingo, Woody**. A local bully. He stole Lewis's first Sherlock Holmes hat in *The Figure in the Shadows*, and later Lewis got in a fight with him and bloodied his nose. He doesn't bother Lewis any longer, though according to Rose Rita, he's still a mean kid.

**Muggins Simoon.** As Jonathan drives it around town, occasionally tooting the horn for no reason other than to hear its deep "Ah-HOOO-gah!" people look at the antique auto with surprised smiles.

**"My Bonnie Lies Over the Ocean."** A traditional Scottish folk song, with a thousand parodies and variants often sung around campfires. Uncle Jonathan plays it on the harmonica for a backyard singalong.

Tidbit about the original: "My Bonnie" is probably a reference to Charles Edward Stuart, "Bonnie Prince Charlie," grandson of James II, the last Stuart king of the United Kingdom. In 1688, James's opponents in England rose against him and deposed him in the Glorious Revolution, replacing him with King William III, a relative of James's and by birth Dutch. James's son Charles Stuart became the Pretender to the Throne, a man who had a claim to become king of the United Kingdom and who had strong support in Scotland

In 1745, the Scots rose up in rebellion against King George II of England (the Jacobite Rebellion, or as the Scots called it, "the 45"). Charles Stuart, whom his father had named as his successor as King of Scotland, led the rebels. After his army was defeated at the Battle of Culloden in 1746, "Bonnie Prince Charlie," as Charles was known, fled into exile "over the sea" to France, and he lived the rest of his days in exile. The Scots had many songs referring to Bonnie Prince Charlie, including "The Skye Boat Song," "Will Ye No Come Back Again," and this one—though with the rebellion of 1745 receding into history, "My Bonnie Lies Over the Ocean" is usually sung as a love song of a man expressing sorrow over his beloved's absence.

*National Geographic.* Trying to help his uncle and Mrs. Zimmermann research, Lewis has looked up all the articles about Hawaii in this magazine. He hasn't found anything that explains what is going on at the Hawaii House, though.

**Naval quotations:** In Chapter 1, Rose Rita reveals she's read a lot about naval warfare and the men who fought the wars. In quick order she quotes Oliver Hazard Perry ("We have met the enemy"), David Farragut ("Full speed ahead"), and George Dewey ("You may fire when ready"). None of these are complete, however.

**New Zebedee Opera House.** Rose Rita and Lewis tell David how they explored it in *Doom of the Haunted Opera* and how it became an auditorium for the town schools—but not about the magic that happened there.

**Night Marchers.** Hawaiian ghosts. Grampa Galway has heard of them. They are the ghosts of great warriors and march only when the moon and sea and stars are in some configuration. In Hawaii, the natives are careful not to build their houses in the path of a Night Marcher trail. And if the homeowner is unfortunate enough to be in the path of the Marchers, they take his or her soul and their numbers grow by one.

**"Old Ironsides."** A poem by Oliver Wendell Holmes, credited with saving the Revolutionary War frigate *U.S.S. Constitution* from being junked. Jonathan recites it as encouragement to Lewis at one point He comforts Lewis by saying one person can make a difference—Old Ironsides was not broken up, but still is afloat in Boston Harbor, the oldest ship still in the Navy.

**Party line.** In the 1950s, for houses outside the city limits, often the cheapest way to afford a phone was to share a line with one or two other households. The Kellers have a party-line telephone.

**Pearl.** A pearl from Hawaii seems to be reclaimed by vengeful island spirits. It bursts into molten flame, like a glob of lava from a volcano.

**Pele.** In ancient Hawaii, the goddess of volcanos. She appears in the novel, manifesting as a beautiful but stern young woman who confronts Mrs. Zimmermann.

**Pete.** "Old Pete" is a grumbling, toothless, elderly man who owns a store in a little village called Crow Corners. It specializes in odd things like buggy whips, screech-owl calls, and hand-cranked apple corers.

**Pottinger, Rose Rita.** In the first chapters, we see her at twelve, or nearly twelve, pretending to be a knight swinging a stick as a sword and beheading burdock weeds and dandelions.

Later, in  the main story, she has a rough first day at school. She discovers she really does not like Home Economics and had rather take creative writing—except the school doesn't offer it. She repeats that one day she wants to become a fiction writer. She recently got a wristwatch for her birthday, and she likes to check the time every five minutes or so just to show it off.

**Prayer.** At a tense moment, Lewis recites a Latin one: *Ab insidiis diabolic, libera nos, Domine . . .* (From the assaults of the devil, good Lord deliver us.")

**Riddle Contest.** Mrs. Zimmermann has a deadly serious one with the goddess Pele.

**Schellmacher, Curt**. An eighth-grade bully, short but husky. He and his friends enjoy pushing other kids around, especially if they're timid or different.

**School**. As part of the transition to high school, that year (Lewis's last in middle school) the students must change classes at the same time. School begins the day after Labor Day. This upsets Lewis a bit because he learns he will have only two classes together with Rose Rita.

**Smoking.** The novel makes it explicit that both Jonathan and Mrs. Zimmermann gave up smoking, though Uncle Jonathan still holds a pipe in his mouth, empty and unlit, when thinking hard. Sometimes he casts a spell so the pipe blows colorful bubbles with little figures inside them: the science teacher wearing a kilt and playing bagpipes, for example, or Lewis riding a bucking horse while juggling three lemon-meringue pies.

**Souvenir of Halifax.** Uncle Jonathan picked up a plush cushion with this embroidered on it. Lewis isn't even sure where Halifax is.

**St. Joseph's Aspirin bottle.** Lewis has one in his desk drawer. Perhaps fittingly, a powerful good talisman is the bottle named for a saint.

**Stevenson, Potsworth Farmer III ("Skunky").** The assistant New Zebedee garbage man. He works for Jute Feasel and drives routes three days a week, collecting garbage. He gets his nickname—well, you can guess why. His family was rich at one time, but Stevenson, though easy-going and good-hearted at first, wasn't smart with money and ran through his whole fortune while still young. The town gave him the job as the assistant sanitation man because everyone felt sorry for him.

At one point in the story, he is terrified when ghostly apparitions chase him from the Hawaii House. In a blind panic, he nearly runs down Lewis, Jonathan, and Rose Rita in his garbage truck, and though Jonathan helps him, he has been horribly shaken by the experience.

*Sword.* The name of a two-masted schooner in a bottle, a model that had belonged to Mr. Chadwick, the builder of the Hawaii House.

**Taubman, Jimmy.** One of the eighth-grade bullies, tall and muscular. He likes to mock weaker kids, imitating the way they talk.

**Thayer, Mrs**. A gray-haired lunchroom lady in the school.

**The Hawaii House.** In Chapter 1, the house is in a state of disorder after having been abandoned. After new owners move in, Lewis gets to see the inside. The house looks three-storied; however, owing to extra-tall walls and high ceilings, it actually has only two floors. The living room has three walls of built-in shelves, some empty and others crammed with mementos from the builder, Mr. Chadwick: wooden ship models, tarnished brass sextants and dividers and compasses, seashells, and other trinkets.

**"The Wreck of Rivermouth."** A poem by John Greenleaf Whittier. Uncle Jonathan memorized it in school and recites a stanza of it.

**Trees.** Oaks and butternuts are indigenous to New Zebedee.

**Twenty Questions.** A guessing game that the characters sometimes play to pass the time.

**"Walloping Window Blind, The."** A song, to the tune of "Ten Thousand Miles Away," lyrics from Charles E. Carryl's poem published in 1885. A rollicking, silly song, it's one of the tunes Uncle Jonathan plays on the harmonica as Mrs. Zimmermann, Rose Rita, Lewis, and David Keller sing along. As Uncle Jonathan suspected, David's stutter vanishes when he sings.

**Westland.** A town between New Zebedee and Detroit. In the book it is the site of a hospital that specializes in treating patients with mental trauma, like Skunky Stevenson, who is sent there.

**Zane, Mrs**. An English teacher at Lewis's school.

**Zenith Stratosphere.** The TV is referenced though again my memory played me tricks and I called it a Stratocaster.

**Zimmermann, Florence.** She carries her umbrella just in case of sudden showers, she says. Readers know the real reason—it's her magic wand. When she steps into the Hawaii House, she says a short prayer of welcoming that, she says, came down to her from her great-grandmother on her father's side. She tests the Hawaii House for curses or evil spells and can't find any, but she tells Lewis she senses the Kellers are in danger from some unknown threat.

◆ ◆ ◆

# Chapter 10: A John Bellairs Mystery:
## *The Sign of the Sinister Sorcerer*
## By Brad Strickland
## Dial Books for Young Readers, 2008

Mrs. Zimmermann had a primo part to play in *The House Where Nobody Lived.* As I planned the next book, I wanted to feature Uncle Jonathan. My tentative title was "The Third Bad Thing," focusing on Lewis's nervous superstition that bad things come in threes. The editor—my fourth since Toby Sherry retired—wanted something zippier, and of the six or seven I suggested, she went with *The Sign of the Sinister Sorcerer.*

For the basic plot hook, I went back to a John Bellairs book, but not one about Lewis. Instead, I remembered that in *The Face in the Frost*, John had mentioned that to become full-fledged sorcerers, two students had to create some joint magical wonder. That bound them together—and if one turned evil, the other had to resist that evil.

The stage was set and for perhaps the last time—it was off to New Zebedee.

**Summary:**

As school ends, Uncle Jonathan hosts a party in the Barnavelt back yard. He even builds a stage to stand on as he does his magic act for Lewis, Rose Rita, and some of their friends from school. One, Hal Everit, is a newcomer to New Zebedee. Rose Rita has a bit of a grudge against him, and he is something of a Doubting Thomas, but Jonathan's spectacular illusions impress even him. One thing provides a note of unease: Lewis could swear he saw a hooded figure lurking nearby during the party.

Soon afterward, while reading a book from his uncle's study, Lewis learns about the old Rule of Three superstition: bad luck always comes in threes. He begins to fret about that. When he, Rose Rita, and Hal Everit watch a baseball game, he gets smacked by a foul ball that bloodies his nose. And then worse things begin to happen . . . as Lewis fearfully waits for the third and most disastrous one. Before it's all over, an evil sorcerer has made an appearance, and Uncle Jonathan has vanished. It's up to his friends to find and rescue him.

◆  ◆  ◆

*Behind the Scenes:*

The new editor was in her twenties and had never read any of John's or my books and had worked mostly on chapter books and picture books. When Jonathan was being held prisoner at one point, she asked, "Why doesn't he just use his cell phone to call for help?"

Because there were no cell phones in the 1950s, I told her. She insisted that she thought she had seen them in old movies, though. Sigh.

There are a few nods to *The Face in the Frost* and to other books by John scattered throughout. The revivification of Selenna Izard is mentioned in the first chapter, along with Tarby. An old fellow who likes to umpire youth baseball games came from out east somewhere and once played on a team called the Spiders—maybe with Johnny Dixon's grandfather as a teammate (*Eyes of the Killer Robot*). And I put in the usual complement of books for Lewis to read.

The time frame of the book is compact, unlike the previous one. The action takes place only over a few weeks in the summer. The writing went faster, too, and from the time I sent in the proposal to the time I submitted the manuscript, no more than seven months went by. However, there were some publishing delays (the recession was really pounding publishers at that time).

Because the editor was overworked, the book went through the publishing process with a bit less oversight that earlier ones had, so I wouldn't be surprised if some typos and editing errors slipped through.

Publication really is a team effort, and every writer needs a good editor and copy editor to backstop the effort.

Baseball, Rose Rita's favorite sport, comes in for some action in this novel. The first bad thing that happens to Lewis is a painful moment when a foul ball smacks his face, bloodying his nose.

It isn't very serious, after all, but being the timid kid that he is, the injury worries Lewis. It's a replay of something that happened to me the year I was a high-school freshman. We went to the gym for PE. We were doing calisthenics, while older kids were practicing basketball on the other half of the court.

I don't recall, but I think we were doing jumping jacks when a basketball thrown hard from the other side of the court suddenly loomed in my vision and then smashed into my face while I was mid-jump. It knocked me out, and the next thing I knew, I was lying on my back with the PE teacher swabbing my face with a cold towel. I had a spectacular nosebleed, my left front top incisor had been broken, and my glasses were smashed to pieces.

They sent me to the school nurse's office, where the nosebleed took half an hour to stanch. They called my home, but my dad was at work and couldn't be contacted. After two hours, my uncle finally drove to the school, collected me, and took me to the family doctor, who determined that my nose wasn't broken. I had a mild concussion, spectacular black eyes, and I was for all practical purposes blind without my glasses (20/400 vision). It took about two weeks for everything to sort out. I channeled that experience, less extreme, for Lewis.

This time around, I dedicated the book "To Jonathan, my juggling son." Jonathan graduated from the University of Georgia, eventually joined the crew of howstuffworks.com, and today is an internet star well-known for his podcasts for *How Stuff Works*. Just look for Jonathan Strickland. I recommend "Why do people in old movies talk funny?"

The cover art is by Jasmin Rubero and shows an evil-looking red-robed wizard swishing his wand through the air, leaving a fiery numeral 3 hanging there and glowing. It is atmospheric and reminiscent of the Edward Gorey illustrations, though it is not in the Gorey style.

As I had suspected it might be, *The Sign of the Sinister Sorcerer* was the twelfth and the final installment in the New Zebedee series. It's possible, of course, that the series could be taken up again, but Dial decided to devote more of its output to picture books and best-sellers, and the Bellairs books, which sold respectably but not spectacularly, did not make the cut.

I can't complain too much. I loved John Bellairs's work, I felt it was a great honor to take up the series he began, and, though I may not have come up to the mark of the master, I always tried my best to do well by him and by his creations, my good friends Lewis, Rose Rita, Uncle Jonathan, and Mrs. Zimmermann. Wherever they are today, I wish them all the best.

◆ ◆ ◆

## *The Sign of the Sinister Sorcerer:* People, Places and Things

**Abacus.** Uncle Jonathan uses one when he's paying bills, and he can calculate on it faster than Lewis can use an adding machine.

**Abomination of desolation.** A biblical reference, to Matthew 24. Its meaning is obscure, but Jonathan takes it to refer to a place of emptiness.

**Barnavelt, Lewis.** Though he is older and more experienced and not quite as timid as he once was, Lewis maintains some of his old habits. In the summer he loves to lie stretched out in a lawn chair in the Barnavelt back yard, reading a book, sipping milk, and snacking on crackers spread with pimento cheese or on chocolate-covered raisins. He also is still a worrywart, always anticipating the worst.

**Bell.** Uncle Jonathan enchants a little hand bell for Lewis to use while he's laid up after his accident in case he needs to call someone. When Lewis rings it, it produces sounds ranging from foghorns to dog barks, and wherever he is, Jonathan will always hear it.

**Bergen, Edgar** (1903-1978). An American actor and entertainer, best known as a ventriloquist. His most famous "partner" was the ventriloquist's dummy Charlie McCarthy, who wore a monocle and a tuxedo but who sounded like a smart-alec American teenager. For many years Bergen and McCarthy were a popular radio act—even though a ventriloquist working in radio is rather strange. Uncle Jonathan references Bergen and McCarthy.

**Bielski, Bobby.** One of the baseball-playing kids. He has a blazing fastball.

**Bowl-Mor.** The local bowling alley, just past the town limits on the west side of town, and near the athletic fields.

*Bruja.* Spanish for "witch." Mrs. Zimmermann mentions this fact.

**Cagliostro, Count.** Hal has heard of him. "Count Alessandro Cagliostro" was a name assumed by the Italian Giuseppe Balsamo (1743-1795), a self-styled student of the occult and, by some accounts, what today we would call a con artist. He traveled widely in Europe, living variously in Russia, Germany, and then France, where he became influential in court affairs and even met Benjamin Franklin. Cagliostro was involved in the Freemasons (later writers credit him with having either created or reformed the basic practices of the group). After Cagliostro fell under suspicion of having participated in a fraud involving Queen Marie Antoinette and a diamond necklace, King Louis XVI exiled him from France. While in Rome, he was arrested by the Inquisition and imprisoned. He died in prison in 1795. Even after his death, some people persisted in believing he was a real sorcerer instead of a clever trickster.

**Capharnaum County Magicians Society.** They have their meeting in the G.A.R. Hall in the novel.

**Captain Midnight Secret Decoder Ring.** Another mention of this token, which listeners to the *Captain Midnight* radio show (and later TV show) could get. Though almost everyone calls it this, really the decoder was a pin or badge, not a ring.

**Card games.** Lewis plays some of Mrs. Zimmermann's trademark goofy card games with her, including "Wild Widow," Spit-in-the-Ocean" and "Pineapple." Lewis also plays a fiendishly complex form of solitaire that Jonathan taught him, "Napoleon's March to Moscow."

**Chilly Willy.** A cartoon penguin in short cartoons by the Walter Lantz studio. Lewis and Rose Rita go to see the movie *Conquest of Space* and one of these cartoons is on the bill. Though not named, it's probably "The Legend of Rockabye Point," directed by Tex Avery.

**Christie, Agatha.** A popular British mystery writer. At one point, Lewis reads one of her novels about the Belgian detective Hercule Poirot.

**Circle, Magic.** Mrs. Zimmermann draws one when she is trying to determine by magic where someone might be.

***Compendium of Curious Beliefs and Superstitions of the Britons, Scots, and Irish, A.*** A fictitious book, written by Theodosius M. Fraser and published in London, 1851. To a degree, it is modeled on *The Golden Bough: A Study in Magic and Religion,* a twelve-volume work by Sir James George Frazer, 1906-1915. However, the *Compendium,* though big and heavy, is in only one volume. One chapter, about death and disaster omens, begins to bother Lewis as he reads.

***Conquest of Space.*** A 1955 Technicolor movie produced by George Pal. Lewis and Rose Rita go to see it in the downtown theater.

**Conwell, Mr.** Uncle Jonathan's lawyer. His last name comes from Bill Conwell, a long-time Bellairs fan.

**Costick, Sandra.** One of the kids at the end-of-school party.

**Deitz, Mr.** Manager of Uncle Jonathan's bank. His last name comes from my friend and fellow fantasy writer, the late Thomas F. Deitz.

**Detmeyer, Mr.** A lanky, bald old man who hangs out at the fire station. In his youth, he played for a minor-league team called the Spiders as a second baseman, and might have made it to the majors, but in an exhibition game, he caught bare-handed a line drive hit by the great Babe Ruth and broke every bone in his right hand. He likes to umpire kids' games, and the players all like him and think he's a good umpire.

**Drinking glass.** When Mrs. Zimmermann needs to locate a missing magical item, she doesn't have a crystal ball, so she uses an ordinary glass of water with one drop of olive oil floating on the surface. It works just as well.

**Elephant.** At the magic show for the end-of-school party, Uncle Jonathan creates a lifelike illusion of a tiny miniature elephant. It later transforms into a pigeon.

**Everit, Hal.** A new kid at school, a recent transfer to New Zebedee. He is very smart at history, and Rose Rita is a bit peeved that he edged her out for the History Medal, because he had a grade of

100, barely beating her 98.5—and she had been in class all year, as opposed to the month or six weeks that Hal had been in school. Lewis had sympathized with Hal because he had no friends in town, and impulsively invited him to the end-of-school party in the Barnavelt back yard. More athletic and raucous than Lewis, Hal can be brash and loud-mouthed, but Lewis makes allowances for him.

He tells Lewis that his dad abandoned the family, his mom lost a good job, and they had to move to New Zebedee where she found another, low-paying one. Now, he says, they must live in a crummy little house.

**Fireworks.** Uncle Jonathan conjures up some splendid ones, though they probably are illusions.

**Fain, Punchy.** A tall, skinny kid about fourteen or fifteen. He's one of the baseball-playing kids and is a pitcher with a good curveball.

**Fuller, Alan.** One of the kids at the end-of-school party. His last name comes from my co-writer on a dozen books, the late Thomas E. Fuller.

**Fuse Box Dwarf.** This magical illusion dwindled and went away over time, because Jonathan didn't renew the enchantment.

**G.A.R. Hall.** Named for the Grand Army of the Republic, the Union Army during the Civil War, it is at the east end of Main Street. It has meeting rooms and a ballroom, and the Capharnaum County Magicians Society sometimes meets there.

**Ghoulies and Ghosties.** At one point, Jonathan quotes an old Scottish prayer, first collected in "The Denham Tracts," a series of pamphlets written by Michael A. Denham between 1846 and 1859 and later published by the British Folklore Society under the editorship of James Hardy (1892). The full text of the prayer is "From ghoulies and ghosties / And long-leggedy beasties / And things that go bump in the night, / Good Lord, deliver us!" Denham also included the word "hobbit" as the name of a kind of fairy, and it's possible that J.R.R. Tolkien found the word in Hardy's published version.

**Gloria.** Lewis remembers the terrible night when he was ten. Gloria was his babysitter, and the police came to the front door with the news that both of Lewis's parents had been killed in a horrible auto crash.

**Granny Weatherbee.** Mrs. Zimmermann recalls that she believed in the Rule of Three and taught her niece magic at the same time she taught Mrs. Zimmermann. The editorial staff for some reason changed the name from the original spelling to "Weatherby" in the published version of this book, perhaps to avoid confusing her with Principal Weatherbee in the "Archie" comic books.

**Hardy Boys.** Lewis references these fictional boy detectives.

*Hechicero.* Spanish for "sorcerer." Mrs. Zimmerman mentions this fact.

**Heemsoth's Rexall Drug Store.** The soda fountain there is one of Lewis and Rose Rita's hangouts. It is described in Chapter 5, and the description is based on my memories of the soda fountain at Whatley's Pharmacy in my home town.

**Helen, Aunt.** Referenced. She is one of Jonathan's sisters, a gloomy woman who does not like children. She and her husband Jimmy live in Osee Five Hills.

**Holmes, Sherlock.** When she and Lewis begin to search for Uncle Jonathan's missing cane, Rose Rita slightly misquotes from Sir Arthur Conan Doyle's Sherlock Holmes story "The Abbey Grange": "Come, Watson, come! The game is afoot." Doyle himself was referring a line in Act 3, scene 1 of Shakespeare's *King Henry V,* as on the verge of a battle with the French, King Henry rallies his British army with a speech that includes the lines "I see you stand like greyhounds in the slips, / Straining upon the start. The game's afoot...." In both cases, the idea comes from hunting: Holmes and Watson, and the British Army in the Shakespeare play, are like hounds; the game animal they seek is already on the run (afoot), so they must hurry. "Slips" are slip collars that the masters of the hounds could release in a moment to let the dogs run to chase the prey.

Later, Hal Everit mentions a story that must be "The Speckled Band," involving a murderer with a unique, living weapon.

**Humphries, Dr.** The Barnavelt family physician comes in when Lewis gets hit in the face by a foul ball. As usual, the doctor is sympathetic, encouraging, and humorous, and very competent at both treating and reassuring Lewis, who escapes a concussion but has two very black eyes and a bloody nose.

**Jaeger, Mrs.** The inept witch whom we met in *The Doom of the Haunted Opera* makes a brief appearance in this novel.

**Jailbird.** The whistling cat, enchanted by Uncle Jonathan, gradually lost the ability to whistle because Jonathan didn't bother to keep the enchantment going.

**Jones, John Paul** (1747-1792). Born John Paul in Scotland, he fled to America after he killed a shipmate in a duel, and during the American Revolution he became a famous captain in the Colonial Navy. During a furious naval engagement with the British ship *Serapis,* the British captain ordered Jones to surrender his ship, the *Bonhomme Richard,* because it was badly damaged. Defiantly, Jones responded, "I have not yet begun to fight!" Mrs. Zimmermann quotes him in this book.

**Keller, David.** David, whom we met in *The House where Nobody Lived,* makes an appearance as a guest at the end-of-school party in chapter 1. He is receiving speech therapy for his stutter, and it is improving.

**Land of Ooze.** Jonathan's phrase for the weird void in which he is temporarily imprisoned.

**Lansing.** State capital of Michigan, about a fifty-mile trip from New Zebedee. Uncle Jonathan drives there to consult his old magic teacher, and Lewis remembers taking a school field trip there.

**Litton, William, Lord.** A member of the Edinburgh branch of the Order of the Golden Circle in 1888.

**Logan, Buzzy.** One of the baseball-playing kids. Bobby Bielski strikes him out.

**Marciano, Rocky.** Rocco Francis Marchegiano (1923-1969), better known by his professional name, was an American heavyweight boxer who became the World Heavyweight Champion in 1952 and who eventually retired undefeated. At one point when Lewis has two black eyes, Rose Rita teases that he looks as if he went a few rounds in the ring with Marciano.

**Marlowe, Philip.** A fictional private detective, created by the writer Raymond Chandler. Lewis mentions him, though he probably knew about him through the movies or a radio show about him.

**Marville, Mundale, Dr.** Formerly a professor of mathematics at Michigan Agricultural College, he was also a practicing sorcerer and taught Uncle Jonathan the basics of magic. Marville had been a member of the Order of the Golden Circle at one time.

Though not an evil magician himself, Marville taught at least one student who turned to dark magic. At the time of the story, Dr. Marville is retired and living in Lansing, MI.

**Mattie, Aunt.** Referenced. She was one of Jonathan's sisters, a spiteful, bad-tempered woman who, Lewis always remembers, used to mock him for being overweight. She has passed away.

**McConnell, Trip.** One of the kids at the end-0f-school party. His last name comes from a college where I taught years ago, Truett-McConnell College (now University). I don't know where his first name comes from, but later we got a dog we named Tripper.

**Mirror, Magic.** In the enchanted mirror in the front hallway of the Barnavelt house, Lewis glimpses a sinister figure in maroon robes swishing a wand that leaves a glowing orange 3 floating in the air. This is the image on the original dust jacket.

**Moreland, Sir Michael.** A barrister (we would say lawyer) who in 1888 was a member of the Edinburgh branch of the Order of the Golden Circle.

**Morgan, Mr.** The basketball coach at Lewis and Rose Rita's school. He is named for Coach "Pete" Morgan, who was the coach at my elementary school and was one of the good guys.

**Museum of Natural History.** The New York landmark. The first time Mrs. Zimmermann sees Lewis after his accident with the baseball, she says she half expected him to be wrapped up in bandages like a mummy in the museum.

**National Museum of Magic.** Rose Rita and Lewis suggest that Hal buy some tricks there when he mentions wanting to learn how to be a magician.

**Nevins, Captain Lewis.** A fictional British Army officer that Lewis reads about in the book on superstitions. The curse of bad things coming in three is illustrated when, all on the same day, Captain Nevins was struck by a cricket ball, slightly wounded when a firearm discharged accidentally, and then after medical treatment fainted at the top of some stairs and fell to his death. Because of his first name, Lewis takes the story to heart.

**Numerology.** The belief that certain numbers have magical or mystical properties. Rose Rita dismisses the idea by demonstrating that someone who's superstitious about the number thirteen can turn practically any number into thirteen by thinking up convoluted ways of doing it. For example, she turns Lewis's street number, 101, into thirteen by adding the two ones to get two, dropping the zero, and then because she dropped one number, putting it before the two to get 12. And then because 12 is one less than zero, she adds the one . . . . It's nonsense, but she makes Lewis briefly anxious.

**Order of the Golden Circle.** Not the Masons' group for women, but a fictitious group of sorcerers, modeled in part on the Hermetic Order of the Golden Dawn, an organization active in the British Isles in the late 19th and early 20th centuries. Hal Everit has read about the group. Lewis later reads that the members of the Order always formed groups of three magicians to perform their researches—the Rule of Three—and sees a photograph of three members of the Order.

Jonathan says the man who taught him magic had been a member of the Order, and that the Order had an American branch at one time. However, after some members turned evil, it disbanded itself in the 1930s.

**Parker, Sam.** The mayor of New Zebedee. Near the end of the book he desperately calls on Uncle Jonathan for some help.

**Picasso.** Jonathan mentions this famous artist.

**Pietra, Mildred.** One of the kids at the end-of-school party.

**Pipe.** Though Uncle Jonathan no longer smokes tobacco, he has kept his pipes, and when he's thinking, he likes to hold an empty, unlit one between his teeth. His favorite is a British Bulldog brier pipe, a curved one like the ones in pictures of Sherlock Holmes. He says it's the perfect thinking pipe.

**Pottinger, Rose Rita.** We learn a few of her superstitions: she has a couple of lucky charms, though she doesn't take them seriously. However, when she plays baseball she always wears her lucky socks and Detroit Tigers cap. Ordinarily, though, she doesn't bother with stuff like worrying about black cats or walking under ladders, because she puts no stock in bad-luck omens.

She also indulges her habit of spinning yarns, telling a whopper in Chapter 7 about the wood used in Uncle Jonathan's wand, ancient Egypt, and King Richard the Lionheart.

**Prospero and Roger Bacon.** Hal knows about these famous medieval wizards. Really, they're both fictional, the main characters in John Bellairs's book *The Face in the Frost.*

**Rule of Three.** Uncle Jonathan explains that when someone wants to learn magic, there are different ways. The student can try to pick up magic from books; or can become an apprentice to a master magician; or, in the time-honored way, can join with another student and study magic with a teacher. Some believe this last way—the Rule of Three, two students and one teacher—is the best, because the personalities balance each other, like the legs of a tripod. Additionally, if one of the students becomes evil, the other two can combat him or her.

**Schlectesherz, Adolfus.** A fellow student of Jonathan's in college, and with Jonathan a student of magic, taught by Dr. Mundale Marville. He chose the dark path. The name in German means "evil heart," which is a tipoff if I ever heard one. Adolfus is about ten years older than Jonathan, and he's carried a grudge ever since college because Dr. Marville refused to grant him a magic wand. Adolfus and Jonathan had cooperated to create a magical item—but Adolfus had been petty, pushy, and nasty during the effort, and so while Jonathan passed the test, Adolfus did not.

**Shakespeare, William.** Two plays are referenced: *Henry V,* indirectly (see "Sherlock Holmes") and *The Tempest.*

**Silver Dollars.** Lewis's allowance is five dollars a week, and Uncle Jonathan gives it to him in big round silver dollars (real silver in those days), which make Lewis feel quite wealthy. At one point in the story, though, he loses his allowance because of a hole in his pocket.

**Spade, Sam.** A fictional private detective, created by the writer Dashiell Hammett, featured most prominently in the novel *The Maltese Falcon.* Lewis mentions him, though he might have known about him through the movies or a radio show using the character.

*Specter from the Magician's Museum.* Rose Rita references it.

**St. John, Aubrey.** A poet, and a member of the Edinburgh branch of the Order of the Golden Circle in 1888. Rumor has it that he lost his mind because of his occult studies. The name "St. John," by the way, is pronounced in the British style: "Sinjin."

**Stamps.** At one point Jonathan is writing checks and mailing them to pay bills. He uses three-cent stamps, because that was the cost of mailing a first-class letter up to 1958. People have actually asked me about that.

**Stereoscope.** Lewis enjoys looking at the old sepia-toned 3D photos with this, which in the book is once more mistakenly called a stereopticon. My fault.

**Tieg, Diane.** One of the kids at the end-of-school party.

**Van Gogh, Vincent.** Jonathan mentions this famous artist.

**Voodoo.** Uncle Jonathan explains that voodoo curses work only if the victim believes in them and knows he or she has been cursed.

**Wands.** Uncle Jonathan says that costumes don't matter much to wizards—they neither add nor take from magical power—but wizards do rely on their wands, which are attuned to their powers and amplify them. Of course, powerful sorcerers like Mrs. Zimmermann can do impressive magic even without a wand, but the wand makes them stronger. At a crucial point in the story, Uncle Jonathan realizes that his own wand, a cane with a crystal knob for a handle, is missing.

**Welsh.** When Mrs. Zimmermann uncharacteristically uses magic to wash up the dishes, she speaks a magic spell in Welsh. This is an oblique reference to the movie *The Sword in the Stone*, where Merlin, a Welsh magician, does the same trick.

***Wolverine, The.*** Yearbook of Michigan Agricultural College, Uncle Jonathan's alma mater. This one is modeled on an actual example of the yearbook from the proper period (1930s).

**Zimmermann, Florence.** She uses her good magic to cast protective spells on the Barnavelt House, and the crystal globe that she received in *The Ghost in the Mirror* gets a specific reference.

◆ ◆ ◆

# Chapter 11: Adventures in Bellairs Land

I was sad, but not surprised, when Dial decided against continuing the Bellairs series after the twelfth book in the New Zebedee series. Publishing had taken a beating during the Great Recession. Readers were turning to electronic books instead of print ones. The whole nature of publishing was changing.

I had regrets. One was that I never had a chance to write an Anthony Monday book. For various reasons, the editorial staff did not care for that series—partly because John had taken the first one, *The Treasure of Alpheus Winterborn,* away from Dial. He resisted making changes that the editor insisted on. He published that book at Random House instead, though it did not find as wide an audience as his earlier books, and he soon returned to Dial.[6] Then, too, my editor felt that Anthony's home life, with the parents always arguing, was distressing.

Over the years I proposed five different story lines for Anthony Monday books, none of which were accepted, though one of them, "The Last Book in the Library" eventually became the Johnny Dixon novel *The Bell, the Book, and the Spellbinder,* with Johnny's friend Fergie taking the role that Anthony would have had.

Another that I really liked but never got to write was "The Gold of Hangman's Key," which like *Treasure* would have been a non-supernatural treasure hunt. In it, Emerson discovers an old diary that includes clues to where a pirate treasure was buried in 1692.

Some Johnny Dixons remained unwritten, too. The one I liked most was "The Trolley to Tomorrow," in which the Time Trolley reappears and takes Johnny and Fergie thirty years into the future—where they meet themselves as adults. My editor said, "No kid wants to read about

---

[6] Dial later repurchased the rights to Alpheus Winterborn so they had the complete Anthony Monday series.

growing up" and nixed the idea. I used just one tiny part of the plot in *The Wrath of the Grinning Ghost.* Another was "Weatherman of Woe," about an incompetent, but not evil, sorcerer who gains control over the weather—with disastrous results. I have four or five more ideas in my files.

For the New Zebedee books, I proposed one I called "The Bone, the Moon, and the Manitou," in which a Native American relic exposes Rose Rita to a magical menace and Mrs. Zimmermann calls on Lewis to help her come to the rescue. My editor was nervous about dealing with Native American beliefs and legends, though (she never wanted to offend any ethnic group), and turned it down. Another was "The Sorcerer's Circle," in which our friends travel to Germany for a two-week vacation and Mrs. Zimmermann discovers that an old adversary of hers is eager to challenge her to a wizard's duel. Others were "The Secret of the Standing Stones," in which a Stonehenge-like circle transports Lewis and Rose Rita to England in the 16th century and they have to find a way back and "The Hag, the Hill, and the Horror," about a deranged witch who controls shadows—but not ordinary ones.

But none of these ever saw the light of day. They remain just what-might-have-beens.

◆  ◆  ◆

Regrets aside, being associated with the John Bellairs series has brought me joy. The fans have always been wonderful. I've appreciated every letter, every speaking opportunity, and every chance to meet the readers. I even discovered in my one extremely brief meeting with J.K. Rowling that she knows and likes the works of Bellairs.

Then, too, the people of Marshall have always been so kind and considerate that I owe them a great debt of gratitude. I've always enjoyed my visits there—even when they encouraged me to climb up into the tower of the Cronin Mansion to peek out of the oval window and I realized I had dozens of small bats for company. But even the bats were amiable. It's a lovely town and the people are marvelous.

In 2017, a long-awaited event finally materialized: Producer Brad Fischer, director Eli Roth, and producer/writer Eric Kripke began production of the film *The House with a Clock in Its Walls.* The "property"—that is, the film rights to the book—had been drifting around for years, bought and sold by one production company after another.

Now not only was it being filmed—it was being filmed in my home state, and not far from me. The main street of Newnan, Georgia, became a good facsimile of downtown New Zebedee. A fantastic recreation of the Barnavelt house interiors became a reality at Atlanta Metro Studio, just south of the city.

Most exciting of all—for me—was that the company invited my wife and me to visit the studio. We returned three separate times, because in Brad and Eli I met two fellow Bellairs fans. We got to meet Owen Vaccaro, who plays Lewis; Jack Black (Uncle Jonathan); Cate Blanchett (Mrs. Zimmermann); and Kyle MacLachlan (Isaac Izard). Everyone was friendly, charming, and enthusiastic, and we enjoyed the experience more than I can tell you.

Also, we were able to meet John's former wife, Priscilla Bellairs, a gracious, good-humored, and brilliant lady who treasures her memories of John and of the books. She came down to Georgia just for the occasion, and we spent two delightful days in her company. I'm very excited by the prospect of a major motion picture based on *House* and have high hopes for it.

◆ ◆ ◆

Since I began working with the Bellairs material, I have discovered that John's work is influential. Bellairs was a pathfinder. His style, blending humor, suspense, and moments of terror, mesmerizes readers. Hundreds of YA stories, featuring mystery, the supernatural, and suspense, echo his work. I see traces of his influence in R.L. Stine, Ransom Riggs, Lemony Snicket, and others. I know three published writers whose work grew out of their love of John's books. Any youngster who reads Bellairs will  remember the stories with fondness.

The cover art, too, has been inspirational. Once or twice I've stopped short while passing a book, thinking, "That's a Gorey cover." But it isn't—it pays homage to Gorey in style. Good art can give a person a goal and a direction. It can make a reader into a writer or an artist.

John's glow touches more than fiction and art. A podcast series out of Chicago, *Our Fair City*, proudly acknowledges him as an inspiration.

Neil Gaiman's *Dead Boy Detectives* comics have distinct Bellairsian overtones. If you look around, I'm sure you'll find many others.

Sometimes I stumble on something that just makes me think of John's work. When I first happened across the cartoon series *Gravity Falls*—the first installment I ever saw was the third-from-last episode— it instantly seemed familiar. The series is about Dipper and Mabel Pines, twelve-year-old twins from California, who spend the summer with their great-uncle Stanford Pines (who is not what he seems, heh-heh) in the weird town of Gravity Falls, Oregon. Stan Pines is gruff, cantankerous, and eccentric. The town seethes with creatures from aliens to zombies; offbeat human characters abound, and mysteries lurk.

For sheer orneriness, Stan could give Professor Childermass a run for his money. I'd bet that he would be a natural poker buddy of Jonathan Barnavelt, and he'd try corny, mushy, unsuccessful pickup lines on Mrs. Zimmermann.

Dipper is insecure, a worrywart, and timid—but he's brainy and intrigued by mystery and brave when he must be. His sister is fun-loving, funny, and concerned for his welfare. Hmm, a lot like Lewis and Rose Rita. Most of all, the vibe is familiar. The setting is a town just oozing with paranormal goings-on. Comfortable scenes of kids enjoying being kids alternate with moments of sheer nightmare. Hilarious humor shades into spine-freezing horror.

Oh, so new and yet so familiar; I'm not sure if the creator of the series, Alex Hirsch, ever read a John Bellairs book in his life—but whether he has or not, the show itself strikes me as very Bellairsian.

But then, John's influence is in the air. Those who breathe it want to live it. True, John is no longer with us, but his words and his works and his influence live on. They will live on for a very long time.

And I, for one, am most grateful for that.

◆　◆　◆

# Acknowledgments

So many people to thank! Where do I begin? Priscilla Bellairs is supportive and always helpful in answering questions. Producer Brad Fischer and director Eli Roth were kind hosts when we visited the movie set for *The House with a Clock in Its Walls*. Jane Reid is a welcome connection to Marshall, Michigan. Angela Semifero, Director of the Marshall District Library, offered wonderful encouragement.

As always, Richard Curtis, my long-time agent and friend, deserves my thanks for all he has done for my writing career, going beyond the call of duty out of friendship. My wife Barbara tolerates my long hours of writing—she says I'm working more now than before I retired. Love you, sweetie.

I still owe Jeanne Sharp a big thank-you for taking time to read and critique three of my earlier manuscripts. Alex DeLuca, S.E. Johnson, and Brigid Burke helped me proofread this book, catching a whole net full of errors, and I give them my heartfelt thanks. The goofs remaining belong to me alone.

Artist and King Kong aficionado Joe DeVito helped with the book's cover design and composition, taking time from his busy schedule. I sincerely appreciate his thoughtfulness.

And, of course, I want to thank the Bellairs family, the people of Marshall, and the wonderful fans who, like me, discovered and loved the works of John Bellairs.

Cheers!

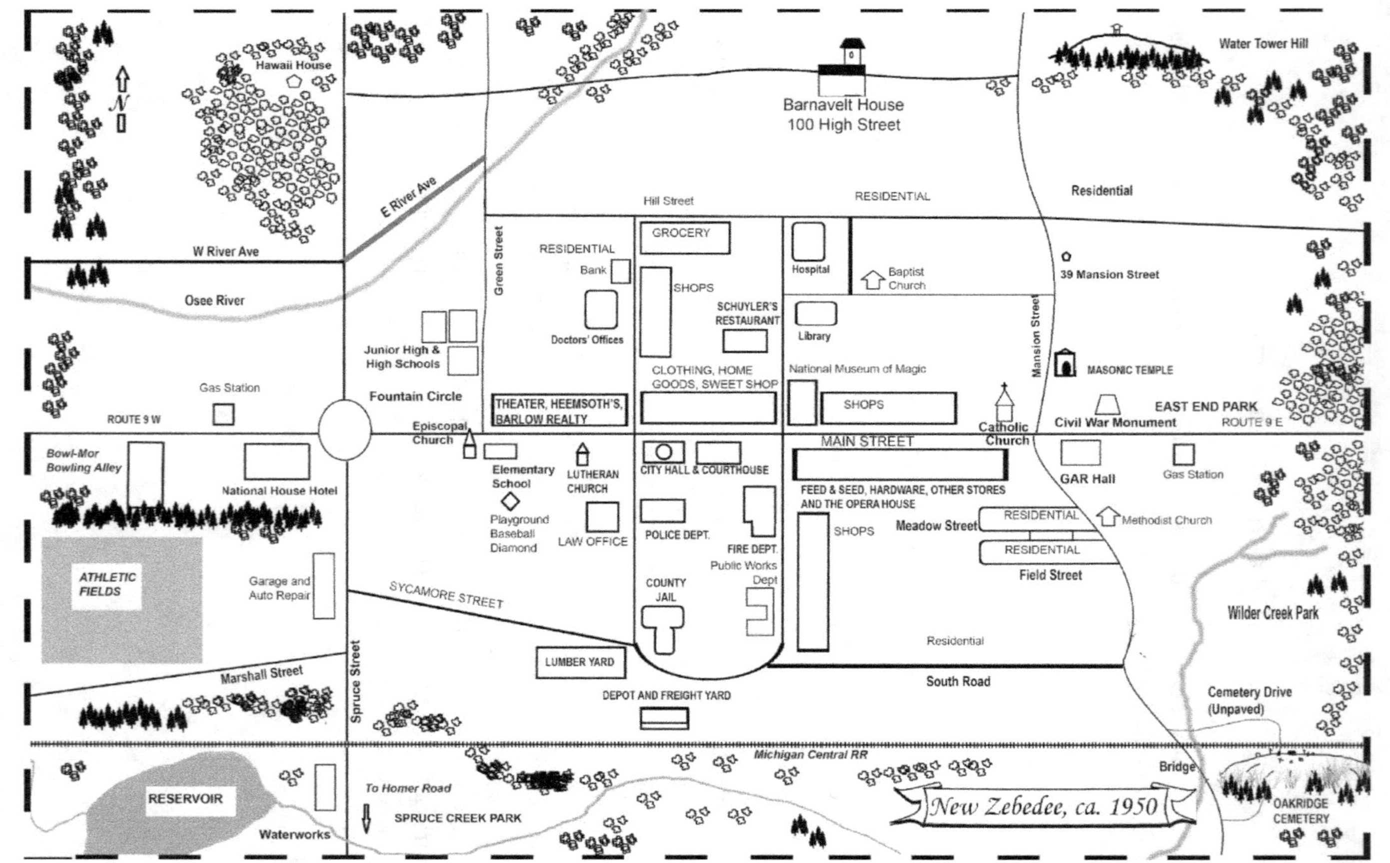
N
Hawaii House
Water Tower Hill
Barnavelt House
100 High Street
E River Ave
RESIDENTIAL
Residential
W River Ave
Hill Street
Osee River
Green Street
GROCERY
RESIDENTIAL
Bank
Hospital
Baptist Church
39 Mansion Street
SHOPS
SCHUYLER'S RESTAURANT
Mansion Street
Doctors' Offices
Library
MASONIC TEMPLE
Junior High & High Schools
National Museum of Magic
Gas Station
Fountain Circle
CLOTHING, HOME GOODS, SWEET SHOP
SHOPS
EAST END PARK
ROUTE 9 W
THEATER, HEEMSOTH'S, BARLOW REALTY
Catholic Church
Civil War Monument
ROUTE 9 E
Episcopal Church
MAIN STREET
Bowl-Mor Bowling Alley
Elementary School
LUTHERAN CHURCH
CITY HALL & COURTHOUSE
GAR Hall
Gas Station
National House Hotel
FEED & SEED, HARDWARE, OTHER STORES AND THE OPERA HOUSE
Playground Baseball Diamond
LAW OFFICE
POLICE DEPT.
SHOPS
Meadow Street
RESIDENTIAL
Methodist Church
ATHLETIC FIELDS
Garage and Auto Repair
FIRE DEPT.
Public Works Dept
RESIDENTIAL
Field Street
SYCAMORE STREET
COUNTY JAIL
Wilder Creek Park
Residential
Marshall Street
Spruce Street
LUMBER YARD
South Road
Cemetery Drive (Unpaved)
DEPOT AND FREIGHT YARD
Michigan Central RR
Bridge
RESERVOIR
To Homer Road
New Zebedee, ca. 1950
OAKRIDGE CEMETERY
Waterworks
SPRUCE CREEK PARK

Your mental map of New Zebedee may differ from mine. This is how I see it, based on the books and on Marshall, Michigan. To put in all the houses, all the bridges, all the features of the town would overcrowd the page.

Feel free to add whatever you think is missing. As John Bellairs always advised—

Let your imagination run wild!

www.ingramcontent.com/pod-product-compliance
Lightning Source LLC
Chambersburg PA
CBHW061504050726

47593CB00002B/437

*9781732457010*